"No doubt about it, we have entered a new our institutions face a myriad of changes, fac need to look beyond traditional instruction emerging organizational development roles. The pressures put on faculty developers during this time of flux are immense. Luckily, this important new book, based on original research and state-of-the-art practice, provides a cogent range of insights into what we are all experiencing. *Coming in from the Margins* is an indispensable and timely addition to the field that takes a hard look at where we are right now, and provides a road map for the future."

Mary Deane Sorcinelli, *Associate Provost for Faculty Development, and Professor, Educational Policy, Research and Administration, University of Massachusetts Amherst*

"This is a remarkable work that clarifies the gradual and important transformation in faculty development that has been under way in American high education for decades, enabling us to learn from and build on the experiences, insights, and practical advice of pathfinders in our field. Dr. Schroeder provides a solid research base to this work, augmented by models, case studies, and reflective practice from many of the leaders in our field who have long understood the importance of framing their faculty development roles as agents of organizational change. Connie Schroeder and her colleagues have charted this new terrain for us, recounting their triumphs as well as their challenges. They offer us a new way of thinking about our field and its future, in the U.S. and internationally. I highly recommend this valuable and thought-provoking new resource for faculty developers and the senior academic administrators with whom they work."

Deborah DeZure, *Assistant Provost for Faculty and Organizational Development, Michigan State University*

"This important volume locates a key player – the faculty development professional – in the distributed leadership needed for institutional change. The authors provide insight into becoming involved in strategic planning, mission statement development, and collaborating with administrators. Schroeder notes the wholesale change in the identity of faculty developers, and identifies key enabling factors that alter faculty developers' role to be more central to institutional direction setting. Comprehensive, practical, inspirational, and timely – a must-have book for anyone in the profession."

Adrianna Kezar, *Associate Professor, Rossier School of Education, and Associate Director, of CHEPA, USC*

COMING IN FROM THE MARGINS

COMING IN FROM
THE MARGINS

Faculty Development's Emerging Organizational
Development Role in Institutional Change

Connie M. Schroeder

WITH CONTRIBUTIONS BY *Phyllis Blumberg,*
Nancy Van Note Chism, Catherine E. Frerichs,
Susan Gano-Phillips, Devorah Lieberman,
Diana G. Pace, and Tamara Rosier

STERLING, VIRGINIA

Published by Stylus Publishing, LLC
22883 Quicksilver Drive
Sterling, Virginia 20166-2102

Library of Congress Cataloging-in-Publication-Data
Schroeder, Connie M., 1957–
  Coming in from the margins : faculty development's
emerging organizational development role in institutional
change / Connie M. Schroeder. – 1st ed.
    p. cm.
  Includes bibliographical references and index.
  ISBN 978-1-57922-362-5 (cloth : alk. paper) –
ISBN 978-1-57922-363-2 (pbk. : alk. paper)
    1. Teachers–In-service training–United States.   2. School
management and organization–United States.
3. Teacher-administrator relationships–United States.
4. Organizational change–United States.   I. Title.
    LB1731.S375 2011
    371.200973–dc22   2010022079

13-digit ISBN: 978-1-57922-362-5 (cloth)
13-digit ISBN: 978-1-57922-363-2 (paper)

Printed in the United States of America

All first editions printed on acid free paper
that meets the American National Standards Institute
Z39-48 Standard.

Bulk Purchases

Quantity discounts are available for use in workshops
and for staff development.
Call 1-800-232-0223

First Edition, 2011

10   9   8   7   6   5   4   3   2   1

DEDICATION AND ACKNOWLEDGMENTS

The 18 case study center directors and their supervisors provided the key evidence that allowed me to begin defining the organizational development role currently emerging among developers. Their visions and models of merging instructional and faculty development with involvement in institutional change initiatives as in particular *organizational developers*—institutional change agents—provided important insight into how this role is enacted. Each of their unique institutional and teaching and learning center contexts helped reassure the reader that variation is possible as an organizational development role comes into greater definition. Their models challenge the existing traditional definitions of this work and bring clarity to working at the institutional level in intentional and effective ways. Thank you for leading the way in making the organizational change role a vivid dimension of this work. I am especially grateful for your sustained commitment to this book during my year delay due to cancer and treatment in the middle of this project. As John Lennon wisely reminded us, *Life is what happens while you're busy making other plans.*

To the directors and colleagues who chose to reveal their identities either through authoring a chapter or narrative, or through interview excerpts, including Leora Baron Nixon, Phyllis Blumberg, Catherine E. Frerichs, Diana Pace, Tamara Rosier, and Susan Gano-Phillips, my deepest thanks and appreciation for hours of dedicated reflection, writing, and editing and in stepping forward to reveal your specific contexts. To the case study participants preferring anonymity, who chose to be unnamed, your words and actions were recorded and shared in numerous places in *Coming in From the Margins* and serve as beacons for change and models for developers. The additional contributing authors, Nancy Van Note Chism and Devorah Lieberman, provided extremely valuable and unique, and not often heard, organizational and administrative leadership perspectives that challenge provosts and deans to consider the deeper shifts needed to enact this change and how they can support this role transformation.

To Leora Baron Nixon, whose passing preceded the writing of her chapter but whose words and ideas within the interview excerpts speak clearly and whose life as a colleague, change agent, president-elect of the Professional and

Organizational Development (POD) Network (2007), and organizational leader speaks for itself—much thanks.

To those who kindly completed the anonymous survey that preceded the in-depth interviews—your collective voice framed the foundational ideas of this book. Your willingness to participate in research helps all of us advance our knowledge and provide the evidence needed to guide and reshape our assumptions and practices.

I was very fortunate to have been granted the funding to take on this research project by the POD Network Grant Committee. My involvement with colleagues in POD has been a constant source of growth, reflection, and development. In particular, Mary Deane Sorcinelli has been a constant role model and source of support and encouragement. Her graciousness is unparalleled and her leadership inspiring.

My thanks to the Stylus Publishing team, foremost to John von Knorring, president and publisher, who approached me with the vision of this becoming a book far before I had imagined it so and whose patience during my illness was exceptional.

My dissertation advisor at the University of Wisconsin–Madison, Carolyn Kelley, shaped my entry into scholarship. Her provocative introduction to organizational change has made all the difference.

My parents, Carl and Lois Schroeder, for their lived and embedded message of "finish what you start," enabled me to press on with passion. Finally, Beverly McKeen, my aunt–friend, who always knew I could do it, whatever it was—thank you.

CONTENTS

PREFACE   *ix*
Connie M. Schroeder

INTRODUCTION   *I*
Connie M. Schroeder

PART ONE: CALLING FACULTY DEVELOPMENT TO REENVISION ITS ROLE

1. FACULTY DEVELOPERS AS INSTITUTIONAL DEVELOPERS
   The Missing Prong of Organizational Development   *17*
   Connie M. Schroeder

2. GETTING TO THE TABLE
   Planning and Developing Institutional Initiatives   *47*
   Nancy Van Note Chism

3. NURTURING INSTITUTIONAL CHANGE
   Collaboration and Leadership Between Upper-Level Administrators and Faculty Developers   *60*
   Devorah Lieberman

PART TWO: EXAMINING THE EVIDENCE OF AN ORGANIZATIONAL DEVELOPMENT ROLE

4. INVESTIGATING INSTITUTIONAL INVOLVEMENT AND CHANGE AGENCY   *77*
   Connie M. Schroeder

5. IDENTIFYING THE FACTORS THAT ENABLE AN ORGANIZATIONAL DEVELOPMENT ROLE   *III*
   Connie M. Schroeder

PART THREE: REPOSITIONING CENTERS AND DIRECTORS ON THE INSTITUTIONAL RADAR SCREEN

6. LEADING FROM THE MIDDLE
   A Faculty Development Center at the Heart of Institutional Change   *143*
   Catherine E. Frerichs, Diana G. Pace, and Tamara Rosier

7. INFORMING AND DIRECTING THE PLANNING OF
   INSTITUTIONAL PRIORITIES AND INITIATIVES   *162*
   Phyllis Blumberg

8. DEVELOPING AND ACTING ON A CENTER VISION   *178*
   Connie M. Schroeder

9. KNOWING AND FACILITATING ORGANIZATIONAL CHANGE
   PROCESSES   *199*
   Connie M. Schroeder

10. OPTIMIZING CENTER STAFFING AND ADVISORY BOARDS TO
    PROMOTE INVOLVEMENT IN INSTITUTIONAL CHANGE   *218*
    Susan Gano-Phillips

11. ALIGNING AND REVISING CENTER MISSION STATEMENTS   *235*
    Connie M. Schroeder

12. EMBEDDING CENTERS IN INSTITUTIONAL STRATEGIC
    PLANNING   *260*
    Connie M. Schroeder

PART FOUR: NEXT STEPS

13. RECENTERING WITHIN THE WEB OF INSTITUTIONAL
    LEADERSHIP   *273*
    Connie M. Schroeder

ABOUT THE AUTHOR AND CONTRIBUTORS   *293*

INDEX   *297*

Connie M. Schroeder

As a "second" career in higher education, my work in faculty development (1999–2010) has included several institutions, the POD Network governing board in which I was actively involved, and other national and international higher education organizations. Very early in my development work, I encountered numerous interpretations of "faculty development work" in the United States and beyond, and a wide range of center missions. Commonly, developers I met and continue to meet are faculty and/or administrative professionals up-to-date on the latest literature, deeply committed to their institutions and to advancing teaching and learning, and engaged in the work of supporting instructors. Everyone is engaged in a wide range of activities and services and passionate about their work.

However, it soon was apparent to me that director position descriptions and center tasks vary enormously between institutions both within and outside of the United States (D'Andrea & Gosling, 2001). In addition, I discovered that this field is often called academic development, academic staff development, or educational development outside of the United States. Given my interest in institutional change, I noticed a large continuum in terms of how involved directors and centers of teaching and learning are at the institutional level, and how much they differ in the importance they place on being positioned visibly within the broader institutional landscape.

Interestingly, some teaching and learning centers (TLCs) are primarily technique-based workshop engines that are hugely productive and serve as a highly valued resource, or in some cases, a barely tolerated draw on resources. Their focus clearly is on instructional development. The *instructional development* role of these centers flourishes and absorbs most of their energy, focus, and resources. The expansion and further entrenchment of active learning pedagogies, distance education and e-learning, and learning outcomes, course and program assessment demanded additional skills and expertise of developers. New variations in center titles came about that emphasize teaching and learning, and center staff positions emerged that newly merged technology, instructional development, assessment, and other assorted responsibilities. For example, some developers hold the title of instructional developer and some specialize in instructional technology. Centers that merge instructional technology development with pedagogical expertise often became specialized as instructional technologists, designers, or consultants. *Faculty development* is still a commonly accepted term, at least in the United States, and these additional areas of expertise continue to maintain significant emphasis on instructional development.

In contrast, I noted other centers and their directors are vibrant actors, wholly embedded in the vital "goings-on" and major institutional initiatives, and are thriving at the core of institutional priorities and strategic plans. Centers such as these continue providing instructional development alongside what is clearly a leadership role in broader issues of teaching and learning. These centers and directors are change agents at a much larger scale, functioning at an organizational level as partners and collaborators as well as instructional developers. They are known institutional leaders involved in curriculum reform, first-year programs, retention plans, broad-scale initiatives, or institutional assessment and accreditation efforts, whereas other centers were more quietly positioned at the fringes of the institution in a well-defined *instructional development* niche. Given the changes needed in higher education, I suspect broad-scale change initiatives will continue to increase, and I see the potential for developers to view and enact a broader role.

As we all did, I witnessed TLCs close while other centers expand their funding and staffing, state-of-the-art technology, and spacious offices, while others extend their reach through the Scholarship of Teaching and Learning (SoTL), assessment, and an extensive array of programs. I noted that when TLCs close, colleagues in this field are deeply shaken, perplexed, and nearly paralyzed with disbelief. Given all that they do and all that needs to be done in higher education, it seems impossible to imagine the rationale that leads to a decision to close a center. Developers may see themselves at the heart of the institution, at an obvious nexus of students, administration, faculty, and staff, but the closing of highly active centers leads one to question how developers and TLCs are perceived and how embedded they are in the core mission and initiatives of their institutions. As I continued to reflect on and observe this field, I casually concluded that centers are more marginalized than they may believe or recognize—marginalized in the sense that they may operate in parallel universes or separate silos, quite apart from the broader institutional priorities. The day-to-day demands on center staffing and the never-ending support needed at the course and individual level can leave a center largely outside of the institutional radar screen with a false sense of importance.

It became obvious to me that faculty development is many things to many institutions, both in the United States and abroad, and prides itself on avoiding a one-size-fits-all model. Initially, I thought the variation in role, function, and mission of directors and centers was due to broad differences in institutional missions, histories, and cultures and that custom-designed roles for developers served the field advantageously. However, I soon began to question the reason for what appeared to be vastly different views of the role of faculty development and TLCs. Do institutional missions or cultures account for all of the variation in how this work is defined or explain the different levels of involvement in broader institutional matters? Was all of this variety evidence of flexibility or a lack of definition as a field, or both, and perhaps an indication that this young field was still evolving? Was lack of a common definition of the field an indication of a void within the field itself— evidence of a disconnection between practice and role definition? Where was this field headed and why? What was going on in this field that I had found as a second career?

It seemed plausible to me that neither this relatively young field nor higher education had articulated a common platform of what faculty development currently is or should be, its common purpose, expertise, or value to institutions, nor had either one articulated a vision for its future. Unfortunately, breadth and variety in this field may have become confused with diversity and inclusion, and further defining the field of developers could be mistaken for a narrowing of the field. Must we be all things to all institutions, and if so, to what cost?

In the summer of 2006, I received a grant from the Professional and Organizational Development (POD) Network in order to investigate the role of directors and centers of teaching and learning in broader institutional initiatives and change. I designed the study, titled "Coming in From the Margins: Redefining Faculty Development's Role Within the Institution," to address questions regarding the current and the future role of developers within institutions facing significant institutional change agendas. I had already investigated a considerable amount of the literature on this field's history (Schroeder, 2002) having migrated to a career in faculty development after 15 years in administration within higher education. With somewhat of an insider's and outsider's lens, I observed, read, and asked a lot of questions as I became acquainted with this field and was able to cast my inquiring glances toward this work with relatively fresh eyes.

My original investigation, *Coming in From the Margins: Redefining Faculty Development's Role Within the Institution*, began the exploration of centers positioned in the center as well as at the margins of institutional missions and change.

References

D'Andrea, V., & Gosling, D. (2001).   Joining the dots: Reconceptualizing educational development. *The Institute for Learning and Teaching in Higher Education and SAGE Publications*, *2(1)*, 64–81. Retrieved October 26, 2009, from http://alh.safepub.com

Schroeder, C. M. (2002). Faculty change agents: Individual and organizational factors that enable or impede faculty involvement in organizational change (Doctoral dissertation, The University of Wisconsin–Madison). *Dissertations & Theses:* A&I, *62*(7), 2361.

INTRODUCTION

Connie M. Schroeder

Multiple levers are exerting pressure on higher education institutions to restructure and change their deeply embedded assumptions and practices regarding teaching and learning. These pressures are keenly felt in the United States and abroad. The world is changing and the landscape of higher education is called upon to change with it. Assessment, learning outcomes and learning-centeredness, technological advances, and changes in student populations have emerged on this landscape, forcing bigger questions about the entire enterprise of learning. Institutions face harsh public criticism and are called to step up to greater accountability, enact reform, and show evidence of advancing learning outcomes at program and institutional levels. In response to the intensity of these current demands and expectations, institutions have launched numerous self-studies, enacted strategic initiatives, and implemented change processes to improve the quality of higher education. Broad-scale change efforts prove challenging in these decentralized organizations that value autonomy and independence and lack experience in collaborative leadership across well-defined academic borders. Many of these change initiatives intersect with matters that directly affect teaching and learning, academic excellence, and the work of academic developers.

Applying an organizational lens to this work led me to wonder how broad-scale changes in teaching and learning are likely to be achieved successfully in higher education. The broad-based, institutional level changes in teaching and learning that are needed and being attempted at institutions require more than an instructional development focus from teaching and learning centers (TLCs). These changes must involve approaches that impact more than one instructor or scholarship of teaching and learning scholar at a time, or attendees of programs or workshops—even though all these efforts to prompt and support change are essential. This nearly exclusive focus on instructional development by TLCs to enact change is largely based on one model of organizational change—by informing and generating new instructional understanding—often at the individual level—enacts only one dimension of this work. Exclusive reliance on individual learning and a grassroots model of organizational change by TLCs is limited and too narrow in scope for the challenges ahead. These challenges require broad-based collaboration among multiple "experts" and shifts in the values, boundaries, and paradigms undergirding the structures and policies that inhibit significant institutional change. As higher education steps up to make broad, institutional level change, TLCs and directors should be prepared to function in partnership, leadership, and collaboration—prepared to impact beyond the workshop, individual faculty, teaching assistant (TA), or department levels. This involvement in institutional level change requires developers to provide a different skill set and areas of expertise beyond instructional development. To be clear, instructional development is not simple; it is clearly complex, but it is simply too narrow as it fails to define the full spectrum of this work and exalts one dimension of this role at the expense of another emerging role dimension.

As higher education increasingly is subject to enormous pressures and expectations to improve and change, the role of TLCs is even more critical. Institutions cannot and should not avoid placing new demands and expectations on teaching and learning centers (TLCs) and developers. However, are developers ready to step up and expand the nature of their work? Given the existing challenges institutions are facing, is maintaining primarily an *instructional development* role the best direction for this field in the decades ahead? Is the institutional role or position of the centers within larger institutional initiatives a critical issue? Has faculty development envisioned or articulated an *organizational development* (OD) role in an effort to help address these broad-scale changes in teaching and learning? What is its *organizational development* role in this context and is it the same type of organizational development originally envisioned when this field began? Why are some TLCs and academic developers existing at the fringes of their institutional radar screens, however unintentional? Can institutions afford to advance initiatives that clearly dovetail with matters of teaching and learning without the directors of the centers seated at the planning table? Some would argue, yes, that the director role and center mission is to serve faculty and improve classroom teaching and learning, exclusively. Some directors advocate that centers "fly below the radar" or maintain a low profile. There is a perceived safety in a certain level of invisibility that is perhaps true, to varying degrees, at each institution. Increasing visibility as a *provider of* resources and services and even expertise at an institutional level inevitably draws greater attention to being a *consumer* of resources. Changing institutional leadership and budget tightening may make this a risk to consider. However, how low centers fly and how low their institutional profile *is* should be a concern if their value to the institutional mission and its strategic priorities is not well articulated or visible.

Emerging Role Change

Fortunately, the evidence gathered supports that a significant change in the role of faculty development is well underway. The growing concern with institutional change is apparent when examining emerging literature, publications, and conference sessions both in "faculty development" and higher education. The traditionally known "faculty development" role, with the current focus on instructional development, is changing and very likely needs to change. However, in a field that values variation, changes within the field can be simply viewed as differences and welcome variation rather than a potential shift at the very core of its role definition. How must this field evolve once again in order to meet the current needs of its time? How is faculty development currently situated in terms of the larger, institutional landscape? A broader institutional role and level of involvement in institutional change is being discussed with greater interest among colleagues well beyond the United States. How extensive or isolated might this broader role shift be within the field? The potential impact of this role change is too significant and far reaching to develop unguided over time, or left to the hope that it occurs while the leaders and professionals in this field are passive spectators. If the change agendas in higher education are to be successful, the vision and partnerships required should prompt all institutional leaders to ask who is to be situated at the table or tables in planning change and how to engage all units as change agents.

For those readers who are institutional leaders responsible for overseeing centers, and for some center directors, an organizational and institutional leadership role for TLCs may be familiar and already being enacted. This book reinforces those existing efforts with evidence and provides a map for further embedding and sustaining the broader role of TLCs in the institutional change agenda. For readers who have yet to explore the institutional leadership role of centers, or who may feel marginalized from larger-scale initiatives but want to test the waters of institutional change, this book offers a much-needed map of the streams and currents the directors can expect to swim in and against in assuming a broader role. Perhaps those waters will become more transparent and less murky or less fraught with "sea monsters"—hidden creatures of resistance brought about by change. The centers suffering from institutional disconnect should pay close attention. For those becoming impatient with the role of the centers and directors in working at change—through one instructor or workshop at a time—this discussion may prompt a significant shift in revisioning this work within the broader priorities of the institution. Perhaps the overall appeal may be that this book confronts a widespread and perhaps gnawing uneasiness within the field—what is our role *now*?

The role that the developers *could* play and are already playing in advancing institutional change *through* institutional level involvement is overdue in being defined, studied, and enacted. It is much too important to guess at or gather opinion of anecdotally. In fact, there is much confusion regarding what is even meant by an *organizational development* role. Due to the pressures and demands in higher education around broader issues in teaching and learning, the implications for proactively defining and preparing for this role are far reaching for this field, students, our institutions, and higher education. However, despite the potential impact of defining and adopting what could be an emerging and significant *organizational role*, this aspect of the field has been less developed. Why?

Coming in From the Margins Study

My research focus since 1999 broadly has been organizational change and, more specifically, institutional change in teaching and learning at the individual, departmental, and organizational level. The lack of evidence, and absence of models to inform and further advance a broader role and involvement of centers in institutional change shaped my efforts to seek funding to investigate current activity in this field more closely. I had done considerable research on the historical development of faculty development and faculty as change agents at the department level for my dissertation 10 years ago. Intrigued by those findings and the considerable amount of articles I had massed on this field, I wanted to delve further into the relationship between development work and broader, organizational level change.

As a starting point, I chose to research the way directors and supervisors of TLCs view their role and identify what factors enable or constrain and their involvement in broader institutional change.

Analysis of center director survey results and in-depth interviews with directors and their supervisors confirmed that the majority of the faculty development directors *are* spending a *substantial* part of their time involved in or with institutional initiatives as coleaders, collaborators, and change agents at the institutional level far more than I had anticipated. The directors also maintained their familiar and established role as *instructional develop-ers*. Additionally, center-, director-, and institution-based factors from both quantitative and qualitative data provided extensive insight into how this role develops and is sustained by the centers and directors in centers and institu-tions of all sizes and types. The design of the study, survey participants, and case study selection are outlined in-depth in chapter 4.

This book makes explicit that an *organizational role* through intentional involvement in broader institutional initiatives around teaching and learning does not involve eliminating the current role of *instructional development*. It is not an either/or proposition or argument. It is a transformation. Balancing existing responsibilities with an even broader role is challenging, as evidenced by the case study directors whose chapters follow. In part 3, case study authors identify strategies for forging partnerships and collaborations in institutional change, while also continuing to direct the center, and in some cases, plan and deliver program and workshops as well as nurture the fledgling new instructor or teaching assistant (TA). Directors are currently weaving the role of change agent into their daily work, are already being seated on multiple committees, and serving as coleaders who work collaboratively with multiple units on broad-scale initiatives to improve the institution and student learning.

This is not surprising. Developers uniquely move between and among many levels and units within an institution and have a critical perspective to provide. Who knows the institutional culture, the national and international landscape of teaching and learning, and the scores of instructors, faculty and non-faculty alike, and can cross the disciplinary boundaries with current knowledge of instructors' concerns and challenges with student learning? At which institutional table is this knowledge and expertise critical?

As a former associate dean at a small liberal arts college, I also wore the director hat for two large units and reported to a dean who also wore the hat of vice-president. It was not unheard of for the president, vice president and me, to sit down, discuss, and map out the general direction of a new initia-tive. Smaller institutions have less hierarchy; administrators and faculty wear multiple hats; and getting to the table isn't a particularly long reach, metaphor-ically or literally. Having worked at three research institutions and two smaller institutions, I recognize that being at the table at large institutions may en-tail sitting down at a lesser size table set for a select few administrators after the initiative has been preliminarily outlined higher up in the organizational hierarchy. However, this second tier of institutional change planning puts flesh on the skeletal frame of an initiative and is an opportune table at which developers should be seated. While planning and forming an institutional initiative, especially linked to teaching and learning, the information gathered, theoretical frameworks accessed, and national or institutional knowledge of teaching and learning collected can often benefit from the developer's theoretical, institution-wide, and practical expertise. This *organizational role* is widely practiced in this field and is quite distinct from an instructional development role. The major difference being, the developer sits at the table, collaboratively planning the initiative, rather than performs the traditional role of programing and consulting *about* these issues at the individual or even department level. Is this what we mean collectively by an organizational development role? Are we talking about something more than attending a few more meetings at the expense of the work of the center?

Beyond Programing and Instructional Development

From the survey and case study data that led to this book, I was able to distinguish this emerging developers' role from the traditional role performed over the past several decades in most TLCs. Traditionally, an OD role has been described vaguely and in terms of generating institutional impact largely through consultations with individual instructors, center programs and workshops, and resource materials. The ultimate impact on the individual instructors who change their practices is organizational change when a critical mass or departmental shift comes about—of one sort. However, this take on the developer's role in organizational change is still embedded within an instructional development mindset or niche and focuses at an individual level of change. In this diffused approach to organizational development, the broader institution may or may not be impacted as reliance on one workshop or instructor consultation at a time. I am struck by this common but limited interpretation of an *organizational role* as simply that of programing, for example, on broad issues such as learner-centeredness, diversity and inclusive classrooms, or hosting campus wide conferences on engagement that indeed, ultimately may have organizational value and impact. The convergence of issues right now calls for redefining an organizational development role beyond these efforts.

Merging Past, Present, and Future Roles

The core argument of this book—that a necessary and significant role change is underway in faculty development—is a call for centers to *merge* the traditional responsibilities and services of the past several decades with a leadership role as organizational developers. This field grew and evolved over decades from that of divvying out individual faculty grants to the establishment of TLCs serving multiple constituents that became hubs of resources, workshops, consultations, and expertise in pedagogy and instructional technology. Faculty developers demonstrated flexibility and adaptive willingness to meet the institution's instructional needs of the time as the learning paradigm prompted significant shifts in higher education, and these qualities within the field again are needed. TLCs cannot expect to do business as usual from the framework of the decades past. Most certainly, faculty development cannot afford to bask in its comfortable niche where it is viewed as primarily existing to help with teaching strategies and techniques. Academic developers cannot get stuck with the misperception that their role is merely to serve, program, and provide resources apart from the critical initiatives the institution has outlined. To be sure, the way this role is seen today will continue to evolve as new challenges confront higher education and teaching and learning. It would be a mistake to view an *instructional development* role as an exclusive definition or final destination of this field.

Based on the evidence collected, current involvement in institutional initiatives entails far more than programing on institutional priorities. Although these efforts impact the organization and are surely essential, they are not the level of institutional involvement made transparent by this book. The centers, directors, and staff of TLCs need to continue to do these things, but not at the expense of or tradeoff from *also* being intentionally involved at the planning table for the broad and changing strategic initiatives at each of our institutions. Directors interviewed for this study revealed an intentional and well-integrated role that was clearly more than a casual notion, individual agenda, or whim on their part or that of a few administrators. However, as a field, collective understanding of this role in institutional change remains rather disjointed and fragmented. Change often happens this way, at the edges of tradition and status quo, hardly noticed at first as a departure from the familiar and lacking in formal description and definition. But for this role to remain undefined and invisible at the field and institutional level out of fear and resistance to change or lack of collective articulation within the field is not acceptable or forward thinking. Other than tradition, there is no reason to be indifferent to and unaligned with the institutional change agenda or to be excluded from helping shape this agenda. Granted, conflicts of interest can arise when faculty governance and strong voices clash with institutional directives or initiatives—TLCs already encounter these conflicts around assessment, pedagogy, and inclusive classrooms. The inherent difficulties in navigating or resolving the implications of this role hardly diminish its importance.

Academic developers have often enabled faculty and instructors to step up to change. This field must not be too busy to step up to its own change and fail to redefine its role for the decades ahead. It must take the time to explore the fear of a collective redefinition of its role and misguided assumptions that doing so will somehow clash with a strongly guarded value of welcoming all backgrounds and perspectives to serve this field is at the expense of clearly outlining common roles and unique expertise, skills, and knowledge. Failing collectively to define and outline the dimensions and expertise of this role puts the centers at risk of not only marginalization but dissolution. Change requires some stepping out into the ambiguity of the unknown, as knowingly as one can and with evidence and models whenever possible. It means encountering the resulting stress as constraints are tested with new definitions and practices. Similarly, professors would never have become disciplinary researchers if changes in the role of faculty had not been accepted and integrated into traditional teaching expectations and roles. The role of students as active, self-directed learners versus passive recipients is changing because of questioning existing paradigms and assumptions, suspending disbelief, looking for evidence, and naming the shortcomings of current practice and the status quo. Roles change as needed or they risk becoming less useful or even extinct. Failing to embrace this discussion of the current and future role of the centers of teaching and learning may mean fewer centers, or centers not seated at the table where institutional change must and will be undertaken.

Making Organizational Development Explicit

Being held accountable and relied upon for an institutional leadership role is a significant shift, carries enormous responsibility, and likely will be controversial for this field. Some would rather leave this role unarticulated and left up to each director, institution or center, or dismiss it as something "more" on an already full plate. For example, in a later chapter, one case study center director admitted that she saw the center and her role as a change agent but more of an "undercover change agent." She wanted to remain in the closet as a change agent, as far as the faculty were concerned, but also maintain the dual role of planning and enacting broader institutional change initiatives. Is this dual role possible undercover? By not embedding explicit institutional involvement expectations into the TLC mission or director position descriptions, this leadership role instead is left up to individual directors' personalities or interests, and is vulnerable to changing leadership agendas. At the institutional level, TLCs may then appear optional and often unappreciated and undervalued. I propose that it is the responsibility of academic development collectively to bring its much needed unique expertise and skills as *organizational developers* into greater clarity, to reinforce their unique value at the institutional planning table, and that it is imperative to do so now.

This book is intended to prompt a wider discussion within faculty, and academic development, and provide a road map for TLCs to use in merging an *organizational role* with their existing roles and center missions. Many centers and directors have moved into this role to varying degrees and with great success. The role transformation has already begun out of necessity. Nowhere in the pages of this book is there a call to stop doing what is needed and successful at the individual, programatic, even department level within the instructional development role. It is a call to go beyond in further defining this role.

Contents of the Book

As a book of multiple voices, *Coming in From the Margins* arranges this discussion into four parts. The interviews, case studies, surveys, and accounts set out the parameters of this new role and point out the speed bumps, potholes, and land mines likely to be encountered. Principles to guide the reader's purposeful and informed transition to leadership and migration from the fringes of institutional radar screens are shared by the authors of each chapter.

Part one, "Calling Faculty Development to Reenvision Its Role," presents key leaders and their visions for this organizational and institutional leadership role. In chapter 1, "Faculty Developers as Institutional Developers: The Missing Prong of Organizational Development," I frame this role change within the historical origins of the field and the context of multiple changes that are exerting pressure on the higher education. In chapters 2 and 3, "Getting to the Table: Planning and Developing Institutional Initiatives," by Nancy Van Note Chism, and "Nurturing Institutional Change: Collaboration and Leadership Between Upper-Level Administrators and Faculty Developers," by Devorah Lieberman, these established leaders and authors in this field develop the book's argument from the perspective of an upper-level administrator and faculty member. Based on their recent experience as directors of centers and in light of their current administrative leadership roles in academic affairs, they provide alternative structural and positional paths that advance a broader role for directors and centers. Their message calls provosts, deans, chairs, faculty, and TLCs to consider the implications and benefits of this role change. Official and structural recognition of this role are essential to move centers from marginalization to active participation in solving complex issues. The administrative power of these leaders entails being a conduit to the core of the institutional priorities and directly impacting center position descriptions, center missions, staffing, hiring, and the credibility of directors.

In part two, "Examining the Evidence of an Organizational Development Role," I present the underlying study design and its qualitative and quantitative results in detail. Beginning with chapter 4, "Investigating Institutional Involvement and Change Agency," I review the primary results from the survey along with the results of the statistical analysis of multiple factors. Significant and selected institution-, director-, and center-based factors are reported. Chapter 5, "Identifying the Factors that Enable an Organizational Development Role," I provide the qualitative results of 18 in-depth interviews and an overview of additional primary factors and conditions that enable or impede involvement in institutional change from the perspective of both the center directors and their supervisors. I compare these qualitative results with the survey results, underscoring the value of a combined study design. Highly consistent across cases, centers, and institutional type, the final results provide a more detailed understanding of how centers move from the fringes while maintaining their instructional development role. The primary factors that emerged were subsequently identified as institution-, center-, or director-based factors and serve as the framework for part three.

Part three, "Repositioning Centers and Directors on the Institutional Radar Screen: Research-based Strategies and Challenges," is comprised of seven chapters, followed by a concluding chapter. The contributing case study authors in this section focus on contextualizing multiple primary director-based, institution-based, or center-based factors that enabled their role in institutional change. From their experiences and insights they provide practical recommendations and strategies for the reader to apply to their institutional and center context.

Chapters 6 through 9 focus on the primary *director-based* strategies, including center leadership, initiating and collaborating in change initiatives, committee and institutional strategic planning involvement, developing and enacting the director's center vision, and director knowledge of organizational change processes. Numerous examples, challenges, and recommended strategies accompany each chapter. Chapter 6, "Leading from the Middle: A Faculty Development Center at the Heart of Institutional Change" by Catherine E. Frerichs, Diana G. Pace, and Tamara Rosier, provides careful accounts of this leadership role and the expertise and skills the authors brought to bear in initiating and collaborating broad-scale liberal education initiative. Phyllis Blumberg in chapter 7, "Informing and Directing the Planning of

Institutional Priorities and Initiatives," provides numerous examples of coming to sit at the many types of tables of initiative planning. I close this section with accounts of directors' use of organizational change processes and models in order to advance institutional change from platforms other than planning programs. The case study authors offer accounts of their role at the institutional level and each chapter offers specific recommendations for juggling these multiple and expanding responsibilities. The success and struggles they experienced illustrate their ability to innovate and develop new strategies. Their thoughtful choices intentionally aligned their work with the broader institutional mission and priorities to impact teaching and learning in ways currently limited by the traditional instructional development role.

Chapters 10 through 12 make explicit the *center-based* factors that enable this role with exemplary models within institutional contexts. Chapter 10, "Optimizing Center Staffing and Advisory Boards to Promote Involvement in Institutional Change," by case study author Susan Gano-Phillips, focuses on factors that all directors mentioned as key challenges to enacting this role. It would be naïve to imagine adding this leadership role to the already demanding workload of directors without considering the implications. How can the developers possibly find more time to attend meetings where deliberations may at times seem abstract and politicized while actual individuals and concrete programs are waiting for them? In the remaining chapters in this section, "Aligning and Revising Center Mission Statements" and "Embedding Centers in Institutional Strategic Planning" (chapters 11 and 12), I discuss the data surrounding revising center mission statements and embedding centers in institutional strategic planning.

Throughout this volume, I strived to extract the factors that helped the directors to reinvent their role by using survey data, case narratives, and interview excerpts in order to provide diverse maps of how to broaden the existing instructional development niche and transform it into a dynamic alchemy of the old and new. Convincingly, the data and voice of the directors illustrate how this work can be done differently, intentionally, and with broader impact. The directors continually reinforced the necessity of clearly and intentionally reenvisioning this role collaboratively with those above the director level in order to garner support at all times. Their recommendations provide senior administrators, faculty and staff, and academic developers with a foundation to reimagine existing models of this work *alongside* the existing roles currently enacted at TLCs. Their actions demonstrate how directors have initiated and successfully advanced collaborations on institutional priorities that cannot escape converging around teaching and learning at the broadest level.

Although this *organizational role* is clearly emerging, this field as a whole seems hardly conscious *collectively* that its role is changing. It appears to have one foot in and one foot outside the threshold between fully stepping forward and maximizing the potential of an institutional leadership role and remaining comfortably in a niche it has successfully carved. Part of silently assuming a broader role without fanfare may be due partly to the "undercover" fear mentioned earlier, but perhaps as well, to the generous and willing nature of the professionals that perform this work. A deep commitment to student learning fuels the developer's efforts, and center directors willingly go to meetings, expand their calendars, and squeeze in additional demands not recognizing they are performing a significant role change. As one center director commented at a conference session geared toward preparing developers for this role, "I didn't know *that* was what I was doing. I didn't know *that* was organizational development." There is a price to be paid as a field for an organizational development role to remain unnoticed and indistinguishable from the instructional work traditionally done. My goal is to prompt informed conversation, exploration, and initiation of purposeful change among administrators, faculty and staff, and academic developers across the field of educational/faculty development. It *is* about helping this field and institutions articulate the timely questions that will guide this transformation.

A secondary purpose is to support those already engaged as change agents by making this role better defined and more transparent. By publishing the results of the study in this book—of both the survey and in-depth interviews—I hope to convince the reader that this work is inextricably linked to the changing context of higher education. "Faculty development" as we have known it must step up to these changes and consider seriously the implications of more visibly and collectively embracing this dimension of its role.

This book challenges not only the developers and directors, but also the senior administrators, as well, to reenvision, integrate, or meld the multiple and levels of functions for TLCs. My intent is to allow the evidence to convince institutional stakeholders—faculty and instructional staff, administrators, and staff of TLCs—that the *organizational role* of change agent and leader is already in progress among them and provide models for enacting this role change successfully. This book and the collective experience of its contributors, trace and expand upon earlier threads of this conversation in the literature about the future of this field. It is a conversation that has been emerging with perhaps more energy and focus abroad than in the United States, and the time has come to bring these threads into a coherent whole that will prompt more serious and widespread discussion as a field that has successfully navigated change in the past. It must continue to merge what is comfortable and known with the less familiar roles made evident by the changing needs of higher education.

When a TLC is busy and in demand, it is hard to believe that it may be, despite all the activity and palpable array of daily outcomes, institutionally marginalized. The actual and increasing potential of marginalization and center closings may help motivate this field to recognize the danger of complacency or remaining stuck in an old paradigm that exclusively defines itself as instructional development or supportive service. Of great concern to me are the marginalized centers, who have kept themselves distant from broader institutional change. In doing so, they have limited the scale of their impact on teaching and learning, and most importantly, on the students who need to learn and be prepared to function as well-educated, self-directed, and life-long learners. The message of this book is to provide a clearer vision, based on evidence and models, of faculty development's *organizational* role in achieving the broad-level institutional changes in teaching and learning that must take place.

If faculty development is truly at a threshold of role change, the first step toward defining this role is to convince directors, administrators, and institutions that this shift in role definition is essential, integral, achievable, and in the best interests of our institutions and students. It is not to advocate one model or route to achieve a balance between traditional responsibilities and this new role. I want the readers to consider the practical implications of this role for center missions, staffing, structures, institutional alignment, and budgets, and to translate new expectations of director skills and expertise, collaborations and services, committee involvement into workload, titles, and future professional development.

In the decades to come, this role will certainly entail an assortment of better-defined tasks and functions for a variety of institutional missions and cultures. This role transformation is one more step in the evolution of this field. The leaders of this field need to thoughtfully ask, "Given that this role change is occurring, what changes must we make to proactively prepare and implement this role effectively?" What will be missed if we do not develop a plan to actualize this organizational development role and integrate this level of involvement across this field?" Underlying this question is the more fundamental one: why do this work at all? Is the *end* faculty development or, is it *the means* to impact student learning and teaching at all levels— through faculty, instructional, and *organizational development*? If so, then centers will have to come in from their institutional margins to participate in a wider movement to define and purposefully integrate faculty development's emerging role in institutional change—even at the risk of becoming "change agents" no longer undercover.

PART ONE

CALLING FACULTY DEVELOPMENT TO REENVISION ITS ROLE

FACULTY DEVELOPERS AS INSTITUTIONAL DEVELOPERS

The Missing Prong of Organizational Development

Connie M. Schroeder

aculty development is poised at the threshold of redefining its role,
if not advancing well into the foyer to embrace involvement at an
organizational level within our institutions. This may be one of this
field's best-kept secrets, but as the data presented in this book indicates, a great
number of center directors are already involved in some of the highest levels
of institutional and strategic planning. Involvement in institutional change is
redefining the organizational development (OD) role left undeveloped since
the beginning of this field. Based on the results of the study in which this
book is based, many directors of teaching and learning centers (TLCs) have
successfully redefined their role to encompass significant OD in their daily
work positioning them at the core of the institution's strategic priorities. On
the other hand, some centers have closed, others have been absorbed into
technology units or assessment, and some have maintained little alignment
with institutional initiatives. Off of the institutional radar screen, as I have
termed them, are marginalized institutionally in terms of being at the table
for planning broad institutional initiatives. In between these centers, a large
number of TLCs are fully tapped and well liked, yet struggle to be valued, are
nervous when budgets are cut, and find themselves asking, "Is that all there
is?" As a field that is striving to be organizationally relevant, the field of faculty
or educational development needs to come to some common understanding
of its role in OD within the institutional context rather than just informally
talk about it, or casually hope for better days, more recognition, more space,
and bigger budgets. In order to do so, a look back at the intersection between

faculty development, organizational development, and significant changes in higher education proves insightful.

Historically, as well as within business and corporate sectors, OD encompasses a set of skills and strategies subsumed under the broader discipline of organizational studies. Does the current organizational role already being performed by the majority of center directors reflect a formal organizational development set of practices? The terms OD, organizational change, improvement, and transformation have been transplanted into higher education and this field without clearly defining these terms and the roles that may enact these practices. Developing a shared language around these terms would begin to decrease the casual use of these concepts and resulting confusion among developers.

This chapter defines these terms both within and outside of faculty development in order to create a common framework for positioning developers' OD role within institutional change processes and to create common language for later discussion. However, this chapter is not an attempt to create an OD primer. An adequate supply of resources for this purpose already exists. The historical summary traces significant changes in the teaching paradigm that influenced tremendous growth and change in faculty development, the evolution of faculty development, and the emergence of organizational development as a field overlapping one another in time. The resulting interesting and thought-provoking examination of the values and practices inherent in development work today as well as the ambiguity and resistance surrounding an organizational development role will make evident the growth of OD as a field at a time when faculty development was also gathering momentum and was clearly influenced by the emergence of that field of study. The retracing of faculty development's history as a field prompts the reader to raise critical questions about the current definitions and assumptions of an OD role.

Organizational Development Role Undefined

Perhaps one of the earliest visions of faculty development as a field had outlined a three-pronged framework that included *individual, instructional*, and *organizational development* (Gaff, 1975). Thirty-five years later, "faculty development" means many different things within the field. The least familiar and developed "prong" has been that of OD (Nelsen & Siegel, 1980). Even this term has multiple interpretations and formally refers to a large scope of literature and practices within the organizational behavior studies field. This book will map out a specific definition of organizational development tailored to the current role of TLCs and center directors involved in broader institutional planning and change. This is a significant departure from commonly known formal OD techniques and practiced today in human resource units.

Although there has been occasional discussion of an OD role for developers in the United States, development colleagues in the United Kingdom, Australia, Canada, and South Africa (Campbell, Schwier, & Kenny, 2009; Collette & Davidson, 1997) have been engaged in more conversations and formal studies around an OD role than their counterparts in the United States (Eggins & MacDonald, 2003; Fraser, 2001; Gosling, 2001). Nevertheless, widescale definition and discussion of this role has been slow in coming. Bath and Smith (2004) remark, "the question regarding how academic developers fit in the world of academia still continues to dangle from the edges of our conceptions of this profession" (p. 9). Part of the difficulty in defining and widely embracing this role shift is due to the lack of scholarly research into the development and implementation of this role. This field lacks research-based evidence to guide a new or seasoned center director who recognizes the potential leadership role they could play at an institutional level. As a result, some center directors have not yet recognized the value of providing their expertise to help inform the institutional initiatives that focus broadly on academic excellence and teaching and learning. Other directors may be unaware of their colleagues' involvement at this level and may even reject the possibility. Others, admittedly, have not acquired the skill sets for enacting a broader, institutional leadership role. One seriously might ask, "Do we need to be doing the organizational development missing 'third prong'?"

Until recently, the strategy of many directors for achieving institution-wide impact or OD has been to provide programs and resources that *support* key institutional initiatives. Rather than assume the role of contributor, leader, planner, or initiator of institutional change initiatives, developers have relied on "attendees" of programs and learning-centered instructors who "get it" to spread adoption of innovative instructional concepts and pedagogical techniques to colleagues, departments, and schools and thereby, contribute to organizational change. Asked if they are involved in institutional or organizational change, most directors would answer "yes," and provide examples of programs aligned with institutional priorities as evidence of their institution-wide impact. Many might make the argument that everything they do is part of changing the organization, improving it, and developing it—*ultimately.*

One of the problems with fitting everything developers do under the OD umbrella is that these efforts become indistinguishable from instructional development. The need for acquisition of new skills or expertise to do institutional level OD is no longer obvious if the work is perceived as "already being done" in daily programing or individual-based consulting tasks. New and seasoned developers end up unprepared for institutional involvement and a leadership role. The field as a whole is portrayed as an inconsistently skilled hodge-podge of hard-working professionals performing a wide mixture of behind-the-scenes tasks, surely anyone can do *that* job.

This book defines and explores an evidence-based portrait of what this organizational development role entails in the unique context of higher education. Several threads of historical development have impinged upon the way faculty development was defined and is currently perceived and practiced. The following discussion will attempt to untangle the entwined developmental threads of changes in higher education, the emergence of OD as a discipline, and the founding of faculty development and TLCs.

Changes in Higher Education

The changing landscape of higher education over the past 40 years has shaped how the definitions and dimensions of the developers' role have evolved. As a result, and rightly so, the field of faculty development has transformed itself and experienced tremendous expansion from its early role and beginnings (see Figure 1.1). It has changed and is still changing. Although newcomers to this field may imagine that "it has always been this way," in truth, this is a relatively young field that has undergone waves of change within its short evolution and expansion. This field has not always been defined by or preoccupied with instruction, pedagogy, and technology. Those who have long served in this field will admit that faculty development has been evolving and shifting continuously over the past half a century and is currently far different in scope and mission than the role performed by the early faculty developers in the United States and at the earliest centers of teaching and learning. Had this field resisted changing its role over the past decades, it would not have expanded into multiple center formats as the majority of institutions in the United States and abroad. Centers of teaching and learning might not even be around today if this field had not responded to changes in higher education by shifting its role primarily from providing faculty professional development through sabbaticals, travel, and grant opportunities to focusing on learning, instructional development, and technology. Without being responsive to the changes in higher education, academic developers would not be doing the things they currently are doing. The field must continue to evolve and change along with the pressures and demands placed upon it by higher education.

As institutions of higher learning face multiple new as well as perennial challenges that converge around the most common point of impact—student learning—they must collaborate and draw on expertise across the silos and barriers that have hampered effective resolution of these issues. Integrating an OD and institutional leadership dimension into the role of center directors can be better understood first by examining the changing context of higher education over the past several decades and how faculty development evolved alongside these changes. This brief recap of the major milestones in higher education and the establishment of and changes in the field of faculty development alongside the growth of OD as a field of study, sets the stage for understanding the lack of attention to OD that has plagued this field. Retracing the emergence of these two fields in the context of national and higher education events makes evident how faculty and OD were knit together historically as both fields developed and grew.

Where is Faculty Development and How Did it Get Here?

Establishment of Faculty Development

Significant increases in federal funding and the substantial growth of faculty during the 1960s resulted in efforts by academic deans and department chairs to support the expanding research efforts of the faculty. Grants and opportunities for sabbaticals, release time, and travel initiated ongoing focus on providing individual faculty with resources and became understood as *faculty development* (Brown, 1992; Eble & McKeachie, 1985; Fletcher & Patrick, 1998). As far back as 1810, the beginning of the first sabbatical leave at Harvard, faculty development referred to support for individual faculty efforts in scholarship and continued as the definition until well into the 1960s (Eble & McKeachie, 1985). The first TLC founded in the country was the Center for Research on Learning and Teaching (CRLT) at the University of Michigan in 1962 (Tiberius, 2002). Meanwhile, another field was emerging that would soon intersect the evolution of faculty development as a field.

Organizational Development Field Emerges

Well before TLCs appeared in the United States, organizational studies had already established a field of inquiry into how organizations work. Organizational studies entail multidisciplinary inquiry that has evolved to include organizational behavior, organizational theory, and organizational change. Under these broader categories of research, the discipline of organizational development has merged with a particular focus on how organizational processes work and improve. Organizational development became more widely applied in the 1950s after the death of its founding father, Kurt Lewin, in 1947. Core concepts, such as group dynamics and action research, were advancing (Gallos & Schein, 2006) and continued to expand in the 1960s and early 1970s (Bradford & Burke, 2005, p. 14). For example, Karl Weick (1976) focused organizational research on organizational culture, further contributing significantly to the OD field.

OD is defined as "an effort, (1) planned, (2) organization-wide, and, (3) managed from the top, (4) to increase organization effectiveness and health through (5) planned interventions in the 'organization's processes,' using behavioral-science knowledge" (Beckhard, 1969, p. 3). According to Bennis (1969), organizational development works at the level of beliefs, attitudes, values, and structures (p. 12) but shares the larger umbrella of planned change models with strategic planning and other scientific management tools, including restructuring and reengineering (Kezar, 2001). OD work is complex, largely group- or team-based versus focused on individual learning, a long-term effort, and will entail organizational reflection, system improvement, planning, and self-analysis (Beckhard, 1969).

Gallos and Schein (2006) further explain that the organization's improvement often entails the "assistance of a change agent or catalyst." Growth in OD research continued into the 1980s when organizational change became a major focus of inquiry. Several disciplines, including anthropology, psychology, and sociology contributed a broad base of research to this field. As one dimension of organizational behavior, organizational change intersects with numerous streams of research, including organizational culture, roles, structures, leadership, and management processes. OD, then, resides within the larger framework of investigation of organizational change processes and is associated with organizational improvement versus transformation (Cameron & Quinn, 1983; Kezar, 2001, p. 16).

The emergence of OD alongside the expansion of TLCs and faculty development as a field yields interesting implications for defining the role of faculty development today.

Faculty Development Intersects With Organizational Development: 1960s and 1970s

In the 1960s, teaching centers numbered between 40–50 nationwide (Graf, Albright, & Wheeler, 1992). As the earlier flow of federal funding dried up, record enrollments of the 1960s declined, and economic factors in the 1970s began to limit the career mobility of tenured faculty. The need for faculty renewal and teaching development became of greater interest during the 1970s and opened a window of opportunity for this field to flourish (Fletcher & Patrick, 1998). The now familiar and well-entrenched term *faculty development* persisted as faculty development offices, directors of faculty development, and faculty development programs were established (Schroeder, 2001, 2002). By the early 1970s, 60% of institutions surveyed had centers or teaching support units (Centre, 1976). *Faculty development* became the broadly recognized umbrella term for work with faculty and their teaching role. The earliest models of this work (Bergquist & Phillips, 1975; Gaff, 1975; Gaff & Simpson, 1994) served to bring about a paradigm shift that would broaden the definition of faculty development work to a "multifaceted view" (Sorcinelli, Austin, Eddy, & Beach, 2006, p. 11).

Having a head start on faculty development centers, the field of organizational studies continued to expand, broadening and deepening its research. Focus on organizational change and OD was significant in the 1980s while faculty development continued experiencing important growth. For example, professional organizations serving the growing field of the faculty development emerged out of the 1970s and 1980s and helped solidify this faculty and educational development internationally and its role in higher education, including the Professional and Organizational Development Network (POD) in 1974; National Council for Staff, Programs, and Organizational Development (NCSPOD) in 1977; and the Society for Teaching and Learning in Higher Education (STLHE) in 1981 (Sorcinelli et al., 2006).

Not coincidentally, during the expanding field of organizational studies and its research field of OD, faculty development in the United States formulated a professional network that included *organizational development* as two of its key words in the naming of its new organization (POD). Given the tremendous growth in organizational studies and organizational development, it is not surprising that the term OD strongly infiltrated the vision of this field, the language used within the field, and how it perceived its role. The nurturing, behind-the-scenes, and service elements of this field are hallmarks of the work being done and still temper the work of instructional development in positive ways. The vision of developers as the interventionists in organizational processes is reflected in the current language of POD's online mission statement in which POD identifies one of its three purposes as "seeking to inform and persuade educational leaders of the value of faculty, instructional, and organizational development in institutions of higher education" ("What Is Organizational Development?" 2007).

The language of OD has influenced and mingled with the vision of professional development broadly and faculty development specifically as centers became more widely established at universities and colleges. For example, the POD website defines its understanding of OD:

> Organizational Development provides a third perspective on maximizing institutional effectiveness. The focus of these *programs* [italics inserted] is **the organizational structure of the institution and its subcomponents**. The philosophy is that if one can build an organizational structure which will

be efficient and effective in supporting the faculty and students, the teaching/learning process will naturally thrive. One activity such *programs* [italics inserted] offer is administrative development for department chairs, deans, and other decision-makers. The reasoning is that these are the individuals who will be making the policies which affect how courses are taught, how faculty are hired and promoted, how the students are admitted and graduated. If those policies allow for growth and flexibility while maintaining standards, the amount of learning, which occurs, will increase. . . . Other activities include helping subunits understand how curricular decisions are made, how courses are staffed, and other organizational matters. . . . Still other *programs* [italics inserted] deal with personnel issues, involving faculty. How are the faculty evaluated and rewarded? How are they prepared for changes in the institution, including their own retirement? Where do the faculty fit into the overall governance structure of the institution? . . . Thus, it can be seen that these *programs* [italics inserted] look at interactions within the institution and how they affect the functioning of the individual as well as the institution. Then they seek ways of making those interactions more humane and more effective. ("What Is Organizational Development?" 2007)

Embedded in this statement are numerous references to influencing policies, structures, processes, personnel issues, and interactions—all of which reflect the language and concepts of the expanding field of OD at that particular point in time. This early coupling with concepts of OD as part of faculty development clearly focused on the building and improvement of the institution's organizational structure and its processes. However, the frequent emphasis on *programs* as the means to impact the broader organization limited the vision of an OD role within faculty development. As an outgrowth of the 1970s and 1980s and a unique intersection in time between OD and faculty development, the initial vision of a particular type of OD role has been all but lost to the next decades of developers. One might wonder, if founded today, would a professional organization such as POD or other international educational development organizations include OD in its very name or even development? Do developers today have this historical insight and do they embrace the OD practices emphasized by this field at a time when the discipline of OD was first becoming entrenched and widely practiced? Is that type of OD role needed today, or is there another way to interpret organizational development within this field?

Despite the early alignment with OD concepts and language, a formal knowledge of OD practices, interventions, and strategies did not become the common knowledge and skill base of developers. Why is that? How did the OD thread become lost or pushed back into the shadows, and what kind of

OD is practiced or needed today? Formal integration of OD practices may very well have become central or at least a major third dimension of this work but for the events and new directions occurring in higher education and significant human resource development in the 1960s that redirected this work.

Several changes in organizations and higher education help explain the "missing 'O' in POD" (Gillespie, Lee, & Tiberius, 2006). Over time, some OD processes through professional development became positioned within human resource development. Interestingly, according to Bradford and Burke (2005), the field of OD is currently being questioned by its own founders in terms of its relevance to organizational change. These changes point toward a thoughtful reconsideration of what OD means to this field at this juncture in higher education. Few developers today would know the actual interventions and strategies that define the field of OD within organizational studies and behavior. Instead, the OD dimension of the developer's role has become vaguely associated with instructional development programing and efforts that ultimately may improve the culture of the institution rather than reflect the linear, rational planning models under which it is best associated (Kezar, 2001, 32–33). The OD dimension shrank back from emphasis in the field as instructional development and the push for learning, assessment, pedagogy, and technology in the recent decades have overshadowed what originally may have been a much different OD vision for this field.

Changes in Higher Education and Faculty Development in the 1980s

Significant expansion of TLCs in the 1980s through the 1990s took place when instructional development demands permeated all types of institutions. The 1980s were an important decade of growth for faculty development in response to several critical reports of higher education in the United States, including *A Nation at Risk* (1983) (Fletcher & Patrick, 1998). Institutions responded to external criticism by devoting more attention and resources toward student learning. Higher education continued to prompt and shape changes in the expanding field of what still was called *faculty development*, but what had become *instructional development*. Several key studies produced evidence for changing institution-wide practices in order to advance student success, including *How College Affects Students* (Pascarella & Terrenzini, 1991). Faculty developers shifted to focus on teaching strategies that would enhance learning (Fletcher & Patrick, 1998). Expansion of the field picked up speed with the new research-based paradigms that emphasized student success and student learning, as opposed to teaching and delivery of knowledge, and developers were called upon to help instructors focus on learning outcomes versus inputs. Once can see how the field shifted to improving or developing the individual instructor (and each institution had many with more hired annually), rather than attend to improving the more abstract institutional structures, personnel interactions, culture, and values. One can almost hear the closing of the OD door in this field.

Inevitably, these paradigm shifts in higher education began to impact the earlier definitions of development work and TLCs. The instructional paradigm understandably riveted the attention of this field toward instruction, classroom, and the instructor level of impact. Students became active agents in their educational experience and expressed their demands and criticisms of all aspects of their education, bringing more attention to the need for instructional improvement measures (Fletcher & Patrick, 1998; Graham & Diamond, 1997). Institutions clearly needed and still need the help of instructional developers to improve instruction and address public criticism and concerns with accountability. However, change at a larger scale is required.

An Instructional Development Role Emerges

With the rapid expansion of more centers of teaching and learning in the 1980s, the field of faculty development continued to establish itself as a common feature at institutions. Center staff became experts in instructional development, offering institution-wide workshops, conferences or programs, and individual as well as departmental consultations (see Figure 1.1). Constant advances in technology and the increasing emphasis on learning outcomes, assessment, and accountability further impacted expectations of institutions and faculty. The general public, accrediting agencies, employers, and legislature pressed for evidence regarding learning and the value-added contribution of higher education. In response, faculty development embraced multiple new learning technologies, acquired and contributed to a vastly growing amount of literature on learning, and applied these theories to impact teaching practices. This expanding research base anchored center workshops, consultations, and programs and provided developers with new empirical evidence regarding what works instructionally and why. TLCs were providers of *instructional development*, but this role did nothing to clarify how an OD dimension of this role might be enacted to benefit institutions. Not surprisingly, OD as an integral dimension of this work was subsumed within the intense focus on improving instruction.

Perhaps due to working harder with less, center directors continued business as usual or even *more* business than usual. The high demand for instructional and technology services led centers to conclude that their role *is* to function at the individual, course, workshop, and department level. Instructional and faculty development meant offering support and "development" through one instructor, consultation, workshop, or Scholarship of Teaching and Learning (SoTL) grant at a time. Center directors may have concluded from their steady and heavy workload that they were situated near or within the center of the institutional radar screen.

Expectations of Teaching and Learning Centers in the 1990s

TLCs continued to expand across all types of institutions and developed a variety of formats tailored to the unique history and needs of their institutional contexts. Even research universities recognized the need to establish teaching and learning centers in order to fulfill institutional missions that demanded excellence in learning while still fulfilling rigorous research agendas. By 1992–1993, the majority of research universities had established faculty development programs (Crawley, 1995). As the language of higher education shifted from teaching toward learning, and very soon to include assessment, the names of faculty development centers noticeably reflected this shift in focus. New and scaled-up faculty development centers became centers of learning, instructional development centers, academic or teaching excellence centers, innovative learning and teaching centers, or distance learning and technology units, or an amalgam of these titles.

Increasing attention to student learning versus teaching delivery permeated higher education and was met with varying degrees of resistance (Barr & Tagg, 1995). The emphasis on learning required institutions to become concerned with "how faculty learn" and could best learn to adjust to the multiple changes confronting them (Fletcher & Patrick, 1998). Instructors often lacked the necessary pedagogical expertise and needed to know more than "the way they were taught" in order to meet the new expectations and demands in course design, technology, assessment, and student learning. The language of learning and assessment was new and not always well received. Instructional and faculty developers were often the translators of this new language and paradigm for both the eager innovators and early adopters of change and the reluctant or resistant faculty and instructors. The unique organizational characteristics of higher education that value faculty autonomy, tenure, and academic freedom, challenged both the institution and developers to find effective strategies that would, in effect, improve the institution and advance student learning through largely voluntary and nonrewarded participation in instructional development.

These changes increasingly demanded enormous support by the staff of TLCs. The work was unending as increasing numbers of teaching assistants, adjunct instructors and lecturers surpassed the number of tenured faculty nationally (American Federation of Teachers, 2009). This trend inevitably added new and changing clientele to the population of new faculty hires and seasoned instructors, also needing the developer's expertise. As faculty developers functioned as brokers (McAlpine, 1992) and conduits of change at the individual and program level, the broader institutional issues were initiated and planned by administrative leaders and planners, but seldom with faculty developers at the table.

Establishing Neutrality and Separation

Centers of teaching and learning worked hard to dispel notions of being a "fix-it" or remedial service in order to avoid any stigma attached to their services and in order to encourage all instructors to seek development. Some continue to struggle with this perception. In response to instructional improvement pressures, centers developed strategies to attract instructors voluntarily to their cutting edge and innovative programs by positioning the TLCs and themselves as neutral service providers that functioned outside of promotion, tenure, and merit systems.

Maintaining some distance from administrative agendas was thought important in order to gain faculty trust and to dispel concern that centers might serve as arms of the suspect administration. Greater involvement in institutional priorities, some claimed, may make developers seem "as the resocialization agency of university administrations" and developers were cautioned against being the "change agents of mandated change" (Knight & Wilcox, 1998, p. 100). This aim for neutral positioning may have created more distance than necessary from the broader institutional picture, and over time, this intentional separation from the institutional agenda may have produced some unintentional effects. Working in its own neutral silo, centers expanded while becoming increasingly marginalized within their institutions—an unexpected price they paid for this neutrality. Perhaps this explains why some centers continue to operate independently from their institutional missions, strategic plans, and current change initiatives. Acting more like satellites revolving around broader institutional priorities, they function as marginalized units in the sense that they lack a role in shaping initiatives, but instead, respond to them. The center or director may be very popular, well-liked, and sought after, but have little input or influence in the decisions and plans for change that are intertwined with teaching and learning at the institutional level.

Despite the increased attention to teaching and learning, some expressed the belief that as long as teaching is marginalized, centers will be too (Gosling, 2001). However, nearly 10 years after arguing this reality-check statement, even research institutions with research-centered missions are joining other teaching oriented institutions with strategic priorities on general education reform and the entire learning environment. Institutions can no longer afford to marginalize "learning," no matter their institutional mission. However, by providing a plethora of information, programs, services, and technological support while maintaining distance from the administration, centers may have defined their role too narrowly as solely instruction-focused professionals.

Instructional Development Service Niche

In hindsight, when classroom learning and work with instructors began to consume the developers' focus nearly exclusively, TLCs blossomed into larger staffs. The original and traditional individual *faculty development* role was no longer the primary function and barely within the collective memory of the changing field.

Many new professionals made their way into this field, including a mixture of faculty and instructional staff ready to help, support, serve, and assist the faculty and the growing number of teaching assistants. Within the expanding but narrow niche of *instructional development*, the perception of this work as primarily instructional development was evident in center mission statements as well (see chapter 11). Faculty development in the United States became widely perceived by others and promoted itself as developers that program, consult, encourage, help, assist, provide, nurture, and support. The interventionist and OD concepts that had intersected this field early on still echoed around these important service-based functions. More often behind the scenes, these actions, though highly valuable for the institution, are usually responsive in nature *to institutional initiatives* and do not suggest a leadership role or developers as change agents and collaborators in institutional initiatives. Centers reinforced this service-oriented perspective through mission statements, position descriptions, activities, and priorities focused on instructional development. Perhaps these service-oriented and traditionally individual- and development-based practices are what appear to clash with the language of change agent and institutional leader.

Just by focusing exclusively on instructional development and often including online instruction, TLCs have more work than they can cope with given the goal to reach all faculty and teaching staff, keep up with the continually changing instructional technology, and embed assessment practices at the same time. As a result, some directors are nearly institutionally passive and function as outsiders to key institutional change agendas and certainly are not leaders or change agents. Fixated solely at the individual and instructional level, centers not only feel overwhelmed but also maintain the illusion of functioning at the center of the institutional radar screen. This unending nature of the role of the *instructional development* is part of what constrains redefinition of this role to reflect involvement with the current needs of institutions.

Within this relatively new instructional development niche that was expanding in multiple directions, the field failed to identify the other dimensions of its role within the larger institutional picture. A clear vision of the OD dimension of this work was left to take form, or not, and often fell to merely hoping and believing in the eventual larger-scale impact of instructional development efforts. During a time of expansion, it may be unreasonable to have expected this field to ask itself, "Is this role too limited in scope and missing the critical dimension of *organizational development*?" Ironically, perhaps at the busiest time thus far in the field, faculty development may have fallen off the institutional radar screen into a narrow crevice of programs and services while it was broadening skills and expertise in instructional design at nearly a frantic pace.

The center staff work long hours to change faculty beliefs and practices, pedagogical methods, and syllabi rather than focus on broad-level changes in teaching and learning. As *responders* to change initiatives, centers of teaching excellence have been at the periphery of the institutional planning process. However, the lack of definition of an OD dimension of this role or perhaps because it became side-tracked, unintentionally discouraged involvement at the institutional level as change agents, partners, collaborators, and initiators of change for too long. The instructional development role and paradigm shifts in higher education were simply too compelling to allow for developing this additional dimension. Uninvited to the table where institutional change initiatives are planned, too many academic developers are unable to influence their institution's far-reaching decisions about teaching and learning despite their unique knowledge and areas of expertise. If center directors are not at the planning table, it's because this field has not clearly and convincingly defined its role and expertise in broader issues of teaching and learning. If center directors are not being asked to help shape and initiate strategic plans and institutional level programs, it's because the field has not made clear that it has a shared knowledge and skill base and a vital and unique organizational role to play.

The lack of a common set of skills is apparent when reviewing director position descriptions. Even within the narrow focus on instructional development, director position descriptions are accompanied by an inconsistent list of expertise areas and fail to communicate the current role many faculty developers are playing in institutional change initiatives. These descriptions continue to reflect an instructional development focus and rarely include qualifications that define the TLC director as a leader or change agent. What a developer can do and bring to the table cannot remain dependent on the vision and interests of the individual professional or left out of position descriptions. Scholars in the field have warned being over inclusive of all backgrounds "undermines our reputation" and "gives the impression that anyone in the academy can do our work" (Hartland & Staniforth, 2003, p. 33). Unfortunately, if educational development allows its role to be determined by individual strengths and weaknesses, or solely defined by each institutional culture, it will inevitably trade off having institutions certain of what expertise to count on from academic developers.

Occasionally, a director position announcement successfully merges a traditional instructional development role with institutional leadership simply by mentioning involvement with institutional initiatives and priorities, membership on strategic planning committees and task forces, knowledge of change processes and national trends, or demonstration of specific leadership skills (see chapter 13). For example, an excerpt from a recent center director position read:

> the Director will create a culture of teaching, respond to individual faculty members for development of teaching skills, advance innovation, and new initiatives in the curriculum (including the use of technology to enhance learning), and **act as an institutional change agent**. (POD Listserve, 2008)

Widespread Role Ambiguity

Similarly, unless center mission statements, performance evaluations, and ongoing professional development reflect the OD role advocated and documented by this book, this work by directors at the broadest level will continue to be done but not institutionalized or consistently sought (see chapters 11 and 12). As the needs of higher education have shifted, so too should the organizational and leadership role of academic developers become legitimized and clearly identified.

Not surprisingly, the lack of role definition and clarity regarding faculty development work has caused uncertainty and debate both within and outside of the United States and North America. Initial findings by researchers suggest that role uncertainty of educational development extends all across the English-speaking world, including the United Kingdom, New Zealand, Australia, and South Africa (D'Andrea & Gosling, 2001). Academic developers in the United Kingdom and Australia continue to debate regarding the "rightful place" of academic developers in higher education and whether academic development is credible or "irrelevant to the real intellectual tasks of academic life" (Rowland, Byron, Furedi, Padfield, & Smyth, 1998, p. 134).

Eggins and MacDonald (2003) made the case that educational development be recognized as a legitimate field and D'Andrea and Gosling (2001) argue that it must define its identity. Bath and Smith (2004) warned that "academic developers are still watching their backs and wondering how others perceive them," (p. 10) and still face uncertainty. Bath and Smith (2004) concur with Rowland's (2002) description of the "fragmentation of higher education" and the warning that "unless academic developers are clear about what the boundaries of the field or the subject matter of academic development are, it is difficult to see what they have to offer academics in the disciplines" (in Bath & Smith, 2004, p. 13). Others in the United Kingdom and New Zealand have wondered if "academic development is presently too diverse and in danger of fragmenting before it has a chance to genuinely establish a language, a theoretical base and an epistemology" (Hartland & Staniforth, 2003, p. 30). Instructional design, often combining technology and online learning with faculty development, may suffer similar identity and credibility concerns. According to researchers in Canada (Schwier, Campbell, & Kenny, 2003), instructional designers "recognize that they have a role to play in the changes currently underway in education, but are less understanding of how to express that role forcefully and demonstrate leadership" (p. 38–39). Something is amiss when developers are this busy but lack credibility when centers perform hundreds of services and programs and are shut down, and when developers are uncertain of their value within institutions and across national boundaries spanning several decades.

Center Marginalization in the Literature

Awareness of the actual and potential marginalization of teaching and learning centers began to be discussed by faculty developers as institutional budgets tightened, centers closed, and new demands on faculty and developers became apparent. Chism (1998) expressed her concern regarding the marginalized role of the teaching centers by pointing out that most centers were actually functioning *"at the fringes of the university fabric"* (p. 151). This concern was echoed later among colleagues in the United Kingdom and Canada who claimed, "our profession is situated on the fringes of serious academic activity" (Hartland & Staniforth, 2003, p. 33). Chism (1998) called faculty development to move "from the basement office" in order to play a pivotal role in institutional change. The "fringe" operation of centers that Chism (1998) warned about is evidenced by the narrow institutional perception of this work and the accompanying ignorance of the expertise and leadership skills of directors of TLCs. Colleagues in the United Kingdom admit, "In many of its incarnations, support for learning and teaching continues to be seen as marginal to the main purposes of higher education" and propose a "major reconceptualization of educational development" (D'Andrea & Gosling, 2001, p. 71).

More than 10 years after Chism's warning, it is obvious that this field has neglected to take up this issue collectively. On an individual center level, many directors have invented or been drawn into a role that situates them at the core of their institution's key priorities. However, many centers have not integrated this organizational leadership role into their existing full plates and may not view leadership at the institutional level as part of their "job" or role. Without serious conversations as a field about this facet of development work, it appears to be an optional aspect of being a director. Failure to initiate or be seen as experts in the current institutional challenges threatens not only marginalization, but also extinction of centers. It is much easier to lop off a center that is marginalized. Randy Bass, assistant provost, Teaching and Learning Initiatives executive director, director of the Center for New Designs in Learning and Scholarship, and director of the Visible Knowledge Project stated during his interview, "I also think that the water level is rising, and I think if we do not actively maintain our position as contributors intellectually in that conversation then we will look like a support for that conversation." Faculty and academic development clearly struggle with an overall role definition, issues of credibility, and fleshing out newly interpreted OD roles in the United States and abroad.

Developers as Change Agents

Scholars have challenged centers to better situate themselves as leaders in institutional change and broader institutional initiatives. As early as 1983, Gaige (1983), Paul (1983), and Rice (1983) prompted consideration of the link between faculty development and academic planning, long-range planning, institutional research, and curricular change (Lee & Field, 1984; Smith, 1988). This broader leadership role or redefined organizational development role may be considered by some as a change agent. Change agents have been attributed with "stirring dissatisfaction with the status quo," to stimulate incremental change and cultivation of a critical mass (Lindquist, 1978, p. 14). Change agency in higher education, in general, has emphasized acquiring knowledge of institutional change strategies and organization dynamics as two of the necessary knowledge areas for change agents for some time (Lindquist, 1978), whereas Farmer (1990) identified playing multiple roles, including catalyst, solution giver, process helper, resource linker, and confidence builder. These findings closely resemble the roles and strategies the case study center directors reported, confirming that they were change agents while others were reluctant to be identified overtly as such.

By the early 1990s, the national concern with changes in higher education and quality management spurred conversation in the development literature in the United States and abroad regarding this field's potential role in institutional change (Brown, 1992; Gaff & Simpson, 1994). Threads of this conversation continued to appear and may have begun to influence the role and work of the centers and their directors. Although a leadership role was not proposed by Nemke and Simpson (1991), the potential of the campus-wide influence of faculty development was discussed. Zahorski (1993) recognized the potential of faculty development's leadership role and the importance of broadening the focus of the field to that of an "institutional change agent." Brown (1992) proposed that faculty development serve as a process and "a tool" for advancing organizational learning (Brown, 1992; Schroeder, 2001-2002). However, defining in what sense a "tool" was left unclear. These threads were never woven into a coherent dialogue about the role of developers that the field fully embraced.

Examples in the literature of faculty development's role in specific institutional initiatives began to emerge as well, including institutional assessment (Sutherland & Guffey, 1997), Writing-Across-the-Curriculum (Cottell Jr., Hansen & Ronald, 1999), freshmen learning initiatives (Middendorf, 2000; Stassen, 1999), departmental program review (Rhodes, 2001), and curricular reform (Cook, 2001). The concept of a learning organization and the link between the individual and organizational learning had swept through corporate organizations in the 1990s (Senge, 1990) and influenced developers. Patrick and Fletcher (1998) discussed faculty development's role in transforming institutions into learning organizations in the late 1990s and Laycock (2000) introduced whole-institutional faculty development in the United Kingdom that stimulates culture change in a constructivist process. Institutional change became a hot topic, and Eckel (2001) offered insight into institutional transformation and change based on a study of 24 institutional change agendas, linking the elements of institutional change to faculty development. Still, it could hardly be said that developers utilized these studies to heed the call for articulating and elevating their role in institutional change.

More recently, the portrayal of the role of TLCs in literature remains inconsistent. This was evidenced in the study by Frantz, Beebe, Horvath, Canales, and Swee (2005) in "The Role of Teaching and Learning Centers." Only one institutional initiative, "Assessment Coordination at the Institutional Level" (p. 77), was reported among the key roles centers played by 18% of the survey respondents (p. 77), reported by Sorcinelli et al. (2006), from a survey of almost 500 faculty developers at 331 institutions, reported eight current institutional issues were currently offered by developers at a slight to moderate degree (p. 72). The *Coming in From the Margins* study results indicate the majority of directors are involved in multiple institutional issues (see chapter 4). Several explanations may explain the lack of consistency in reporting this level of involvement by directors. First, the measurement of the work done at the institutional level is less concrete and may be harder to document when compared with reporting the number of workshops or number in attendance. Second, this work may be highly invisible, with only a select few around a planning table or on subcommittees. Finally, the satisfaction level for instructional development is high, and the results begin to be apparent nearly immediately and continue on as courses are modified and instructional change becomes observable. Perhaps, in contrast, the work of institutional change is less rewarding, more challenging, and less measurable. Contributions are less attributable and more collaborative, and success is a long way off.

Despite the reluctance to embrace this role more explicitly, the role of TLCs in institutional change has been gaining stronger attention in scholarly work both within and outside the United States and emerging within the POD Network (Baron, 2006; Diamond, 2002). For example, Lieberman and Guskin (2002) argued for new higher education models based on the changing education environment and the impact on faculty. In this literature, an important distinction becomes evident. Some leaders in the field would argue the extent of faculty development's necessary role change stems from a call to meet the changing needs of *faculty* in the context of a changing institution and changing faculty roles. While it could be argued that focusing on the changing needs of faculty may indeed be part of the developer's role, the OD *role* advocated in this book entails *also* developing and impacting teaching and learning through leadership and involvement in broader institutional initiatives by *developers*. Some of the persisting notions of territories valuing faculty versus administrative status, and an us-versus-them mentality in which advancing "administrative" agendas is suspect, need to be questioned. The changes required in higher education call for dissolving fragmented silos in order to make learning effective. Developers in search of new words to replace "faculty development" or ways to translate OD into the current context of their work may recognize themselves as change agents working at multiple levels within the institution. What might this look like (see Figure 1.1)? The progression of the developer's role as the needs of higher education change can be better understood, perhaps, from a visual representation that tries to capture the distinct merging practices of the multilevel change agent. Are *faculty* still "served"? The answer is yes, but through a role that includes impacting a broader constituency and broader issues at multiple levels.

FIGURE 1.1
Developers as multilevel change agents

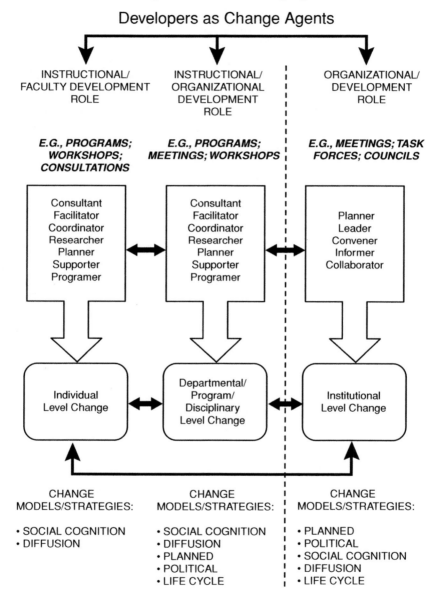

Developers as Change Agents

INSTRUCTIONAL/ FACULTY DEVELOPMENT ROLE	INSTRUCTIONAL/ ORGANIZATIONAL DEVELOPMENT ROLE	ORGANIZATIONAL/ DEVELOPMENT ROLE
E.G., PROGRAMS; WORKSHOPS; CONSULTATIONS	*E.G., PROGRAMS; MEETINGS; WORKSHOPS*	*E.G., MEETINGS; TASK FORCES; COUNCILS*
Consultant Facilitator Coordinator Researcher Planner Supporter Programer	Consultant Facilitator Coordinator Researcher Planner Supporter Programer	Planner Leader Convener Informer Collaborator
Individual Level Change	Departmental/ Program/ Disciplinary Level Change	Institutional Level Change
CHANGE MODELS/STRATEGIES:	CHANGE MODELS/STRATEGIES:	CHANGE MODELS/STRATEGIES:
• SOCIAL COGNITION • DIFFUSION	• SOCIAL COGNITION • DIFFUSION • PLANNED • POLITICAL • LIFE CYCLE	• PLANNED • POLITICAL • SOCIAL COGNITION • DIFFUSION • LIFE CYCLE

Developers as Multilevel Change Agents

The issues confronting higher education institutions, more often than not, will interface with some element of teaching and learning in classroom and online environments. At some point, institutional planning for broad initiatives, such as retention, diversity and inclusion, access, assessment, or general education reform, all intersect with the process of learning and have important implications for teaching. If defined and staffed appropriately, directors of TLCs would bring important expertise to the table when these initiatives are first considered and plans are outlined. Australian colleagues point out that developers can "play a pivotal role in meaning making for institutional committees" because of their local knowledge, and "assist with the interpretation, contexualisation and implementation of strategic priorities" (Fraser, 2006, p. 12). Fraser offers a model at Macquarie University, Australia, of a holistic, integrated, and interrelated collaborative model with levels of micro, meso, and macro development. Taylor and Schönwetter (2002) insist that the changes confronting higher education "offer faculty developers exciting opportunities to optimize the leadership potential of the faculty development role" (p. 648), and they further argue, "Faculty developers are often called upon to facilitate institutional problem solving and change" (p. 647). Their work focused discussion on a framework for conceptualizing and approaching leadership that is consistent with the work of faculty development, arguing that faculty developers' expertise and skills position them to provide leadership "to build community problem-solving capacity" (p. 652). Their work describes a "sophisticated leadership role" based on Parker Palmer's (1992) facilitative and collaborative nature of leadership. In order to effectively facilitate change, they offer a discussion of change processes and conditions for systemic institutional change. Taylor's (2005) research of Australian academic developers noted an increasing recognition of being seen as integral to the campus and positioned on important committees (p. 35) and Fraser (2006) reports an increasing role in key policy and planning groups. Fletcher and Patrick (1998) argue, "As higher education in the United States faces political, social, and technological challenges, faculty developers must play a more active role in institutional transformation" (p. 39).

One of the boldest statements that failed to stir controversy in this field stated that leadership should be "an inherent role in faculty development practice" (Taylor & Schönwetter, 2002, p. 647) and suggests an institutional leadership role is a "third wave of evolution" in this field (Fletcher & Patrick, 1998). Diamond (2005) suggests the option of "expanding the role of faculty, instructional, and teaching centers" to "serve in the role of change agents"

(p. 33). Diamond (2005) advocates for a new structure or agency located within academic affairs that would provide an integrated model of academic reform (p. 30). Within this coordinating unit, multiple services including professional development, assessment, course and curriculum design, and facilitation would be provided. An alternative, he suggests, may involve "expanding the role of faculty, instructional, and teaching centers" to "serve in the role of change agents" (p. 33). Diamond's recent passing did not allow him to see actualization of his integrated center model and widespread adoption of faculty developers as "change agents."

Structural changes have helped to advance a "whole-institutional approach" to educational development in the United Kingdom when many educational development units became managed by the vice chancellors (VC) with better access to important decision-making and institutional structures (D'Andrea & Gosling, 2001, p. 66). These units in the United Kingdom were surveyed regarding their institutional role and identified multiple strategies for embedding change (Gosling, 2001). A recent Australasian survey and interviews among educational developers reported evidence of shared conceptions of institutional change involvement that included, "to implement or decide on strategic changes" (Fraser, 2001, p. 38).

However, Sorcinelli et al. (2009), in *Creating the Future of Faculty Development*, identified institutional challenges affecting faculty and the implications for the future of faculty development. They recommended institutional leaders and center directors to question whether or not the current focus of their center and work, expertise, mission statements, and roles are in alignment with the needs of higher education and its current challenges, and to prepare proactively for the vision and future role of faculty development supported by this research. These authors point out,

> If institutions recognize developer's expertise . . . faculty development will be well positioned to support not only individual faculty development but also institutional decision-making. Faculty development will be far from marginal and optional. (p. 169)

They further insist that developers will be called upon to preserve, clarify, and enhance the purposes of faculty development, and to network with faculty and institutional leaders to respond to the institutional problems and propose constructive solutions as we meet the challenges of the new century (p. 28). They clearly stated the importance of an OD role: "We believe that faculty development is a key strategic lever for ensuring institutional quality and supporting institutional change" (p. xi). They reinforced their belief in this role with the statement, "We hope that our findings will further encourage universities and colleges to give developers a central role in relation to strategic institutional planning, management, and leadership." Fortunately, the data reported in chapters 4 and 5 document the institution-, director-, and center-based factors that enable directors to provide the leadership and expertise to successfully become collaborators in large-scale initiatives.

Implications of Today's Higher Education Challenges

Now, well into the twenty-first century, higher education may be facing its greatest constellation of changes ever seen (Oblinger & Ruth, 1997; Plater, 1995). As higher education tries to change and implement broader-scale initiatives that affect teaching and learning in the classroom and across the institution, TLCs and their directors *are* offering their expertise, assistance, and leadership in ways not widely known or considered a key function of their role in earlier decades (see chapter 4). This role shift from traditional *faculty development* and even from *instructional development* entails involvement at the institutional level and effectively merging a redefined OD role with the two already well established dimensions of this work (see Figure 1.1).

Conclusion

For much of its history, faculty development has played a supportive but nondirective role in colleges and universities in the United States: "For the most part, faculty developers have been reactive, generally responding to questions from faculty, not initiating them" (Fletcher & Patrick, 1998, p. 39). What evidence do we have of the migration of "faculty development" toward an institutional and organizationally focused role? What are the challenges, conflicts, and gains experienced by directors and centers well engaged in institutional initiatives and change? What are the tradeoffs and adaptations necessary to accommodate this role? If directors of teaching and learning centers recognize the value of and opportunity for broader institutional involvement, how does this role develop and what factors enable or impede the success of involvement in institutional change? What models of faculty development and TLCs today can portray these expectations and make visible the realities of leadership, change agency, and involvement at the institutional level of change? How do we define our expanding role as change agents and organizational developers and integrate these responsibilities into the existing essential services? What expertise would developers bring to the table? How would institutional planners know this? Are we facing a serious divide within our field, between those who institutionally lead versus those who do not; those who are marginalized or defined by instructional development, effective as they may be, from centers that are situated and aligned with the institutional mission and priorities? It is time now to sort through the changes in higher education, practice of educational or faculty development, and determine how to define OD within the scope of a developer's role and in the context of higher education's current needs.

No matter the institutional culture, size, and mission, and despite the size of centers, staffing, and budgets, could not all centers and directors infuse institutional involvement to some degree? Would this role definition not only better anchor and secure the center and its staff's value and existence, while more importantly influence the structures, programs, and initiatives that impact teaching and learning systematically? There is considerable resistance to define what is common about this field out of a fear that a cookie-cutter definition would rigidly inhibit a field that has welcomed and benefited from a wide background among its developers. However, based on the results of the study shared in chapter 4, it is not the background of developers as much as it was proven to be what they do in their positions, and a variety of other primary factors, which enable this leadership role. Somewhere between extreme role flexibility and institutional variability, and a rigid definition of our field, lies a more coherent and consistent academic developer's role. Lacking intensive professional development that targets these abilities, areas of expertise, and knowledge required, centers of teaching and learning have already missed opportunities to help lead institutions to broadly realign their initiatives and planning to effectively improve student learning. To continue in this narrow niche may work for a while at some institutions, given the unique structures and histories that exist. However, based on the results of the study, an overwhelming majority of centers and directors are significantly involved at the institutional level and have enormous value to contribute.

Forecasting the challenges and directions of higher education should continue to prompt this field to modify itself accordingly and to be fast on its feet in providing the expertise, knowledge, and leadership it uniquely can provide and to prepare itself explicitly for this leadership role. Have developers paused long enough to catch their collective breath and critically consider, "What are we doing?" and "How could we be doing it?" "Do we want to know how we fit into the institutional radar screen or impact broader-scale initiatives?" Being convinced once again of the importance in adapting this field to reflect the future directions of higher education, how does a field go about reinventing its role or a director in realigning a center that is marginalized? Kay Gillespie, CKF Associates, Lion Gardiner, Rutgers University–Newark, Virginia,

Virginia S. Lee & Associates, and Richard Tiberius, University of Miami, Miller School of Medicine presented a session at the 2007 POD Conference, *The "O" in POD: Organizational Development—Retrospective and New Perspectives*, in which they reviewed the role of OD within POD in the past and discussed current and future understandings of this aspect of development work. Much more attention is needed.

Coming in From the Margins is aimed at determining how faculty development is currently situated in terms of participation and leadership within institutional initiatives and decision-making structures. Rather than remain a "missing prong," a vibrant OD role has evolved quite differently than originally envisioned well before organizational change became a driving dimension of organizations during the last several decades. The organizational role that directors of centers have stepped up to (and into) arises out of the complex issues facing higher education and the need for broad changes in teaching and learning. This OD role has taken shape and been defined by centers and institutions that are collaborating and partnering in new ways, across traditions, tables, and hierarchies. Together, as authors, we present the evidence, models, and strategies that demonstrate change in the role of directors of teaching and learning centers and argue that this role change may very well be necessary in order for institutions to achieve their intended transformations (Schroeder, 2006). Continued discussion across the field should be able to move developers toward shared meanings and collective understanding of an organizational role.

References

American Federation of Teachers. (2009). *American academic: The state of the higher education workforce 1997–2007*. Washington, DC: American Federation of Teachers.

Baron, L. (2006). The advantages of a reciprocal relationship between faculty development and organizational development in higher education. In S. Chadwick-Blossey, & D. R. Robertson (Eds.), *To improve the academy: Yearbook of the Professional and Organizational Development Network in Higher Education, Vol. 24* (pp. 29–43). Bolton, MA: Anker.

Barr, R. B., & Tagg, J. (November, December, 1995). From teaching to learning. *Change*, 13–25.

Bath, D., & Smith, C. (2004). Academic developers: An academic tribe claiming their territory in higher education. *International Journal for Academic Development, 9(1)*, 9–27.

Beckhard, R. (1969). *Organization development: Strategies and models*. Reading, MA: Addison-Wesley.

Bergquist, W. H., & Phillips, S. R. (1975). Components of an effective faculty development program. *Journal of Higher Education, 46*(2), 177–215.

Bradford, D. L., & Burke, W. W. (Eds.). (2005). *Reinventing organization development.* San Francisco: Pfeiffer.

Brown, H. (1992, Spring). Staff development in higher education: Towards the learning organization. *Higher Education Quarterly, 46*(2), 174–190.

Cameron, K. S., & Quinn, R. E. (1983). The field of organizational development. In R. E. Quinn, & K. S. Cameron (Eds.), *Classics in organizational development* (p. 42). Oak Park, IL: Moore.

Campbell, K., Schwier, R. A., & Kenny, R. F. (2009). The critical, relational practice of instructional design in higher education: An emerging model of change agency. *Educational Technical Research Development 57*, (pp. 645–663). (DOI 10.1007/s11423-007-9061-6)

Centre, J. A. (1976). *Faculty development practices in US colleges and universities.* Project Report 76–30. Princeton: Educational Testing Service.

Chism, N. (1998). The role of education developers in institutional change: From the basement office to the front office. In M. Kaplan, & D. Lieberman (Eds.), *To improve the academy: Vol. 17. Resources for faculty, instructional and organizational development* (pp. 141–154). Stillwater, OK: New Forums Press.

Collette, P., & Davidson, M. (1997). Re-negotiating autonomy and accountability: The professional growth of developers in a South African institution. *International Journal for Academic Development, 2,* 28–34.

Cook, C. E. (2001). The role of a teaching center in curricular reform. In D. Lieberman & C. Wehlburg (Eds.), *To improve the academy* (Vol. 19, pp. 217–231). Bolton, MA: Anker.

Cottell, P. G. Jr., Hansen, S., & Ronald, K. (1999). From transparency toward expertise: Writing-Across-The-Curriculum as a site for new collaborations in organizational, faculty, and instructional development. In M. Kaplan & D. Lieberman (Eds.), *To improve the academy: Vol. 18. Resources for faculty, instructional and organizational development* (pp. 164–180). Bolton, MA: Anker.

Crawley, A. (1995). Faculty development programs at research universities: Implications for senior faculty renewal. In S. Chadwick-Blossey, & D. R. Robertson (Eds.), *To improve the academy: Vol. 14. Resources for faculty, instructional and organizational development* (pp. 65–90). Stillwater, OK: New Forums Press.

D'Andrea, V., & Gosling, D. (2001). Joining the dots: Reconceptualizing educational development. *The Institute for Learning and Teaching in Higher Education and SAGE Publications, 2*(1), 64–81. Retrieved October 26, 2009, from http://alh.safepub.com

Diamond, R. M. (2002). Faculty, instructional, and organizational development: Options and choices. In K. H. Gillespie, L. R. Hilsen, & E. C. Wadsworth (Eds.), *A guide to faculty development: Practical advice, examples, and resources* (pp. 2–8). Bolton, MA: Anker.

Diamond, R. M. (2005). The institutional change agency: The expanding role of academic support centers. In S. Chadwick-Blossey, & D. R. Robertson (Eds.), *To improve the academy: Vol. 23. Resources for faculty, instructional and organizational development* (pp. 24–37). Bolton, MA: Anker.

Eble K., & McKeachie, W. (1985). *Improving undergraduate education through faculty development*. San Francisco: Jossey-Bass.

Eckel, P. D. (2001). Institutional transformation and change: Insights for faculty developers. In D. Lieberman, & C. Wehlburg (Eds.), *To improve the academy: Vol. 20. Resources for faculty, instructional and organizational development* (pp. 3–19). Bolton, MA: Anker.

Eggins, H., & MacDonald, R. (Eds.). (2003). *The scholarship of academic development*. Philadelphia: The Society for Research into Higher Education and Open University Press.

Emmanuel College (2008, September 17). [Electronic mailing list message]. Retrieved from http://www.podnetwork.org/listserv.html

Farmer, D. (1990). Institutional improvement and motivated faculty: A case study. In D. Steeples (Ed.), *Managing change in higher education: new directions for higher education, Vol. 17* (pp. 87–95). San Francisco: Jossey-Bass.

Fletcher, J., Patrick, S. (1998). Not just workshops any more: The role of faculty development in reframing academic priorities. *International Journal of Academic Development, 3*(1), 39–46.

Frantz, A. C., Beebe, S. A., Horvath, V. S., Canales, J., & Swee, D. E. (2005). The role of teaching and learning centers. In S. Chanwick-Blossey, & D. R. Robertson (Eds.), *To improve the academy: Vol. 23. Resources for faculty, instructional and organizational development* (pp. 72–90). Bolton, MA: Anker.

Fraser, K. (2001). Australasian academic developers' conceptions of the profession. *International Journal for Academic Development, 6,* 54–64.

Fraser, S. P. (2006, May). Shaping the university curriculum through partnerships and critical conversations. *International Journal for Academic Development, 11*(1), 5–17.

Gaff, J. (1975). *Toward faculty renewal: Advances in faculty instructional and organizational development*. San Francisco: Jossey-Bass.

Gaff, J., & Simpson, R. D. (1994, Spring). Faculty development in the United States. *Innovative Higher Education, 18*(3), 167.

Gaige, F. H. (1983). Long-range planning and faculty development. In M. Davis, M. Fisher, S. C. Inglis, & S. Scholl (Eds.), *To improve the academy: Vol. 2. Resources for faculty, instructional and organizational development*. Stillwater, OK: New Forums Press.

Gallos, J. V., & Schein, E. H. (2006). *Organization development: A Jossey-Bass reader*. San Francisco: Jossey-Bass.

Gillespie, K., Lee, V., Tiberius R. G. (2006, October). The missing "O" in POD. Presentation at the Professional and Organizational Development Network Conference, Portland, Oregon.

Gosling, D. (2001). Educational development units in the UK—What are they doing five years on? *International Journal for Academic Development, 6,* 74–90.

Graf, D., Albright, M., & Wheeler, D. (1992, Fall). Faculty development's role in improving undergraduate education. *New Directions for Teaching and Learning, 50,* 101–109.

Graham, H. D., & Diamond, N. (1997). *The rise of American research universities.* Baltimore: Johns Hopkins University Press.

Hartland, T., & Staniforth, D. (2003, May/November). Academic development as academic work. *International Journal for Academic Development, 8*(1/2), 25–35.

Kezar, A. (2001). Understanding and facilitating organizational change in the 21st century. *ASHE-ERIC Higher Education Report, 28*(4), 1–147.

Knight, P. T., & Wilcox, S. (1998, November). Effectiveness and ethics in educational development: Changing contexts, changing notions. *International Journal for Academic Developers, 3*(2), 97–106.

Laycock, M. (2000). QILT: An approach to faculty development and institutional self-improvement. In M. Kaplan (Ed.), *To improve the academy: Vol. 18. Resources for faculty, instructional and organizational development* (pp. 69–93). Stillwater, OK: New Forums Press.

Lee, R., & Field, M. (1984). Hidden opportunities for faculty development and curricular change. In L. C. Buhl, L. & A. Wilson (Eds.), *To improve the academy: Vol. 3. Resources for faculty, instructional and organizational development* (pp. 95–98). Pittsburgh: Duff's Business Institute.

Lieberman, D. A., & Guskin, A. E. (2002). The essential role of faculty development in new higher education models. In C. M. Wehlburg, & S. Chadwick-Blossey (Eds.), *To improve the academy: Vol. 21. Resources for faculty, instructional and organizational development* (pp. 257–272). Bolton, MA: Anker.

Lindquist, J. (1978). *Strategies for planned change.* Berkeley, CA: Pacific Sounding Press.

McAlpine, L. (1992). Cross-cultural instructional design: Using the cultural expert to formatively evaluate process and product. *Educational Training Technology International, 29*(4), 310–315.

Middendorf, J. (2000). Finding key faculty to influence change. *To improve the academy: Vol. 17. Resources for faculty, instructional and organizational development.* (pp. 203–224). Stillwater, OK: New Forums Press.

National Commission on Excellence in Education (1983). *A nation at risk: The imperative for educational reform: A report to the nation and the Secretary of Education* (p. 65). Washington, DC: United States Department of Education.

Nelson, W. C., & Siegel, M. E. (1980). *Effective approaches to faculty development.* Washington, DC: Association of American Colleges.

Nemke, M., & Simpson, R. D. (1991). Nine keys to enhancing campus-wide influence of faculty development centers. In K. J. Zahorski (Ed.), *To improve the academy Vol. 10 Resources for faculty, instructional, and organizational development* (pp. 83–88). Stillwater, OK: New Forums Press.

Oblinger, D. G., & Ruth, S. C. (Eds.). (1997). *The learning revolution: The challenge of information technology in the academy.* Bolton, MA: Anker Publishing.

Palmer, P. (Mar/Apr 1992). *Divided no more. Change Magazine, 24*(2), 10–17.

Pascarella, E., & Terrenzini, P. (1991). *How college affects students.* San Francisco: Jossey-Bass.

Patrick, S., & Fletcher, J. (1998). Faculty developers as change agents: Transforming colleges and universities into learning organizations. In M. Kaplan (Ed.), *To improve the academy: Vol. 17. Resources for faculty, instructional and organizational development* (pp. 155–170). Stillwater, OK: New Forums Press & POD.

Paul, C. A. (1983). The relationship of institutional planning and institutional research to faculty. M. David, M. Fischer, S. C. Inglis, S. Scholl (Eds.), *To improve the academy: Vol. 2. Resources for faculty, instructional and organizational development.* Stillwater, OK: New Forums Press.

Plater, W. (1995). Future work: Faculty time in the 21st century. *Change, 27*(3), 203–220.

Rhodes, F. H. T. (2001). *The creation of the future: The role of the American university.* Ithaca, NY: Cornell University Press.

Rice, R. E. (1983). Linking faculty development and academic planning. In M. Davis, M. Fisher, S. C. Inglis, & S. Scholl (Eds.), *To improve the academy: Vol. 2. Resources for faculty, instructional and organizational development.* Stillwater, OK: New Forums Press.

Rowland, (2002). Overcoming fragmentation in professional life: The challenge of academic development. *Higher Education Quarterly, 56*(1), 52–64.

Rowland, S., Byron, C., Furedi, F., Padfield, N., & Smyth, T. (1998). Turning academics into teachers? *Teaching in Higher Education, 3,* 133–141.

Schroeder, C. M. (2001/2002). Faculty change agents: Individual and organizational factors that enable or impede faculty involvement in organizational change (Doctoral dissertation, University of Wisconsin–Madison, 2001). *Dissertations & Theses: A&I, 62*(7), 2361.

Schroeder, C. M. (2006). Evidence of the transformational dimensions of the scholarship of teaching and learning: Faculty development through the eyes of SoTL scholars. In S. Chadwick-Blossey & D. R. Robertson (Eds.), *To improve the academy: Vol. 23. Resources for faculty, instructional and organizational development* (pp. 47–71). Bolton, MA: Anker.

Schwier, R. A., Campbell, K., & Kenny, R. (2003, September). *Instructional Designers' observations about identity, communities of practice, and change agency.* Retrieved March 20, 2010, from http://homepage.mac.com/richard.schwier/schwier.ca/pubs/idcop04.pdf

Senge, P. (1990). *The fifth discipline.* New York: Doubleday Currency.

Smith, B. L. (1988). The Washington Center: A grass roots approach to faculty development and curricular reform. In J. G. Kurfiss (Ed.), *To improve the academy: Vol. 7. Resources for faculty, instructional and organizational development* (pp. 165–177). Stillwater, OK: New Forums Press.

Sorcinelli, M., Austin, A. E., Eddy, P. L., & Beach, A. L. (2006). *Creating the future of faculty development: Learning from the past, understanding the present.* Bolton, MA: Anker.

Stassen, M. (1999). It's hard work! Faculty development in a program for first-year students. In M. Kaplan (Ed.), *To improve the academy: Vol. 18. Resources for faculty, instructional and organizational development* (pp. 254–277). Bolton, MA: Anker.

Sutherland, T., & Guffey, J. M. (1997). The impact of comprehensive institutional assessment on faculty. D. Dezure (Ed.), *To improve the academy: Vol. 16. Resources for faculty, instructional and organizational development* (pp. 151–164). Bolton, MA: Anker.

Taylor, K. L. (2005, May). Academic development as institutional leadership: An interplay of person, role, strategy, and institution. *International Journal for Academic Development, 10*(1), 31–46.

Taylor, K. L., & Schönwetter, D. J. (July, 2002). *Faculty development as institutional leadership: A framework for meeting new challenges.* HERDSA Conference, Australia.

Tiberius, R. G. (2002). A brief history of educational development: Implications for teachers and developers. In D. Lieberman, & C. Wehlburg (Eds.), *To improve the academy: Vol. 20. Resources for faculty, instructional, and organizational development* (pp. 20–37). Bolton, MA: Anker.

Weick, K. (1976). Educational organizations as loosely coupled systems. *Administrative Science Quarterly, 21*, 1–19.

What Is Organizational Development? (2007) Retrieved March 20, 2010, from Professional and Organizational Development Network website: http://www. podnetwork.org/faculty_development/definitions.htm

Zahorski, K. (1993). Taking the lead: Faculty development as institutional change agent. In D. L. Wright, & J. P. Lunde (Eds.), *To improve the academy: Vol. 12. Resources for faculty, instructional, and organizational development* (pp. 227–245). Stillwater, OK: New Forums Press.

2

GETTING TO THE TABLE

Planning and Developing Institutional Initiatives

Nancy Van Note Chism

S everal years ago, while considering the role of faculty developers at the institutional level, I wrote a piece subtitled, "From the Basement Office to the Front Office." I talked about the importance of bringing faculty development from the periphery to the center of focus on organizational as well as individual development (Chism, 1998). In the intervening years, I did get to the front office. I would like to use this opportunity to develop my earlier thoughts through my more recent personal experiences, hoping to abstract from them some insights for my colleagues who want to "get to the table" and arguing that it is important to do so.

At the institution where I first worked in faculty development, the site of that first basement office, my role as an instructional development specialist was fairly limited to the work of consulting with individual faculty members and teaching assistants (TAs). Although I progressed from specialist to director and from that basement location to a suite in a run-down but centrally located academic building and almost (I left too soon) to a lovely suite in a new building that I helped to design, my role remained somewhat bounded. It was fine for me (and expected of me) to provide leadership for the new faculty and TA orientations, but the deans' and chairpersons' workshops had to be organized by higher ups. I could institute faculty learning communities, workshops on teaching topics, and issue a teaching handbook, but I was never asked to chime in on the design of classrooms or articulation of expectations for teaching performance in the promotion and tenure process. I could teach as an adjunct and serve on the committees of many doctoral students (and win awards doing those things) but could not have "real" faculty status—until

I had an offer from another campus. In short, I was appreciated and given resources to be supportive, but very kindly kept in my place.

Certain exceptions come to mind. I was consulted in the development of a program for departmental teaching awards. I did participate in the revision of the student evaluation of teaching form. I attended and staffed the Provost's External Advisory Board on Teaching. I felt very needed and respected and never thought I would leave my job, although there were some instances that made me unhappy, like the time when I was asked to leave a meeting before a vote because "I wasn't faculty," the time when I was cautioned not to do too much publishing, or the time when my suggestion to expand my title and responsibilities within academic affairs was met with surprise that I had such aspirations, followed by a gentle denial.

But then came an offer to change institutions, an offer that I first brushed aside. When my future boss was persistent in arguing why I should make the change, I began to see my situation in a new light. I noticed my constraints more regularly, and though it was a very difficult decision to leave my first university, I made the leap. In my new position I still had responsibility for faculty development, but I also had the title of Associate Vice Chancellor for Academic Affairs and Associate Dean of the Faculties. I had resources to restructure and expand the professional development units on the campus as well as to provide leadership for discussions on student retention and instructional technology. My role continually expanded and soon I was helping to draft the promotion and tenure regulations, which was influencing decisions on learning space construction and renovation, and I had a seat at more tables than I ever had envisioned. And I had faculty status. Did I become smarter and more effective overnight? I do not think so. I was simply positioned differently.

As I reflect on this difference, I can say that getting to the table can certainly involve having to change institutions in order to lose your taken-for-granted status. But more than that, it is about becoming more confident about how you can contribute, articulating that confidence, and finding a champion in the central administration who believes in you. Had I been more assertive and intentional, I might have gotten to the table at my first university.

I am more aware now of the importance of being involved in central decisions affecting faculty work and broader initiatives of student learning and the ways in which this involvement can be approached. In what follows, I'll try to abstract from my experiences to address five questions: What is the "table"? Who is at the table? What's so hot about being at the table? What can developers bring to the table? and How does one get to the table?

What Is the "Table"?

When the focus of faculty development is defined most inclusively, it is aimed at teaching and learning and faculty work at the institutional level rather than only on the instructional development role. Within this broad scope, the "table" is the metaphor for those activities that influence the decisions surrounding teaching and learning and conditions of faculty work as well as the work itself. In change theory terms (Bergquist & Phillips, 1995; Bolman & Deal, 1997) this means focusing on institutional arrangements and organizational structures that influence how decisions and initiatives get done. Activities that focus more broadly on faculty work at the institutional level range from revising appointment policies, developing the general education plan, making budget decisions, and setting academic schedules to allocating research seed grants and defining expectations for campus service. Those activities that focus broadly on student learning initiatives include deciding how to approach solving institutional problems or improving aspects that affect student learning. Because most of these activities involve meetings, the conference table arises as a salient image. In addition, some activities occur "offline" or through the efforts of the individuals; these may be conducted at coffee tables, lunch tables, or "virtual" tables. These "tables" will be included in the discussion here as well.

Who Is at the Table?

Major types of actors participating at the institutional level regarding faculty work and broader institutional initiatives include members of governance or monitoring committees, administrative unit officers, and policy and project development task forces.

Members of Governance or Monitoring Committees

At most campuses, a faculty governance group addresses crucial issues pertaining to faculty work. There may also be special oversight groups, such as advisory committees on the academic calendar, committees on academic misconduct, and the human subjects review committee. Leadership seems to be a key element: the groups can be active or lethargic, depending on the motivation of those charged with convening them. Sometimes a special incident, such as a lawsuit or a breach of the campus technology security system, can occasion high activity, while at other times, a chairperson who is especially interested in a particular issue can trigger more proactive work. An example of such a committee on most campuses is the faculty affairs committee, which in more routine modes appoints members of grievance committees, reviews policy revisions on evaluation of teaching or faculty appointments, and responds to other issues that arise concerning faculty appointments. In proactive mode, this committee might examine the current system of evaluation of teaching and propose a new one, argue for specific guidelines on faculty workload, or establish a conflict of commitment policy. Membership on these groups is usually appointed. If the group is situated within the faculty governance organization, members are routinely from that group, which would entail faculty council member status. For special activities, however, the groups often invite resource people, advisors, or outside consultants, creating an entrée for the developer.

Administrative Unit Officers

Whether at the institutional or college level, school, department, or program level, administrative units are the locations for much academic decision- making concerning teaching and learning beyond the classroom level as well as faculty work. Depending on how authority is shared and input valued, these units convene groups of people to do work that impacts faculty members as well as student learning in important ways. At the central administrative level, such activities as establishing priorities for a development campaign, restructuring academic support units, choosing a new dean, or cutting the library budget can have far-reaching consequences for faculty and student learning. Often, groups of central administrators make these decisions after consulting with faculty or administrators, on-campus experts, or external consultants. Developers have the advantage of being relatively neutral politically for these consulting roles since they have a campus-wide reach and are not usually aligned with particular disciplinary units.

Within academic units, similar situations occur that affect structures, policy, curriculum and practice and that intersect around matters of teaching and learning. For example, when the department of psychology decides to require senior faculty to teach at least one course of introductory psychology, repercussions affect nontenured faculty members as well as the senior faculty, students, faculty development unit, and others. When nursing requires two service learning experiences for graduation, nursing faculty and students, community members, and service learning support staff are affected. Curricular and workload initiatives, such as these can result from a mandate by the leader, but often have been vetted by a faculty committee convened for the initiative or by advisors invited to provide opinions and ideas on an informal basis. Membership in these advisory groups may be confined to members of the unit, but often include invited participants with special expertise on the topic. Developers can serve this function well, advocating for the faculty and guiding decisions that impact student learning rather than simply reacting after the decision has been made.

Policy and Project Development Task Forces

Usually in conjunction with an idea arising from administrators or the faculty governance body, task forces are convened to develop policies or institutional initiatives. These vary widely in scope, independence, time span, resources, and membership. The charge given to these groups is often specific, but open-ended, affording them the opportunity to be creative, participative, and influential. For example, a general education curriculum development task force or a project on diversifying the faculty can stimulate major changes that influence faculty, teaching and learning practices, programs, and practices that affect student learning. Depending on their leadership, task forces charged with developing policies or projects are usually open to broad membership, drawing from academic, staff, administrative, students, and community populations. It is not uncommon for developers to serve on these groups.

Across all these types of "tables," membership rules may be restrictive or nonexistent. Getting to the table requires determining a feasible and influential role that can be assumed. For example, a developer can always seek to be included as an expert, but if group membership is confined to tenured members of a unit or elected position holders, more extensive involvement is precluded. Ways of participating will be explored later. First, it's important to consider why one would want to be a part of these groups.

What's So Hot About Being at the Table?

As the variety of activities and projects already listed indicates, strikingly influential work occurs at these tables. A vivid memory resurfaces from my days as a consultant while helping a steady stream of new teaching assistants who struggled with the teaching of an introductory course. They were berating themselves, desperate for advice on how to teach well. In reality, the course design was the root of the problem, but they all had to use the existing course design and syllabus. My uninvited inquiry to the course leader was met with the argument that the expectations for the course goals, and methods were determined by a department committee, which in turn was being responsive to the general education committee at the university. I realized that if I wanted to be truly effective, I needed to work at the institutional level to change the idea that cramming vocabulary and theories into an introductory course would lead to effective learning. Instead, I was spending my time consoling the teaching assistants and helping them to develop workarounds or minor adjustments to a major design flaw. By contrast, one of my first acts at my second institution was to use money that could have been spent on student remediation to instead pay the airfare for a large group of our math faculty to travel to Virginia Tech's Math Emporium to look at a model for changing our approach to mathematics teaching. Although both types of efforts were perhaps necessary, each had far different levels of impact.

These two contrasting examples of development work illustrate key points about getting to the table. Besides the main advantage of providing the opportunity to make changes at fundamental levels (resources, policies, and assumptions) of the institution, being a part of key decision-making groups elevates the status of faculty development to include a leadership level instead of exclusively functioning at the service level. Status in itself is not a lofty goal, but the power it brings is the key to effectiveness. If we as developers allow ourselves to be consigned to the fringes, content with quietly nurturing skills or coordinating programs and events as our sole occupation, we marginalize ourselves. We must couple this important behind-the-scenes work with work that is more publicly influential, thereby elevating the whole enterprise of development to a more central position rather than a subservient status. And as Diamond (2005) and Lieberman and Guskin (2003) pointed out, people who are good developers have the background and talent to be leaders.

Cultivating visibility through being at the table promotes deeper understanding of the work of development. Interactions with decision-makers who may not come into direct contact with the services of a development unit help create loyalty and advocacy for the unit or center. These interactions also provide the opportunities to dispel misconceptions about the unit's functions and even to garner new resources or to expand the client base. Casual conversations before or after a meeting with a dean, for example, might later prove their worth during the budget hearings or discussions of the need for a development unit or center.

Finally, getting to the table can reap benefits in personal growth of the developer as well as the co-leaders and decision-makers. Working on the multitude of issues that face academic decision-makers requires knowledge of practices at other institutions, insights into the areas of knowledge that may be new to the developer or administrators and colleagues, and refinement of interpersonal and political skills. Developers at the table have to think about practicalities and navigate conflicting goals and opinions, providing a "get real" factor to the implementation of their ideals.

What Can Developers Bring to the Table?

As Fletcher and Patrick (1998) point out, the higher-education environment is currently too turbulent for institutions to navigate without help. Members of campus communities who can help with identification of issues, ideas for strategic approaches, research skills, and skills for facilitating communication and collaboration are sorely needed. With the understanding that developers vary in their backgrounds, levels of knowledge and skills, and motivational and personal qualities, it is still clear that the professionals in the development positions have much to offer during these challenging times. Lieberman and Guskin (2003) state this well:

> Faculty developers must perceive themselves as institutional change agents. Rather than directing support activities to individual faculty, faculty developers will also need to take responsibility for supporting administrators and faculty leaders, who have some sense that significant change is needed, by providing access to new conceptions of educating students, new institutional forms to enable them to occur and the change process needed to accomplish both. (p. 263)

My earlier writing on this topic (Chism, 1998) illustrates the roles I envision for developers working at the institutional level (see Appendix). Based on an action learning approach to change, I describe how organizations perceive and engage problems or possibilities for improvement and work to arrive at and implement solutions. I connect the needs that the organization has at each phase of the change process with an indication for how the developers can help and what role they might play (see Appendix).

Briefly, the roles that the developers can take on and the strengths they possess for these roles include the following:

- Because developers have knowledge of assessment strategies, teaching approaches, and communication skills, they can serve as

- ○ Assessment resources: Suggesting sound ways for making judgments about the quality of the current state (institution, higher education, teaching and learning)
- ○ Researchers: Helping to locate information about the current or desired state of the organization (research-based best practices in teaching, learning, change processes, retention, curricular reform, assessment, trends etc.)
- Because developers work from a sincere concern about the organization; have cultivated personal habits of honesty, tact, and courage; and continually use networking skills, they can serve as
  - ○ Friendly critics: Pointing out limitations of current practices and arrangements with the good of the institution at heart
- Because developers have pursued knowledge of national models and trends, involvement in national networks, organization and communication skills, they can serve as
  - ○ Messengers: Bringing news of the outside world to the campus
  - ○ Translators: Taking studies and information and putting them into terms that the administrators and faculty can understand
  - ○ Impresarios: Finding good talent (experts in higher educational issues) and bringing it to the campus
  - ○ Travel agents: Alert and initiate faculty and administrators to go to conferences, meetings, and other events where they will develop new understandings
  - ○ Networkers: Knowing people to contact for various pieces of information; putting people in communication with each other
- Because developers have worked to establish their personal self-understanding and vision and have established interpersonal skills, they can serve as
  - ○ Nurturers: Helping the organization to take risks
  - ○ Partners: Contributing time, energy, and other resources
  - ○ Coaches: Supporting and championing change

Baron (2006) lists additional attributes that she thinks faculty developers can bring to the table: entrepreneurship, risk-taking, collaboration, neutrality, strategic planning ability, and initiative.

In short, by virtue of the needs that attracted developers to their work, the qualities they brought with them or developed on the job, their scholarship, often educational preparation in programs such as Higher Education Administration, and the connections and knowledge base they have established, they have much to offer as colleagues.

How Does One Get to the Table?

Despite strong arguments for the importance of working at the institutional level and the fit between the competencies of developers and organizational development, discussion of developers' involvement in key initiatives or decision-making functions are not commonplace and invitations to the table vary across the field. How does one get to the table? Here are nine different ideas.

1. **Define your position carefully when you first accept it.** Negotiating a job offer is perhaps the situation in which you have the most leverage you will ever have. Whether you are being recruited from within or through an external search, it is important to create the understanding with your prospective manager that to do your development job well, you will have to be a part of groups that make the key decisions that impact upon broader issues that affect students learning and faculty work. Making this point early on and specifying the names of the committees or task forces that are important to your role establishes you as an important player for the future. It is also important to ensure that you will have regular meetings with your supervisor and that the agenda for these meetings includes your hearing about and responding to future initiatives that the supervisor is thinking about.

2. **Prepare yourself for influence.** In your own professional development efforts, make reading widely and staying current on higher education issues a priority. Even if topics seem outside of your interest, for example, case-study method or service learning, understand that changes in the faculty composition, endowment spending, general education models, or research compliance rules across the country are things that you should know about. Also cultivate practices of effective group leadership and membership—good teamwork skills, time management, and delegation. Having a "big picture" perspective and good group skills make you much more attractive as a member of a campus planning or action group.

3. **Look for hot button issues.** Baron (2006) talks about "hot button" issues as those that will have a long lifespan, need to involve the whole institution, are complex and multilayered, and create controversy. As examples, she lists accreditation, retention and graduate timelines, learning technologies integration, diversity, and community engagement—issues that are ripe for involvement of the faculty developers.

Land (2001) calls the cultivation of the attitude of seeking these opportunities for participation one of vigilant opportunism (Land, 2001) the orientation toward recognizing important topical events and opportunities and using them strategically. The advantage of locating these issues is that engagement in them puts you at the heart of important continuing work that influences teaching and learning in the broadest sense and that is central to the institution's success.

4. **Volunteer to work with key groups.** Instead of waiting to be appointed or invited, you might send a note or make a call to the chair of a committee or leader of an initiative to which you can make a contribution. While your offer might be refused, you at least have taken the opportunity to point out that you believe the undertaking in question is important and that you have expertise in the area. If the offer is accepted, you are at the table.

5. **Create a track record for being useful.** The leaders tend to remember those who have been able to provide them with timely and accurate information, good advice, or contacts with others who can help them. To establish your usefulness, you might do things, such as pass along good articles in the literature, names of consultants you've found helpful, or ideas about new developments in higher education that institutions need to consider. While these actions alone do not get you to the table, they ensure that you exert some indirect influence and create the possibility that your name will come up when future decision-making bodies are formed. I still smile when I hear the administrators use expressions such as "making the campus sticky" or "digital immigrants," knowing that I originally introduced them to these terms.

6. **Make friends in high places.** Establishing a personal connection with known leaders is an important part of the developer's work. This does not mean engaging in social climbing or flattery, but rather getting to know the people who are influencing the conditions under which you and the faculty work. Inviting the president of the faculty council to lunch, talking with the budget director at the supermarket, and taking advantage of other informal opportunities to get to know campus leaders as people can help you to do your work better, but also has the side advantage of raising your profile as a potential member of future decision-making groups.

7. **Market yourself and your center.** Carefully considering the way in which your website, brochures, or other communications are framed

is essential to establishing connections that get you to the table. It is extremely important not to foreground yourself, yet the opposite—making yourself invisible—is also a problem. Talk with the communication and marketing staff at your institution about how the work of you and your center can be used to enhance the reputation of the institution as progressive: this will create internal recognition as well. Conduct personal visits with deans and other decision-makers to establish a personal connection.

8. **Understand who might be dismissive of or threatened by you or your center.** Cataloging resistance helps to anticipate factors that are blocking your access. For example, many developers do not have tenured faculty positions: the faculty members who are most protective of their status regard tenure as a central qualifying condition for membership at the table. Deans may regard the development center as doing work that should rightly be done only within the academic unit and may resent budget expenditures that support the center. They may not want rival voices in decision-making situations. While it is not possible to dispel misconceptions and jealousies or prevent exclusionary practices, it is good to understand what these are in order to circumvent them.

9. **Do not overlook the "factory virtues."** Showing up on time, coming prepared, speaking respectfully, and being organized are all important qualities for successful membership in decision-making groups. While exceptions to these rules are perhaps tolerated more in academia than other contexts, it is still worth the effort to become known as someone who remembers when meetings are scheduled, follows up on tasks, and is dependable. These qualities may give one the edge when group membership is being decided.

In sum, the challenges that face higher education are too important to be faced without appropriate diagnosis, information, and judgment. Faculty developers offer their institutions knowledge and skills that can help produce transformative change. They owe it to their institutions and to themselves to be at the many tables where decisions about the future of institutions and students learning are being made. As Baron (2006) points out, "The effectiveness of faculty development, and sometimes its very survival, is dependent to a large extent on its ability to influence and participate in organizational development outside its own confines" (p. 29).

References

Baron, L. (2006). The advantages of a reciprocal relationship between faculty development and organizational development in higher education. In S. Chadwick-Blossey, & D. R. Robertson (Eds.), *To improve the academy: Vol. 24. Yearbook of the professional and organizational development network in higher education* (pp. 29–43). Bolton, MA: Anker.

Bergquist, W., & Phillips, S. (1995). *Developing human and organizational resources: A comprehensive manual.* Peter Magnusson.

Bolman, L. G., & Deal, T. E. (1997). *Reframing organizations: Artistry, choice, and leadership* (2nd ed.). San Francisco: Jossey-Bass.

Chism, N. (1998). The role of educational developers in institutional change: From the basement office to the front office. In D. Lieberman (Ed.), *To improve the academy: Vol. 17. Yearbook of the professional and organizational development network in higher education* (pp. 141–153). Stillwater, OK: New Forums.

Diamond, R. M. (2005). The institutional change agency: The expanding role of academic support centers. In S. Chadwick-Blossey (Ed.), *To improve the academy: Vol. 23. Yearbook of the professional and organizational development network in higher education* (pp. 24–37). Bolton, MA: Anker.

Fletcher, J. J., & Patrick, S. K. (1998). Not just workshops any more: The role of faculty development in reframing academic priorities. *International Journal of Academic Development, 3*(1), 39–46.

Land, R. (2001). Agency, context, and change in academic development. *International Journal of Academic Development, 6*(1), 4–20.

Lieberman, D. A., & Guskin, A. F. (2003). The essential role of faculty development in new higher education models. In S. Chadwick-Blossey (Ed.), *To improve the academy: Vol. 21. Yearbook of the professional and organizational development network in higher education* (pp. 257–272). Bolton, MA: Anker.

Appendix

Developers' Roles in the Change Process

Organizational Task	How the Educational Developer Can Help	Role of the Educational Developer
Consider present effectiveness	• Assist in articulating assessment models • Assist in implementation of assessment methods	Researcher Assessment resource
Embrace "hitches"–problematic areas	• Help decision-makers to reflect on results of assessment • Create a community of inquiry	Friendly critic
Generate possibilities for change	• Help create awareness of new ways of thinking about the work of higher education	Messenger Translator Impresario Travel agent Networker
Try out some new possibilities	• Provide process consultation • Contribute labor • Give psychological support	Nurturer Partner Coach
Collect data on the effects of these changes	• Assist with assessment (as above) The cycle repeats	Researcher Assessment resource

Source: Chism, N. (1998). The role of educational developers in institutional change: From the basement office to the front office. In D. Lieberman (Ed.), *To improve the academy: Yearbook of the Professional and Organizational Development Network in Higher Education:* Vol. 17. (pp. 141–153). Stillwater, OK: New Forums Press. Reprinted with permission of John Wiley & Sons, Inc.

3

NURTURING INSTITUTIONAL CHANGE

Collaboration and Leadership Between Upper-Level
Administrators and Faculty Developers

Devorah Lieberman

T
raditionally, the questions we, as professional educators, ask about
curriculum and pedagogy have been deeply rooted in our strong desire to improve student learning. For decades, the development of
skills and abilities of faculty that were intended to accelerate student achievement has been ad hoc and the research results related to student learning have
had scattered venues for dissemination. In addition, for many years structured
faculty development activities were not a primary academic concern. Seldom
was institution-wide faculty development integral to internal or external systems of accountability. Similarly, confusion was common about the purpose
and the role of the individuals tasked with, or who chose to be the leaders in
"faculty development." Rarely was there a direct connection between institutionalizing a faculty development position, and when others lobbied for new
positions in academic departments or administrative offices. Though faculty
development has come to be considered "important," it is far from being
deemed "critical" to the faculty or the institution.

The Need for Centers for Teaching and Learning

In the last quarter of the previous century many colleges and universities began
to realize the importance of systemic and strategic faculty development. That
responsibility was placed in Centers for Teaching and Learning. Such centers

tended to be separated from the mainstream of institutional endeavors and often were funded by time-limited foundation grants or as a "pet project" for a particular administrator or senior faculty member. Centers for Teaching and Learning were then understood and positioned as sources of assistance to faculty who had specific questions about improving their own capacity to teach. Mission statements of many of these centers often focused only on providing assistance for improved or remedial pedagogical strategies (see chapter 2).

My first foray into faculty development began in the 1990s at my former institution, a large public university. I had been teaching in a tenure-track position within a traditional department. Recognizing my deep interest in student learning, the provost appointed me to a new position: director for teaching and learning of a newly created Center. Opinions about the need, value, and relevance for the Center were widely diverse. The mere establishment of the Center was seen by some as a statement that my colleagues on the faculty were not good teachers. Others, to be sure, hailed the center as an important resource. Shortly after assuming the directorship, I contacted each department chair to discuss the new Center's mission and to receive feedback about the services the Center could offer. Upon the introduction of the new Center and me, one department chair emphatically stated: "Your Center is a cancer upon the institution. It gives nothing; it only uses our resources in ways that do not benefit us." I was shocked!

It was astonishing for me to learn that this Center, which was created to provide what the provost and I thought were critical resources to enhance student learning, was perceived to be a drain of the precious resources and provided nothing of value to the university. Five years hence, when the institution was facing serious budget constraints, the administration announced that any department or program that was neither revenue-producing nor academically critical to the institution's mission would face the deepest revenue reductions or would be eliminated entirely. Through many internal discussions with Center staff and larger discussions with the budget committee, we were able to position the Center as a unit that, though not revenue-positive, was the recipient of sizeable external grants and provided services to the faculty that were accessed by hundreds of full-time and tenure-track faculty. The Center survived.

Revenue-positive and mission-critical are vitally important criteria in determining a program or center's value. Yet, standards of valuation are so subjective that a case can be made for or against almost any institutional endeavor! I believe that Centers for Teaching and Learning and institution-wide faculty development are mission-critical. Are we as professional educators not in the business of providing students the best possible education through experiences that expand both their knowledge, and more importantly, their abilities to learn? As has been documented, the correlation among student success, retention, and positive revenue is quite strong (Pascarella & Terrenzini, 2005).

The purpose and need for centers for teaching and learning often continue to be misunderstood. Part of the confusion may lie in the name: "Center for Teaching and Learning." This name implies that the sole purpose of the center is to provide assistance for teaching and learning as opposed to the broader purposes aligned with the institutional mission and institutional change. It is a mystery to me how the centers can be perceived as nonessential to the mission of the institutions that were founded on providing excellence in student education. Perhaps this lack of recognition lies partially with the center leadership, names of the centers, and the ones who craft the center's mission.

The mission statements of many centers position them as supporting the academic process through ancillary activity—a place to go when you or somebody else thinks you need help. Such language fosters the perceptions that the center is all about remedial and individual level assistance. Often, centers of this ilk do not perceive themselves as entrepreneurial and, consequently, do not take the initiative to create significant roles for themselves in support of either the central mission of the university, in academic departments, or in future visioning for the institution. They wait for the faculty to come to them with questions about teaching and learning or for administrative directives around which to focus their programing. Leadership of the most effective centers is almost evangelistic in their advocacy for improved pedagogy.

Positioning the Center's Role in the Institution

More than ever before, institutions, faculty, and students are facing pressure for increased accountability from accrediting agencies and sources of public and private funding. Accreditors, funding sources, legislatures, parents, and students themselves are intensively focused on the return on their investment of money, effort, and time. All press for data defining learning outcomes and long-term impact. Many of their questions are the same that faculty development advocates have been asking for decades. Yet, now these questions are being asked in contexts that are more systemic, systematic, and rigorous. These questions are forcing us, as institutions and as professional educators, to create a campus culture of assessment and accountability that includes and extends well beyond the classroom. External and internal constituencies insist that we examine our own institutions, our missions, our learning outcomes, our commitment to the greater good, and our own performances. No longer is accountability an issue that arises only during deliberations of budget or promotion and tenure. New insistence on accountability is forcing continuing and broad-based professional development among faculty in order to ensure, as best as we can, that they possess the skills and perspectives required for demonstrable and pervasive achievement of the institutional mission in a climate of rapid social, technological, informational, and scientific evolution.

With the onset of increased accountability and transparency, every institution seeks to establish its brand as credible, dynamic, and distinctive. Prospective and current students, faculty, staff, and donors—those constituencies that provide the human and financial resources on which an institution thrives—insist that institutions deliver on the promises articulated in its brand. As we know, the core of every institution is its ability to deliver learning. Centers for Teaching and Learning must perceive themselves and be perceived by others as absolutely essential elements of this institutional endeavor and become those units that have the skills, knowledge, and ability to holistically assist the campus achieve its institutional mission and articulated strategic goals. The push for accountability provides the opportunity for centers to become intentionally "mission critical." In other words, without the existence of a center for teaching and learning it would be difficult (and in some cases impossible) to achieve the mission of the institution.

Staff of such faculty development centers must seize the opportunity and become engaged collaborators, part of the institutional team that helps to create, implement, and assess the institution's strategic and tactical academic and co-curricular initiatives. Faculty development officers and staff simply cannot afford to stand in the wings, waiting to be invited on stage. They must align themselves as members of the upper administrative team and assume leadership roles in the following endeavors:

- Shaping the institutional mission
- Shaping and informing the strategic planning process
- Assessing student learning
- Helping to develop and assess disciplinary programs
- Campus accreditation processes
- Assisting with institutional organizational development
- Furthering initiatives to support the institutional mission, that is, distance education and general education reform
- Bridging the institution with the national dialogue

- Disseminating information about the institution through conferences, publications, and off-campus site visitations
- Connecting the campus units and departments to one another and to the institutional initiatives
- Providing input into the faculty-adopted promotion and tenure guidelines
- Shaping and supporting the campus culture
- Developing and securing external grant support
- Mentoring new faculty and adjunct instructors
- Mentoring academic department chairs
- Furthering campus wide diversity initiatives
- Furthering campus wide internationalization initiatives
- Providing graduate assistant support
- Providing E-portfolio development and support

Faculty Development in the Learning Organization

Ideally every college or university, no matter its scope or franchise, should function as a "learning organization" (i.e., a group of colleagues who are continually enhancing their capabilities to deliver the institution's mission). Simplistically stated, upper-level administrators are responsible for sustained institutional visioning while concurrently creating a highly inclusive institutional infrastructure that supports this vision. It is they, with the concurrence of the governing board, who design institutional infrastructure and the processes by which it operates. The way in which they do this determines institutional culture. The most effective institutions intentionally adopt the practices of the learning organizations (Kezar, 2005; Lieberman, 2005).

In this environment, faculty development thrives. Individuals charged with faculty development easily cross position title and responsibility boundaries. What do I mean by this? The faculty often see their roles and responsibilities as related directly to their specific individual disciplinary teaching, research, and committee work. Deans, associate deans, directors, etc., often perceive their roles and responsibilities related directly to overseeing and advocating for specific programs. In contrast, the administrative staff of teaching and learning or faculty development Centers serve many departments and across all academic programs. Their perspective encompasses a broad view, a view from the trenches, and a view that the very necessary hierarchy of an institution inhibits. One of the most apparent markers is that the faculty developers' view is not only informed by their historical relationship with colleagues in the disciplinary trenches, but also their concurrent foray and participation in the national and international conversations and understanding of the related literature. While living in both worlds, they can more easily earn the credibility and the trust of the faculty at large as well as the upper-level administration. Positioned as such, and if provided appropriate latitude, an institution's faculty development team can develop an encompassing perspective on the academic process, and thus serve as internal consultants for specific departments and programs as well as the institution at large.

Taking these perspectives into account, here are the most typical structures for faculty development activities and centers:

- An identified center for teaching and learning with a director and staff
- A full-time staff or faculty member who individually coordinates faculty development
- A part-time staffing arrangement
- A council, academy, or teaching committee for one or a system of institutions
- An institutional commitment to the faculty development with no centralized support structure—faculty development responsibilities are shared by many throughout the institution

There is no optimal infrastructure that dictates the most effective organizational design for faculty development. Typically, the primary faculty development officer serves as a senior member of the staff of the chief academic officer. To avoid the problems posed when faculty development is perceived to be a service rather than a strategic function, the chief academic officer should make it a standing practice to engage the faculty development director in substantial and public decision making regarding evolutions of curriculum and pedagogy and the broader teaching and learning initiatives. In this manner, a commitment to enhanced capacity for teaching and learning can be seamlessly integrated into sustaining institutional vision and its implementation.

Upper-Level Administrators' Engagement of Faculty Developers and Centers for Teaching and Learning

The structure I suggest and have found the most effective ensures that the principal faculty developer will blend into the team of upper-level administrators primarily responsible for implementing institutional vision. As the current provost and vice president for academic affairs at Wagner College, a private liberal arts-comprehensive institution, I have the luxury of working closely with the president and the senior staff to further strategic initiatives to support the mission of the institution. My own academic and professional background has also helped to shape what I believe are significant areas of responsibility and formal positions needed to achieve the institution's strategic and tactical objectives. My own scholarly and academic growth came from following a traditional tenure-track faculty position in an academic department and then selecting to pursue faculty development within the same institution. These various vantage points shaped my perceptions of the importance of bringing the voice and experience of faculty development into the process and product of institutional change.

Though Wagner College does not (yet) have a centrally located or singularly identified center for teaching and learning, we are deeply committed to the learning community model for faculty development, and provide a stipend to a faculty member who serves as the Faculty Scholar for Teaching and Learning. The Faculty Scholar for Teaching and Learning reports directly to the provost and understands that her role is to further the goals in the campus-wide strategic plan, which are associated with "teaching excellence." In particular, this position focuses on furthering a campus climate that places student learning and sound pedagogy at the pinnacle of respect for faculty, administrators, and students. The Faculty Scholar for Teaching and Learning is responsible for three primary objectives: (a) to assist with student recruitment and retention activities associated with faculty teaching, students learning, and deeper student connections with faculty; (b) to assist with engaging all full-time and tenure-track faculty in self-examination of pedagogical principles and strategies; and (c) to address any and all individual faculty questions, concerns, and curiosities about their own teaching practice and student learning.

The Wagner Plan is the core undergraduate plan for the campus. For further information about this, refer to www.wagner.edu. The Faculty Scholar for Teaching and Learning brings her faculty development efforts to bear on her charge and to supporting the Wagner Plan goals, as stated below.

To Deepen the Wagner Plan for the Practical Liberal Arts by:

- Increasing the learning outcomes of Wagner students in core areas of knowledge acquisition, effective communication, and problem solving
- Increasing student learning outcomes by integrating fieldwork, classroom instruction, and applied learning
- Increasing size of full-time faculty and rebalance responsibilities of faculty to meet educational goals of the Wagner Plan
- Enhancing and sustaining the effective use of information technology

- Institutionalizing the use of effective learning outcomes assessment
- Increasing the scholarly development and professional profile of the Wagner faculty through a sustained program of support for scholarly work
- Continuing to increase both the academic quality and overall diversity of the student body
- Increasing professional credentials and diversity of faculty and administration

Collaborators and Coconstructors of Institutional Change

Based on the case above, I believe that faculty developers have a critical role to play in furthering institutional transformation and institutional initiatives. In order to achieve sound, systemic, and continuing change it is important to identify faculty, staff, and administrators who have the potential to become active collaborators in leading and participating in this same process. Some of these may assume faculty development as their primary responsibility, while others may assume faculty development responsibilities in conjunction with the other institutional roles.

Foremost among collaborators are, ideally, the provost's direct reports and includes: the Associate Provost, Associate Dean of the Faculty, Coordinator of Grant Activities, Dean of Academic and Career Development, Dean of Campus Life, Dean of the Library, Dean of Learning Communities and Experiential Learning, Director for the Center for Leadership and Service, Director of Instructional Technology, Faculty Scholar for Teaching and Learning, and the Registrar. Members of the Provost's Council serve as co-constructors of the institutional vision and change process. Wagner College (similar to many other institutions) participated in a lengthy process to identify strategic objectives to support the institutional mission. Annually, the Provost's Council collaboratively designs lengthy objectives to help meet these institutional goals. These goals are reviewed, edited, modified, and adjusted by the faculty and the Board of Trustees. The Faculty Scholar for Teaching and Learning participates directly in this process, contributing a voice, an opinion, and ongoing feedback.

Recognizing the Faculty Developer's Roles and Responsibilities

When the faculty developer is recognized as a critical resource person, he or she will provide and staff a regularly scheduled series of activities to enhance student learning through more effective pedagogy. In addition, it is important that faculty development staff be nimble and able to be considered "go to" professionals who can address needs from the perspectives of the individual faculty member or administrator, a department or other institutional unit, or the college or university as a whole.

Annually, Wagner College schedules a day-long faculty development event entitled "Focus on Faculty" during which all full-time and adjunct faculty are invited to meet and focus on a mission-critical issue. This year we chose to concentrate on student retention and related variables. Because the Faculty Scholar for Teaching and Learning is considered an expert in areas related to teaching and learning as well as responsive to the campus needs, she took the lead and established the theme "Connecting With Students: Improving Student Retention." In order to create campus-wide support for the event, she convened an array of collaborators from different departments to conceive, structure, and deliver the day's program. Working with her were the Dean of Academic and Career Development, the Director for Instructional Technology, the Associate Dean for the Faculty, the Dean for Campus Life, and the Provost. All the organizers felt mutual involvement in the event and the outcomes that emerged.

No matter how gifted, a single staff person cannot facilitate faculty development for an entire campus, irrespective of the size of the campus, nor is it wise to attempt to do so. We feel that it is essential that multiple faculty assume leadership in ongoing faculty development activities. It is important to note that faculty development activities are assumed by faculty who conjoin these activities with their traditional faculty roles.

Because every institution has different personalities and compositions, I recommend that the campus conceive of their "faculty development structure" in a way that works best with the particular campus. However, please note that faculty development activities should be present, thoughtfully designed, and aligned with the longer-term vision of the campus. Wagner College is known for its culture of closely knit faculty collaboration, which gives rise to our feeling that it is best to have decentralized faculty development. Though these faculty development activities are decentralized, those who take the various leads on each contribute voices and assume roles in shaping annual goals and institutional mission.

A list of strategic faculty development activities could go on and on. Examples of decentralized faculty development activities at Wagner College include, but are not limited to:

- The Coordinator for Faculty Grants facilitates regular workshops on grant writing, facilitates a year-long grant writing faculty group entitled "The Grant Circle," and assists faculty individually with grant questions.

- The Dean for Learning Communities and Experiential Learning over-sees monthly faculty development activities for all faculty teaching undergraduate learning communities.
- The Faculty Scholar for Teaching and Learning assists faculty with their pedagogy and student learning and organizing on-going faculty development activities. She is readily available to all new and junior faculty as a resource and as a class observer.
- The Associate Dean of the Faculty organizes mentor–mentee collab-orations and events for the new faculty, their department chairs, and experienced faculty.

Faculty development can also be intentionally embedded in specific pro-gram initiatives created to advance institutional change. One of the campus-wide initiatives at Wagner College (as it is for most colleges) is to increase and enhance globalization and internationalization in the student body, the faculty, the staff, and the curriculum. When this goal was originally identified, it was necessary to create a process by which it could be achieved. This process needed to have campus leadership that included administrators, faculty, and students. We thought it critical to create and appoint an Internationaliza-tion Action Council that would represent campus voices, create a campus blueprint, and continue to oversee the blueprint so that the outcomes became a reality.

Embedded in this blueprint are faculty development activities aligned with the goals of the Council and the institutional mission. Examples of faculty development activities in the blueprint include: train-the-trainer domestic and international diversity training for all faculty and staff at the college, specific mentoring for all international faculty (in teaching, scholarship, and acclimation to campus culture), and embedding internationalization into course curricula.

Similarly, professional development for the faculty and staff has been integrated in our Diversity Action Council, with representation from student, faculty, administrative, and staff personnel. Examples of faculty development activities in this area include assistance in successfully integrating diversity activities into all the first-year program courses, hosting monthly "Social Justice luncheon topics," creating a Center for Intercultural Advancement to further these and additional activities.

Both the Internationalization Action Council and the Diversity Action Council are co-chaired by an administrator and by a faculty member with the understanding that their roles are to be the campus leaders and faculty developers in shaping and supporting the domestic and internationalization goals, activities, and outcomes for the campus.

Positioning Faculty Development as Change Agents in Learning Organizations

Faculty development is a salient ingredient for institutional progress. Yet faculty developers are not considered, normally, among an institution's "change agents." They should be, however, because their work can have such a dramatic impact on the central role of most colleges and universities. Following are several recommendations that will help establish faculty developers in this, one of their most important roles. I have gathered these ideas through many discussions with professionals in the faculty development, chief academic officers and provosts, and presidents.

1. Negotiate for a title that communicates broad campus responsibility. Typically the faculty developers assume the title of the director or coordinator. This immediately places the center and the director in middle management. If possible, negotiate for a title equal to vice provost, associate provost, or dean. Why is this important? If this position reports directly to the provost, then this individual will consistently be perceived as providing a central voice in shaping institutional strategic and tactical goals.
2. Work closely with the provost to design the faculty development position description and responsibilities. The position description and responsibilities should articulate the faculty developer as an active participant in the shaping of the academic affairs goals and vision. This provost will then perceive faculty development as central to the development of the mission and not merely a support role. In addition, this raises credibility and helps to educate other administrators and faculty to the same.
3. Place the center close to the heart of the campus. If the campus supports a physical center that assumes faculty development responsibilities, the geographic location of the center is critical. The center should be located in as close proximity as possible to the provost's or the president's offices. This communicates metaphorical proximity to the mission of the institution. In addition, the center furnishings, and so forth, should communicate stature within the institution. If this is not possible, I would recommend that the center exists in the library, which is understood as a primary focal point of scholarship

at most institutions. This communicates centrality to the institution's mission. In my opinion, virtual centers do not communicate sustainability. Having a visible center contributes to its substance in thought and in action.

4. Choose a leader with perceived credibility. The individual who directs faculty development for the campus should have established credibility among the faculty, staff, and administrators. This credibility can be derived from any of several different sources. First, if the developer is from among the faculty, this person should be an established scholar and recognized professor of excellence. If the faculty developer is not from the faculty ranks, this person should have an established record of excellence from her or his area of academic expertise. This is a critical element in this equation. If faculty developers do not have perceived credibility, they will consistently be marginalized and their contributions undervalued.

5. Assume a leadership role in student-learning assessment. Be available and become critical to the central team appointed to the institution's accreditation process. In addition, become the perceived "go to person" or "go to office" for departments who have their own individual accreditation process (e.g., Departments of Nursing, Business, Physician Assistant, Chemistry, Architecture).

6. Assume a leadership role in the specific area for which the institution strives to be unique. At my former institution, after several years as director of teaching and learning, I negotiated to be appointed as a vice provost for academic affairs with responsibilities for the faculty development. In this position, the faculty development center assumed campus-wide leadership in areas in which the institution intended to establish itself as excellent and unique: teaching/learning, community-based learning, and assessment. With this in mind, the center was not perceived as the teaching and learning center, but rather the center that provided leadership with my fellow vice provost colleagues, providing both input into shaping vision as well as faculty, administrative, and student support to help achieve these goals. When faculty developers have a title analogous to director or coordinator and directly report to a vice or associate provost, they may be caught in the position that serves only a particular area of the campus, for example undergraduate studies, graduate studies, continuing education, etc. This automatically places limits on the perceptions of campus-wide support as well as minimizes opportunities for providing leadership and input into institutional vision or mission.

7. Provide "nontraditional" faculty development services that are per-ceived as indispensable to campus climate and success. At my previous institution, the faculty development office not only supported teach-ing and learning, community based learning, and assessment, but also provided the following: credit bearing courses for graduate assistants, portfolio development for all graduate students, portfolio assistance for all faculty, and dossier review for the faculty who were submitting materials for promotion and/or tenure (several departments made this a requirement and others made this optional).

8. Continually seek external funding to support initiatives that are part of the institutional mission and further institutional change. This will further deepen the perception that the faculty development officer(s) and/center are integral to the mission of the institution and ongoing institutional change.

Lessons Learned About Inclusion in Institutional Change: Anticipate Needs, Identify Needs, Position Yourself to Meet These Needs

For faculty developers who find themselves in positions where they believe that they are perceived as important but not critical to the institution, I would suggest considering the following as a means to move from the position of important to *critical*:

1. ***Identify and anticipate needs.*** The more you can anticipate the leadership and support needs of the campus, the more likely the provost and president will position you and/or the center in a central position. Become active and visible in the national higher education conversation.

2. ***Become active and a leader in national professional development organizations.*** Engaging with peers in efforts to enhance professional development nationally will open a vast network of professionals and examples of best practices that can help accelerate accomplishment of institutional goals for improvement of teaching and learning. Become active in the Professional and Organizational Development network in higher education. The Association of American Colleges & Uni-versities is broadly known for its outstanding services in academic administrative and faculty development. *EDUCAUSE* advances high education by promoting intelligent use of information technology.

Programs and publications of Higher Education Research and Development Society of Australia are also highly regarded. Leadership in a national or international organization will lend additional credibility to your voice within your own campus.

Conclusion

As institutions of higher education strive to be more efficient and more effective in times when they are being held more accountable by peer institutions and external constituents, it is imperative that faculty developers and administrators seize this opportunity to create the optimal organizational infrastructure and institutional climate. It is the marriage of upper-level administrators and faculty developers that will help to make this optimal environment a reality. It is the mutual respect, collaborative interactions, and complementary contributions to the institutional strategic vision that will increase the personal and professional successes of students, faculty, administrators, and the institution as a whole and, last but by far not least, individuals who have chosen to wear proudly the mantle of *Faculty Developer.*

Note

The author would like to thank John Ross (Rosswrites) for his generous and thoughtful edits and additions to this chapter. They are greatly appreciated.

References

Kezar, A. (Ed.). (2005). *Higher education as a learning organization: Promising concepts and approaches.* New Directions for Higher Education, No. 131. San Francisco: Jossey-Bass.

Lieberman, D. A. (2005). Organizational learning in higher education. In A. Kezar (Ed.), *Beyond faculty development: How centers for teaching and learning can be laboratories for learning* (pp. 87–98). Wilmington, DE Wiley Periodicals, Inc.

Pascarella, E. T., & Terrenzini, P. T. (2005). *How college affects students: A third decade of research.* San Francisco: Jossey-Bass.

PART TWO

EXAMINING THE EVIDENCE
OF AN ORGANIZATIONAL
DEVELOPMENT ROLE

I n part two, the investigation, *Coming in From the Margins,* is outlined, and the quantitative and qualitative results of the survey and case study interviews are presented. This evidence serves as the foundation for the strategies discussed in each of the ensuing chapters throughout the remainder of the book. What were the common factors prevalent among the directors and centers functioning as key leaders in institutional initiatives? What can a director and center do to shift an existing instructional development role to include significant involvement in larger institutional initiatives? This section will address these questions in-depth and identify the best practices in adopting this broader role and common strategies within the cultural and institutional contexts of each center.

As a foundation for the remaining chapters of the book, chapter 4 begins this section by defining the parameters, design, and methods of the study. Of additional interest to the reader is the summary provided of the center-based, director-based, and institutional-based factors tested for the significance of their relationship to each director's level of involvement in institutional initiatives. As little has been done in the way of factor analysis of this leadership role, the factors that enable or impede the director and center involvement at the institutional level were difficult to predict. Not surprisingly, few of the predicted center-, director-, and institution-based factors from the survey data were found significantly related to the level of involvement in institutional initiatives. However, a new set of primary director-, center-, and institution-based factors emerged quite strongly from the 18 in-depth case study interviews of center directors and their supervisors.

Chapter 5 concludes part two with a thorough review of 27 primary director-, center-, and institution-based enabling and impeding factors that emerged from the 18 case study interviews. Although several of the survey factors also surfaced among the case study directors and supervisors, a substantially larger and different set of primary factors were revealed using qualitative methods. Qualitative evidence from the case study interviews is provided in the form of excerpts to support these unpredicted findings. The value of a combined method's approach is apparent in studies such as this when breaking new ground in understanding an experience using qualitative data to identify and map unknown factors, and using quantitative methods to track their prevalence and significance. As a result, the previously unexamined organizational development role, now prevalent among the center directors, becomes more transparent to this field and more easily shaped through professional development.

INVESTIGATING INSTITUTIONAL INVOLVEMENT AND CHANGE AGENCY

Connie M. Schroeder

Academic developers have access to more journals, books, and conferences than they could skim or attend in a lifetime. Given the continuously expanding nature of instructional development and the accompanying literature, academic developers are tapped to their limit in their practice and to stay current. Despite the fact that instructional development is the result of a widespread role transformation itself a few decades back, it is now the central focus of most centers. As centers expanded across the United States during the 1970s, they continued to struggle with issues of credibility at many institutions, even while demand for instructional development grew and contributed to this widespread establishment. Where did TLCs become positioned within the institutional landscape and why? Somewhat of an odd duck, situated between the faculty and the administration, some centers thrived and became significantly important while others managed to maintain their role, although positioned somewhat off of the institutional radar screen, and still others closed.

The struggle for TLC legitimization versus marginalization has ebbed and flowed across many types of institutions and eroded away even the strongest of centers. Perhaps this has created a defensive posture or resistance to change, or made it difficult for the field to question itself. The practices, assumptions, and expectations of any role can become so well established that an opportunity for further role transformation is missed or resisted. Therefore, it may be difficult to rally widespread reflection on the additional organizational dimension of this work. Sandwiched between one more take-it-or-leave-it piece of anecdotal advice on how to do this work and evolving concerns with assessment, technology advances, and funding cuts, a role transformation might fail to grab a developer's instructionally focused attention. How often does the field reflect on itself and collectively look to the future of the field?

Firmly entrenched within an instructional development role with responsibilities that are never done, an awareness of yet another dimension to this role—an institutional leadership role already permeating this work—is sorely lacking. As a result, the scope of this organizational development role and the accompanying unique practices largely are undefined and lack systematic study. Several lone organizational development voices in and outside of the United States (see chapter 1) have questioned the nearly exclusive instructional development dimension of this role and called developers to look more closely at institutional leadership as a significant dimension of this field (Baron, 2006; Brown, 1992; Chism, 1998; Diamond, 2005; Lieberman & Guskin, 2002; Taylor & Schönwetter, 2002).

Despite some discussion among the academic development leaders who have called attention to the organizational dimension of this role, there is little data upon which to guide this discussion and make efforts to reposition this role collectively. Without research-based inquiry and evidence, this rhetoric will bear little impact on the academic development field. When the full scope of this role change is realized collectively, the directors determined to integrate instructional *and* organizational development roles should not be left without a compass. A far better understanding of an institutional change agent role and the factors that enable or impede this involvement is critical in order to base these discussions on more than opinion.

The study *Coming in From the Margins*, funded by the Professional and Organizational Development (POD) Network in 2005, addresses this void by examining the following research questions regarding the current practice of this role:

- What are the levels and type of involvement of teaching and learning centers and directors in institutional initiatives?
- In which institutional initiatives are directors and teaching and learning centers involved (over the past five years)?
- What factors enable or impede the centers' and directors' participation in institutional initiatives?

- How do the enabling or impeding factors work to impact the director and center's involvement in institutional initiatives? How does the process of involvement in institutional initiatives develop? What does an involved center and director look like?

The results of both the survey and interview data are presented in the following two chapters in an effort to provide some of the much-needed direction for developers to navigate a broader role within their institutions. The data presented in this chapter provide a quantitative skeleton of factors as one type of evidence and are followed by a chapter of additional evidence in the form of rich descriptions. The quantitative results reveal surprising factors that enabled and impeded this role. Conflicts of interest, challenges to tradition, and comfortable assumptions and habits rose to the surface when this role was integrated alongside the developer's existing responsibilities and functions. The results presented in this volume may raise more questions than are answered as this field struggles to grapple proactively with the challenges facing higher education. The results of this study, followed by others, can prompt the much-needed discussion of a redefined organizational dimension of this role already underway and help make transparent the implications for centers of teaching and learning, academic developers, faculty, institutions in higher education, and most importantly, students.

Design and Methodology

Upon institutional review board approval, several types of data from multiple sources were collected to better understand the role of teaching and learning centers and directors in institutional initiatives and change. The study aimed to describe institutional involvement of centers and directors at multiple levels, from *marginalized* (defined as not involved in institutional planning or initiatives) to *key leaders* (consistently involved in broader teaching and learning initiatives), and identify the primary factors that enable or impede this role. Quantitative and qualitative methods were used to collect broad-based data from across the field of faculty development through surveys and in-depth interviews with center directors and their supervisors. The combined methods approach served to triangulate the data and increase the credibility of the results.

Survey Design

An anonymous online survey (see Appendix A) was constructed with survey design consultation. Due to grant constraints, the population surveyed was limited to members of the Professional and Organizational Development (POD) Network who were center directors. The total director population at that time, based on the POD executive office records, was 477. An initial e-mail letter with an overview of the study was disseminated electronically by the POD executive director through the POD members only reflector and made accessible to POD members online from January 10, 2006, through February 10, 2006. Invitation to participate in the survey was limited to members who met the criteria of being both a center director and a POD member during that window of time. Directors who met the criteria were asked to visit the embedded web page link provided and to indicate their consent by completing the anonymous online survey.

The survey was comprised of 17 quantitative and qualitative questions regarding the current role that both the directors and centers of teaching and learning play in institutional initiatives. The survey focused on variables predicted as factors affecting the level of institutional involvement such as length of directorship, director background, and status, age of center, and so forth. These variables were later tested for significance in relationship to the level of director or center institutional leadership involvement. The key issue of involvement in institutional initiatives was investigated by embedding several types of questions throughout the survey to enhance the survey validity. Short answer, multiple choice, ranked options, and Likert Scale formats were used. The key phrase "involvement in institutional initiatives" was defined on the survey as "being on an institutional planning group, committee, or task force implementing an intervention or strategy" to distinguish this role from center programing on topics related to institutional priorities. *The Continuum of Center Involvement* diagram included on the survey helped respondents differentiate between the levels of involvement in institutional initiatives from, "marginalized" to a "key leader," and self-identify their involvement level and that of their center (see Figure 4.1).

The survey was divided into two parts. Part I of the survey entailed eight questions. Six multiple-choice questions requested institution, center, and director information. Respondents were given the option of *other* in the multiple choice questions in part I and provided space to include a short answer. The remaining two short-answer questions in part I asked respondents to provide their center mission statement and describe the events prompting the origin of the center (see Table 4.1).

In part II of the survey, participants were asked to complete nine quantitative and qualitative questions. Six multiple choice questions asked respondents to choose from lists and scales that defined or identified the daily work performed, focus of the center, institutional initiatives, level of involvement,

FIGURE 4.1
Continuum of center involvement in institutional initiatives

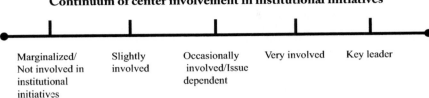

| Marginalized/ Not involved in institutional initiatives | Slightly involved | Occasionally involved/Issue dependent | Very involved | Key leader |

and factors that enabled or impeded their involvement. The respondents were given the option of *other* and provided space to include a short answer. The three open-ended, short answer survey questions in part II asked the respondents to define the role of institutional involvement, how their broader involvement was initiated, and what it entailed for the center and director. In this section, participants identified:

- Level of involvement (director and center)
- Type of daily work (director and center)
- Focus of the center
- Key institutional initiatives
  - Level of involvement in each initiative
  - Role of the director in each initiative
- Factors enabling or impeding institutional involvement
- Initiation of institutional involvement

The survey participants selected which factors listed had enabled or impeded their involvement in institutional initiatives. The frequency results of their factor selections were compared with the significance analysis of director and center variables in relation to level of institutional involvement to

TABLE 4.1
Institution, center, and director survey variables

Institution-Based	*Institution Type*
Director-based	Length of directorship
	Status (faculty, administrator, both) and professional background
Center-based	Age of center
	Origin of center
	Staff size/titles and advisory board/council
	Reporting line
	Center mission

identify the most important factors across the two types of questions and methods used.

At the end of the survey, participants were invited to contact the researcher if they were interested in being considered for selection as one of the eight institutional cases for in-depth interviews that would soon follow.

Case Study Design

A case study design was selected based on the research questions and purpose of the study (Yin, 1989; 1994). The purpose of this research study was not only to *describe* the role of the faculty developers in institutional initiatives but also to allow for "fine-grained analyses of the interaction between the organizational setting and the individual behavior" (Corbett, Dawson, & Firestone, 1984, p. 24–25). Additionally, the in-depth interviews provided interpretative and explanatory rich descriptions to serve later as case study models. Efforts to understand the subjective world of the subject and the meaning and interaction within the subject's context reflect phenomenological research methods (Bogdan & Biklen, 1992). From this data, the researcher identified primary factors that both enable and impede the level of institutional involvement and constructed an evidence-based understanding of how this role is initiated and sustained (Huberman & Miles, 1994; Lincoln, & Guba, 1985; Merriam, 1988).

Theoretical propositions are an established part of qualitative case study design and allow the researcher to examine the theoretical replications across cases (Bogan & Biklen, 1992; Yin, 1989; 1994). Therefore, a set of theoretical propositions typically are developed by the researcher and function as guiding predictors of the results. Based on the relevant literature, important variables are often identified and help direct consideration of possible data to collect. As a design method, the predictions help refine the research questions, shape the collection of data, and define alternative explanations (Yin, 1994; p. 112). The role of involvement in institutional initiatives as an organizational development dimension has not been widely examined and scant literature is available in this field. However, role change, founding leaders, leadership role factors, and organizational change are discussed extensively in the broader organizational literature.

Therefore, this study's theoretical predictions arose from a careful review of the relevant but limited literature in this field and outside of higher education in order to identify possible factors that enable or impede a leadership role in institutional change initiatives (see Table 4.2 and 4.3). In this investigation, the researcher used the theoretical propositions to guide the survey design and case study investigation.

TABLE 4.2
Theoretical propositions

Predicted Extent, Level, and Degree of Involvement

Extent	At least 50% of the directors surveyed are involved at some level in institutional initiatives
Level	30% of the center directors involved in institutional initiatives are *key institutional leaders* or *highly involved* in institutional initiatives
Degree	At least 30% of directors' daily work is devoted to involvement in institutional initiatives (for the majority of directors)

Case Study Selection

In qualitative research, theoretical sampling is a method used to select the study subjects based upon the value of their contribution to understand the problem being researched (Bogdan & Biklen, 1992, p. 71). The case study pool included 57 volunteers after completing the survey. The case study pool was narrowed based on the following criteria: (a) consent to interview from *both* the faculty development director and the directors' supervisor before selection, (b) variation in the level of involvement in institutional initiatives, and (c) variation in institutional type. The first criterion aimed to increase the credibility of the qualitative data collected from two colleagues at each institution. Prior to final selection, directors were asked to reconfirm their level of involvement in institutional initiatives in order to ensure varying levels of institutional leadership. Preference was given to selecting two teaching and learning centers from each of the former Carnegie Institutional Classification categories.

TABLE 4.3
Predicted variables as enabling factors

Institution-based	Institutional type: Centers at liberal arts/or comprehensive institutions will have greater involvement than research-based institutions
Director-based	Length of directorship: A longer span of directorship will enable institutional involvement
Center-based	Center age: Center longevity will enable involvement in institutional initiatives
	Center mission statement: Broadly articulated center missions will enable involvement
	Staff size: Larger center staffs and advisory boards will enable broader director involvement
	Reporting Line: Direct reporting line to academic affairs will enable involvement

After meeting the above criteria, final case study selection was based on achieving further variety based on the following characteristics:

- Institution type
- Institution size
- Length of directorship
- Center founder/Not founder
- Director status/Background: faculty/administrator
- Center age
- Level of institutional involvement

A combined total of 18 in-depth case study interviews from eight institutions were completed: eight center director interviews; eight center director supervisor interviews; and two interviews with the superiors of two directors' supervisors (by the directors' request) (see Table 4.4). Case study participants were interviewed using an interview protocol via phone or in person (see Appendix B). All interviews were recorded and transcribed by a transcriptionist.

The final case study participants included three research institutions, three comprehensive (one with a strong liberal arts history and emphasis), one liberal arts college, and one two-year college. Four had student populations of 20,000 or more, two had between 10,000–15,000 students, and two institutions had student populations of 1,000–5,000. Three of the directors were the founding director (and 5 were not), 3 had been a director between 6 and 10 years, and 5 had been center directors only 1–5 years. The teaching and learning centers also had been in existence for varying lengths of time—from 1–5 years to more than 20 years.

As the level of institutional involvement was a key aspect of the investigation, effort was made first to select cases from multiple levels of institutional involvement (see Table 4.4). Although most of the cases reflected a moderate to high level of involvement in institutional initiatives, purposeful selection of "negative" cases is important for contrasting results and influenced the inclusion of centers and directors who were occasionally involved or had been marginally involved (Bogdan & Biklin, 1992, p. 72; Yin, 1994). Two center directors viewed themselves as *key leaders*, including one that had moved from *marginalized* to a *key leader*; three were *very involved* (including one that had advanced from being *marginalized* to a *very involved*); and one center that was *somewhat* or *occasionally involved*. None of the *marginalized* centers from the survey volunteered to be case study participants. Additionally, four of the directors were tenured and four were not; five were center founders and three were not.

TABLE 4.4
Case study subjects

Case	Institutional Type	Institutional Size	Center Age	Director Years	Director Status	Center Founder	Level of Involvement
A	Comprehensive	20,000+	10–20	6–10	Faculty tenured	No	Marginalized to Key Leader
B	Liberal arts	1,000–5,000	1–5	1–5	Administrator	Yes	Very involved
C	Research	20,000+	10–20	1–5	Administrator	No	Very involved
D	Comprehensive	1,000–5,000	10–20	1–5	Administrator	No	Occasionally
E	Comprehensive	10,000–15,000	6–10	1–5	Faculty tenured	No	Somewhat/Key Leader
F	Two-year college	20,000+	1–5	1–5	Faculty tenured	Yes	Marginalized to Very Involved
G	Research	20,000+	20+	1–5	Administrator	No	Very Involved
H	Research	10,000–15,000	6–10		Faculty tenured	Yes	Key Leader

Analysis

Survey Analysis

The analysis of short answer survey questions involved using the qualitative method of content analysis to examine and code center mission statements and open ended comments about the origin of the center. Initial categories were created for coding the data and were expanded and collapsed based on content analysis. Patterns and themes that emerged from the coding were analyzed for commonalities and differences using the qualitative software program Nud*ist.

The information collected from survey questions in parts I and II were assigned to one of the three categories: center-based, institution-based, or director-based. Each of the 14 institutional, center, and director characteristics from part I of the survey was analyzed for its relationship to the level of involvement in institutional initiatives. The services of a statistician were secured to apply inferential statistics to the survey results. Chi-Square analysis and selection for cross tabulations were used to determine significance among the center, director, and institutional variables as enabling or impeding the level of involvement in institutional initiatives. An alpha level of $p < .05$ was used for all statistical tests. In addition, directors selected enabling or impeding factors from a list. A frequency analysis was completed to compare these responses with the significance analyses of the survey results. The frequency of these factors and the significance of their relationship to involvement in institutional initiatives were then compared with the primary center, director, and institutional enabling and impeding factors that emerged from the case study data (see chapter 5). A compilation and summary of the survey and interview results were compared with the original theoretical propositions in order to conclude whether they had been either confirmed or disconfirmed.

Case Study Interview Analysis

Individual institutional case study analyses and cross case analyses were completed using content analysis techniques and the qualitative software program to identify patterns, themes, and commonalities or differences between cases and to provide a basis for comparison with the survey results (see chapter 5) (Strauss, 1987). Qualitative excerpts from the transcripts and summaries of analysis used as evidence of the enabling and impeding factors were sent to each case study director for confirmation of accuracy and interpretation. In qualitative research, this process of confirmation is a "member check" and contributes to the credibility of the qualitative results (Bogdan & Biklen, 1992; Yin, 1994). Finally, grounded theory methods were employed to construct an emerging theory of how the factors enable and impede the developers' involvement in institutional change and the interaction of these factors in the process of institutional involvement (Bogdan & Biklen, 1992).

Chronologies and Time Series Analysis

Based on the interview transcripts, a chronological time line was constructed for each of the institutional case studies that highlighted key center, director, and institutional initiatives and events. Time series analyses and chronological analyses are appropriate methods used to understand the experiences of the subjects (Yin, 1989). Each time line and summary of the case study interview was sent to each director and supervisor interviewed in order to confirm or modify for accuracy and served as a member check. Further time series analyses were performed with each of the case study authors in part III in order to map in greater detail the organizational change processes and theorize how factors and conditions interacted to enable or impede involvement in broader institutional initiatives. The analysis of the qualitative data sources used to propose an initial grounded theory of how developers construct an institutional leadership role (Glaser & Strauss, 1967). The results of these analyses are discussed in further detail in chapter 5 and most fully in chapter 13.

Survey Results

Four hundred and seventy-seven TLC directors received an online survey via e-mail based on the 2006 list of POD member directors. The response rate was 32%, or 149. The established standard response rate for web surveys is anywhere from 14% to 50%. For the purposes of the study, leadership involvement in institutional initiatives served as the main definition of the organizational development role. Supported by survey evidence, the multidimensional nature of the developer's role encompasses more than instructional development through programing, resources, and consultations. Although instructional development is not void of institutional level change, it is more likely to be *in response* to broader institutional priorities and in support of initiatives rather than provide the *leadership for* planned institutional level change. Therefore, the organizational development dimension is distinct from the instructional development dimension based on the level of impact and type of work.

The key finding of the survey indicates that the majority of directors are spending substantial portions of their time engaged in larger institutional initiatives that advance the quality of teaching and learning at their institutions. Therefore, the center directors' identified level and overall extent of

TABLE 4.5
Level of involvement in institutional initiatives

Level of Involvement	Frequency	Percentage of Respondents
Marginalized	8	6%
Slightly Involved	5	4%
Occasionally Involved/Issue Dependent	33	24%
Very Involved	45	33%
Key Leader; Consistently Involved	45	33%

involvement in institutional initiatives and summary of the common institutional initiatives are presented first to frame the results. A list of the common institutional initiatives in which centers and director were involved follows to further frame the survey results.

Extent and Level of Involvement

Two of the key findings of the study identified the overall extent and level of director involvement in institutional initiatives. The total extent of director involvement in institutional initiatives at all levels and across all types of institutions was reported as 90% (see Table 4.5). This confirmed the predicted level and extent, but this surprising finding far exceeded the threshold estimate of at least 50% involvement to varying degrees.

However, the combined reported level of involvement in institutional initiatives as *key leaders* or *highly involved* was 66%, and therefore, exceeded the original theoretical proposition estimate of 30% involvement at the levels of *very involved* or *key leader*. Only 6% of the respondents were identified as *marginalized* or *not involved* in institutional initiatives. This finding confirms that the role of institutional leader and change agent is not merely an emerging role for center directors but currently is a significant part of the center director's role and the way they perform their role.

Key Institutional Initiatives

The survey design posed several questions to determine the institutional initiatives in which TLCs and directors were involved. The respondents were asked in which key institutional initiatives they, as directors or the centers, were involved. The survey provided the respondents a list of 13 institution-wide initiatives and asked, "In the past five years, what have been the key institutional *initiatives* in general on your campus (*initiative* was defined as a planning group/committee or task force or implementation of an intervention or strategy)?"

A pattern among the most frequently selected initiatives emerged (see Table 4.6). The five most frequently selected initiatives included: program assessment (108); retention (81); online/distance education (74); general education reform (72); learning-centered teaching (71), and scholarship of teaching and learning (66) followed close behind. These frequencies suggest that the type of involvement and areas of focus are relatively common across a wide variety of center and institutional types. This data can greatly assist TLCs, directors, administrators, and organizations in preparing for this role.

TABLE 4.6
Involvement in key institutional initiatives (*N* = 149)

Key Institutional Initiative	Frequency	Percentage
Program assessment	108	74.5
Retention	81	58.3
Online/Distance education	74	50.3
General education reform	72	49.0
Scholarship of teaching and learning	66	48.5
Learning-centered teaching	71	48.3
Interdisciplinary collaboration	57	38.8
Service learning	53	36.1
Curriculum reform	53	36.1
Graduate student education	39	26.5
Peer review	28	19.0
Community-based research	23	15.6
Other	25	17.0

Director and Center Involvement in Initiatives

When asked to select the key institutional initiatives in which they, as directors of the center or the centers, were involved, program assessment (69), online/distance education (54), retention (53), and scholarship of teaching and learning (44) were the four most frequently selected. Interestingly, retention, multiculturalism, and curriculum reform moved further down on the list of initiatives when compared with the selected general institutional initiatives selected earlier. Over time, this list is likely to change for both the director and the institution.

The surveyed directors were asked in which initiatives the center was involved as an effort to compare the involvement between the directors and entire centers. The four most frequently selected institutional initiatives were learner-centered teaching (45), scholarship of teaching and learning (40), program assessment (36), and online/distance education (34). All but learner-centered teaching were the most frequently selected initiatives for center director involvement. Noteworthy as well, retention ranked higher in terms of director involvement than as an initiative for the TLCs.

In Table 4.7, the differences in the initiatives in which directors versus centers were involved are readily apparent. The level of involvement by the directors is more or nearly double than that of the center involvement. This suggests that involvement in institutional initiatives clearly stems from the *role of the director*. However, as the case study data and later chapters make explicit, integrating institutional involvement into the director's role requires adaptation and forethought of the impact on the entire center and staff (see chapter 10).

TABLE 4.7
Center and director involvement in the top seven selected institutional initiatives

Institutional Initiatives	Directors	Centers
Program assessment	69	36
Online/Distance education	54	34
Retention	53	20
Scholarship of teaching and learning	44	40
Multiculturalism	43	19
Learner-centered teaching	35	45
Curriculum reform	33	19

Factors Enabling and Impeding Institutional Involvement

The 14 institution-based, director-based, and center-based characteristics of 149 total survey respondents included wide variation and were reported as frequencies and percentages. All characteristics were tested for the significance of their relationship to the level of involvement in initiatives identified by each director on the survey (see Table 4.8).

Each of the 14 variables were cross tabulated to determine if they were significantly related to the level of involvement in institutional initiatives selected by each director. From this analysis, a list of significant enabling or impeding factors was determined. In summary, only 6 factors among the 14

TABLE 4.8
Analysis of variance between factors and level of involvement ($N = 104$)

Enabling Factors	df	x^2	P
Institution-based enabling factors			
Institutional leadership	4	15.198	.004*
Institutional priorities	4	23.152	.000*
Type of institution	16	26.165	.052*
Center-based enabling factors			
Center leadership	4	22.405	.001*
Age of center	16	22.044	.142
Center staffing	4	4.159	.385
Center advisory board/council	4	2.059	.725
Center reporting line	12	18.150	.111
Center focus	8	15.442	.051*
Center mission	4	4.950	.292
Percentage of daily center work	2	16.616	No significance
Director-based enabling factors			
Length of directorship	16	12.191	.731
Director status	4	2.988	.560
(Administrator/faculty)			
Percentage of director's daily work on	4	1.682	.158
institutional initiatives			

Impeding factors			
Institution-based impeding factors			
Institutional leadership	4	19.761	.001*
Institutional priorities	4	23.855	.000*
Center-based impeding factors			
Center mission	4	2.385	.665
Center resources/staffing	4	1.581	.812

*Note. $p < .05$

institutional, center-based, and director-based enabling or impeding factors were significantly related to the level of involvement in institutional initiatives (see Table 4.9).

Institution-based Factors

The type of institutions represented varied among the survey participants (see Table 4.10). When the level of involvement was analyzed according to type of institution, a significant relationship was reported. Overall, directors that are *key leaders* are more frequently from liberal arts (47%) or comprehensive institutions (44%). Research institutions had the fewest percentage of *key*

TABLE 4.9
Summary of significant enabling and impeding factors

Enabling Factors	Center-based	Institution-based	Director-based
	Center focus Center mission statement Center leadership	Type of institution	
Impeding Factors	Center-based	Institution-based	Director-based
		Institutional leadership Institutional priorities	

leaders—by nearly half, and were the most *occasionally involved* and *very involved* (see Figure 4.2). This confirmed the theoretical proposition that linked institutional type and mission to the level of involvement in institutional initiatives.

Several institution-based factors were identified as impeding the level of involvement. Institutional priorities and institutional leadership were significantly related to the level of involvement in institutional initiatives as impeding factors. Nearly 43% of the centers that reported their level of institutional involvement as *marginalized/not involved* also selected institutional leadership as a factor impeding their involvement in the institutional initiatives. Conversely, only 11% of the *key leaders* reported institutional leadership as a factor that impedes. The manner in which the institutional leadership can function to impede director involvement is made further evident in the discussion of case study results in chapters 5 and 6.

A significant relationship also exists between the factor institutional priorities and the level of institutional involvement. Among the respondents,

TABLE 4.10
Survey participants by type of institution
(*N* = 134)

Type of Institution	Percentage
Research	36.6%
Comprehensive	33.1%
Liberal arts	11.7%
Two-year institution	9.0%
Historically black	9.7%

FIGURE 4.2
Institutional type and level of involvement*

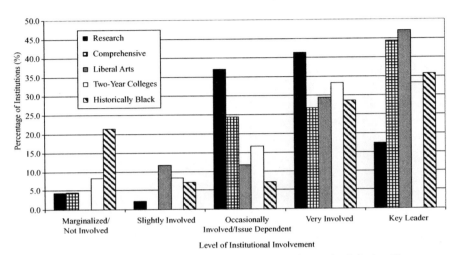

* *The author would like to thank William C. Schroeder for assistance in designing Figure 4.2.*

57% of the *marginalized* centers reported institutional priorities as impeding, whereas only 14.3% of *key leaders* reported being impeded by institutional priorities. This pattern suggests marginalized center directors view factors outside their control as important impediments to their involvement in institutional initiatives.

Center-based Factors

Data about nine center-based variables were collected, including center age, staffing size, advisory board, mission, center focus, center origin, type of work, reporting line, and leadership. Only the variables, focus of the center, percentage of daily work, and center leadership were found to be significantly related to the level of involvement. Those centers that had selected the focus of their daily work as institutional-level, versus departmental or individual, also had a higher level of involvement in institutional initiatives. A significant relationship was found between the selection of center mission as an enabling factor and those with a daily focus on institutional level initiatives. The remaining center-based variables on the survey, including the center staffing size, having an advisory board or council, the center origins, the age of the center, and the reporting line did not have a significant relationship to the level of involvement in institutional initiatives.

Center mission statements were provided by 109 of 149 survey respondents. This large collection of center mission statements was analyzed in-depth using the following three categories: center purpose, center constituents, and center goals. Center mission statements were not significantly related to the level of involvement in institutional initiatives. However, directors who reported that their center mission enabled their involvement spent a higher percentage of their daily work on institutional initiatives (mean percentage 21.25% of daily work) than those who reported their mission did not enable their involvement (mean percentage 28.36%). This difference was significant ($t = -2.350$, $p < .05$). Therefore, we can conclude that there is a significant difference in the time spent on institutional initiatives based on whether the center mission was viewed as an enabling factor. A detailed analysis and summary of the results and discussion of center mission statements as an enabling factor are found in chapter 11.

Analysis of the overall focus of the center provided additional understanding of the way this leadership role is performed by directors within the center context. The respondents selected one of the following as the primary center focus: an individual focus (individual consultations, faculty one-on-one grants and support, etc.), a departmental or school/college focus, or a broader, or institutional level focus (see Table 4.11). More than half of the directors reported having a broader, institutional level center focus (69%) versus individual or department/school focus. The level of institutional involvement was found to be significantly related to the daily focus of the center work (see Table 4.11). More than 61% of *key leaders* reported their center focus as institutional while only 12% of *marginalized* centers reported having an institutional focus. *Marginalized* centers more often reported that their center's primary focus was on individual faculty or instructors (62.5%). This result may reflect a more traditional instructional development role. Very few center directors involved as *key leaders* reported the center focus as primarily individual.

Another survey question examined the type of center daily work based on the categories: Individual faculty/staff/graduate, student teaching/learning work, departmental/unit teaching and learning work, institutional level

TABLE 4.11
Focus of center and involvement level respondents ($N = 133$)

Focus	Frequency	Marginalized	Key Leaders
Individual focus	33	62.5%	20.0%
Institutional focus	69	12.5%	60.0%
Other	33	25.0%	17.8%

TABLE 4.12
Age of teaching and learning centers

Center Age	Percentage
2 years	21.2%
2–5 years	21.9%
6–10 years	21.9%
11–20 years	26.0%
> 20 years	8.9%

involvement, or *other*. There was a significant relationship between the type of center work and the level of institutional involvement reported. This finding suggests a constellation of factors—the center mission statement, the focus of the center, and type of center work, intersect around the overall purpose of the center to significantly impact the level of involvement.

The age of the centers spanned from less than 2 years to more than 20 years with similar percentages of survey respondents in each category except the oldest group of centers. Overall, nearly half of the centers were less than 5 years old. Only 9% of the respondents were at centers older than 20 years (see Table 4.12). Important to note, *key leaders* and *very involved* directors were at very young as well as at well-established centers. However, contrary to the predicted pattern, no significant relationship was determined between the age of the centers and the level of involvement in institutional initiatives, although the results reported a higher percentage (73%) of the *key leaders* and *very involved* centers were less than 10 years old. The few *marginalized* centers that participated in the survey were also at centers that were 1–5 years old and a very small amount from 11–20 years old.

Survey participants selected reasons for the origin of the teaching and learning center from among a list of 14 (see Table 4.13). The most frequent reason for the origin of the center was due to faculty initiative, closely followed by grant acquisition or the consolidation of existing activities into a center. None of the reasons for the origin of the center were found significantly related to the reported level of involvement.

The variable of center resources/staffing was analyzed for its relationship to the level of institutional involvement. No significant relationship was found between the center staffing and the level of involvement in institutional initiatives. Among the centers surveyed, 87.8% had full-time directors, 23.1% had part-time directors, 10.2% had full-time assistant directors and, 19% had associate directors. More than half of the directors indicated that they had other staff, and the mean number of full-time "other staff" was three. More

TABLE 4.13
Origins of centers ($N = 136$)

Reason or Source	Frequency
Faculty-based (faculty, faculty senate, union or individual faculty)	28
Grant/Funding	19
Consolidate or coordinate existing activities	18
To address a specific issue, concern, or complaint	11
Administrative sources	10
External recommendation	<10
Combination of faculty and administrative sources	<10
General need	<10
Specific leader	<10
Institutional mission; changes in mission	<10
Expanding existing services	<10
Curricular	<10
Strategic plan	<10

than 25% of the directors employed a graduate assistant in the office and nearly 35% had a program assistant. Less than 20% had center fellows. Particularly interesting was that staffing was selected most frequently as a key impeding factor elsewhere on the survey and surfaced again in the qualitative interview data as a primary impediment to their involvement.

The most common center reporting line was to academic affairs, in general (75.5%), followed by other (24.5%). These selections were followed in frequency by the provost, a vice president, vice chancellor, associate vice president or chancellor, or a dean. To whom the director reported was not found significantly related to the level of involvement in institutional initiatives.

Surprisingly, 67.3% of the centers participating in the survey did not have an advisory board. This was not found to be a significant factor nor selected by directors as one of the enabling or impeding factors. However, because a number of the case study directors involved their advisory boards in their efforts to broaden their role, a more thorough discussion of center staffing, advisory boards, and councils is provided in chapter 10.

Director-based factors

The five director-based survey factors included the length of directorship, status, professional background, type of daily work, and time spent on initiatives. Among the director-based characteristics tested, daily work focus significantly enabled involvement whereas the length of directorship, the

TABLE 4.14
Amount of time spent by directors on
institutional initiatives

Time Spent on Institutional Initiative Work	Percent of Respondents
0–5% of time	10%
6–25% of time	45%
30–50% of time	36%
More than 50% of time	11%

professional status, and background of the director were not significantly related to involvement in initiatives.

Forty-seven percent of the directors reported spending at least one third to more than half of their time on institutional initiatives. This result surpassed the predicted amount of daily time spent (at least 30%) by the majority of directors in the original theoretical propositions (see Table 4.14).

When the relationship between the percentage of the director's daily work on institutional level initiatives and the focus of the center was tested, a significant relationship was found ($F = 3.031$ with df $= 2$ and $p = .052$). However, no relationship was found between the percentage of daily work on institution level initiatives and the length of time the director has been at the center (df $= 3$, $F = 1.418$, $p = .241$).

The respondents also reported the type of daily work the director performs as estimated percentages (see Table 4.15). Based on mean percentages, the two types of work most performed by the directors were institutional initiatives (30.35% mean average of director time) and institution-wide center-based programing (mean average of 30.2% of their time). Compared with the centers'

TABLE 4.15
TYPE OF DIRECTOR DAILY WORK

Type of Work	Director Mean Percentage	S.D.
Institution-wide center-based programing	30.4	21.67
Time spent on institution initiatives	30.35	19.86
Individual faculty, staff, graduate student instructional work	26.0	17.5
Course teaching/instruction related work	19.42	14.27
Departmental/Unit curricular work	14.89	12.51
Department teaching	14.83	12.27
Other work	18.3	-

type of work, institutional initiatives were estimated to use on average 23.8% of the centers' time. More importantly, the greatest mean percentage of hours for directors was institutional initiatives whereas the centers' highest mean was institution-wide programing (32.6%). These results indicate that the directors' role is distinct from the centers' role in institutional initiatives, and the directors are more involved in institutional initiatives. This suggests that integrating the role of organizational development through involvement in institutional initiatives is concentrated more concretely into the daily work of the directors' and his or her role than the centers.

Most likely a shift has occurred in how directors spend their time in response to the multiple pressures on higher education. Institutions cannot ignore the multiple pressures to improve and assess the quality of learning through initiatives focused on the curriculum, student learning outcomes, assessment, campus climate, retention, diversity, and access and are steadily involving directors to accomplish these efforts.

The overall length of directorship among the respondents was rather short. More than 70% had been directors less than 5 years. Specifically, more than 22% have been directing a center less than 1 year and nearly 49% of this group has been a director more than 1 year. The percentage of directors between 5 and 10 years was more than 22% and those between 10 and more than 20 years was only over 6%. Interestingly, the mean number of years the directors had worked elsewhere in faculty development was only 2.3 years.

In terms of status, most of the surveyed center directors were faculty (69.4%), 30% did not identify as faculty, and 54.4% identified themselves as administrators, indicating some were both faculty and adminstrators. The directors' administrative and faculty background data was collected. Slightly more than the total majority had been in full-time administration less than 10 years, although the mean was 10.5 years. Conversely, the mean number of years as full-time professor was 15.45.

The length of the directorship and the director status were investigated for their relationship to the level of involvement in institutional initiatives. Neither the length of directorship nor the directors' status as faculty or administrative staff, or both, had a significant relationship to the director's involvement in institutional initiatives. Contrary to the theoretical proposition, faculty or administrative status and length of directorship were not enabling factors and were unsupported by the survey data. This also runs contrary to opinion that faculty status is necessary to be TLC directors or involved in large-scale teaching and learning initiatives. Although no significant relationship was determined, a pattern was discernable between having less than 10 years as director and reporting a higher level of institutional involvement.

In summary, none of the director-based variables on the survey were found to be significantly related to the level of involvement other than center leadership, which may refer to and have been interpreted exclusively as the director's leadership, or include past center leadership, center founders, or center supervisors. However, when the directors selected enabling or impeding factors from a list of factors, several different factors emerged. These self-reported factors more closely matched the primary factors identified from the case study interviews and are discussed in-depth in chapter 5.

Director Selected Enabling or Impeding Factors

In part II of the survey, the respondents were asked which factors, among a list of 10, enabled or impeded their institutional involvement. Center leadership (74.1), institutional leadership (63.8), institutional priorities (57.7), and center mission (51.7) were selected by more than 50% of the respondents as key factors *enabling* their involvement. Center staffing/resources (75%) was selected by the highest majority of directors as a factor impeding their involvement (see Table 4.16). The two factors that directors selected but that were not identified by statistical analysis as significant were the center staffing/resources impeding factor and the enabling factor of the center leadership. Interestingly, the center staffing factor was discussed by nearly all of the case study directors and

TABLE 4.16
Comparison of selected enabling and impeding factors and statistical significance

Factors	Frequency	Percentage	Significance
Selected enabling factors			
Institutional leadership* (presidents, chancellors, vice presidents, deans)	95.0	73.1	.004
Center leadership*	82.0	71.4	.001
Institutional priorities*	65.6	57.7	.000
Center mission statement*	59.5	51.7	.292
Center resources/staffing	44.0	33.6	.385
Other	10.6	9.4	-
Selected impeding factors			
Center resources/staffing	80.0	74.8	.812
Institutional priorities*	86.0	65.6	.000
Institutional leadership*	27.0	25.2	.004
Other	26.0	24.3	-
Center leadership	4	2.1	-
Center mission	3	2.0	.6665

Note. Factors determined significantly related to level of institutional involvement.

supervisors as a clear constraint of the enactment of a broader dimension to the director's role. The interpretation of the center leadership likely refers to the leadership effort of the director, and often includes the founding or director's vision of the center. The potential role of a center founder is discussed at length in the case study interview discussions (see chapters 5 and 8). Case study directors also frequently cited the important role of the center supervisor and this may be part of the high rating of center leadership on the survey.

When the entire list of factors selected by directors was compared to the variables tested for significance, only three of the majority selected factors— center mission, center leadership, and institutional leadership—were also found to be significantly related to the level of involvement in initiatives (see Table 4.16). Because center mission statements strongly emerged from *both* to determine key factors impacting involvement, chapter 11 is devoted to a close analysis of more than 104 center mission statements provided through the surveys. Additionally, center leadership, selected by 74% of the directors as an enabling factor, is one of several factors repeatedly emphasized in the chapters on director vision, strategic planning, organizational change, and center mission (chapters 2, 3, 8, 9, 11, and 12).

Of the directors who reported that their leadership had enabled their involvement in institutional initiatives, 84% saw themselves as *key leaders* of institutional involvement.

Of the three most *frequently* selected impeding factors, center staffing, institutional leadership, and institutional priorities, only institutional priorities and institutional leadership were found to be significantly related to involvement in institutional initiatives and are discussed in several of the case study chapters (chapters 6, 7, and 10). Important to note as well, although center resources/staffing was selected most often by directors as an impeding factor for their involvement, no relationship was found between the center staffing and the level of involvement in institutional initiatives. However, due to it being the most prominent factor selected by directors surveyed, it is discussed in further detail in chapter 10.

Comparison of Factors With Theoretical Propositions

Based on the overall survey results, the theoretical propositions outlined at the beginning of the study and reported earlier in this chapter were either confirmed or not confirmed as follows (see Table 4.17). Four of the nine characteristics predicted to enable the director and center's involvement in institutional initiatives were significantly related to the level of institutional involvement and only two of the predicted factors significantly impeded the level of involvement.

TABLE 4.17
Theoretical proposition results

Predicted Extent, Level, and Degree of Involvement		*Survey Results*
Extent	At least 50% of the directors surveyed will be involved at some level in institutional initiatives.	94% (exceeds)
Level	30% of the center directors involved in institutional initiatives will be *key institutional leaders* or *highly involved*.	66% (exceeds)
Degree	At least 30% of directors' daily work is devoted to involvement in institutional initiatives (for the majority of directors).	30.4%

Predicted Institution-, Director-, and Center-based Factors		*Survey Results*
Institution-based	Liberal arts/or comprehensive institutions will have greater involvement than research-based institutions.	Confirmed
Director-based	Length of directorship: A longer span of directorship will enable involvement.	Denied
Center-based	Center age: Center longevity will enable involvement in institutional initiatives.	Denied
	Center mission statement: Broadly articulated center missions will enable involvement.	Partially Confirmed
	Staff size: Larger center staffs and advisory boards will broader director involvement.	Confirmed *(enables and impedes)*
	Reporting line: Direct reporting line to academic affairs will enable involvement.	Denied

Discussion

The design and results of the 2006–07 study, *Coming in From the Margins: Redefining Faculty Development's Role Within the Institution* helped advance the understanding of the center and director involvement in institutional initiatives. A number of methods and approaches were designed to identify the factors that most impact this role, including quantitative and qualitative analysis of multiple types of survey questions and frequency and statistical analysis. In addition, the qualitative interview data provided additional evidence of the way the primary factors interact within the context of the center and director's role.

In particular, the survey results confirmed that involvement in institutional initiatives are well within the director's role at centers of teaching and learning, and that the majority of directors are spending a large proportion of their time on high levels of institutional involvement. Although this role has not been well understood or examined, it is not emerging—it *has* emerged.

The perception of the center of teaching and learning or director's role as that of primarily programing, consulting, providing support and resources, and so forth does not match the actual role performed, according to the center directors surveyed. Important to note as well, all types of institutions reported being *highly involved* or *key leaders* in institutional initiatives.

Several predicted enabling and impeding factors were confirmed using multiple methodological strategies and by posing more than one survey question. Surprisingly, most of the factors predicted to affect involvement in institutional initiatives were not significantly related to the actual level of involvement, and only five of the theoretical propositions were confirmed by the survey data. Nevertheless, from the survey, six institution- and center-based factors significantly related to the level of involvement. Additional important factors were identified by the directors based on their selection from a list of potentially enabling or impeding factors. However, an even deeper understanding of how this role is developed and what additional factors impact this development was obtained through the case study interviews (see chapter 5). The significant and selected factors were compared later to the qualitative data from center director and supervisor interviews (see chapter 5). In this way, the lived experiences of the directors' involvement in institutional change further triangulated the data across multiple methods of inquiry.

Together, these multiple efforts to identify the most important variables that impact this role have successfully pinpointed commonalities that enable and impede functioning at the institutional level, bringing some of the earliest and evidence-based knowledge of an organizational development role to this field. New developers, professional development efforts, and administrators are able to utilize these factors as evidence to support key decision making.

There was a time when faculty development focused on grants and sabbaticals. Later, an instructional development set of practices emerged that became all encompassing based on the paradigm shift inching its way into higher education and that has now defined development work as largely programing, consultations, grant-securing, individual consultations, and gathering and disseminating resources related to teaching and learning.

Given the survey findings that underscore the prevalence of institutional level work, the lack of attention and discussion to the organizational development aspect of this work is perplexing. The considerable time invested in this leadership role and involvement at the institutional level with an identifiable pattern of key initiatives has important implications for this field that will be discussed in each of the chapters that follow. These implications include the need to reexamine position descriptions, center mission statements, overall center assessment and center staff evaluations, professional development avenues, and define more clearly the definition and expectations of the center director and his or her position within the institutional framework.

The next chapter provides rich descriptions of this role to hang on the skeletal framework of factors that were identified using quantitative methods of the study.

Note

The author wishes to acknowledge the assistance of graduate student Leslie Mason, M. S. Sociology, UW–Milwaukee, for her statistical testing expertise.

References

Baron, L. (2006). The advantages of a reciprocal relationship between faculty development and organizational development in higher education. In S. Chadwick-Blossey, & D. R. Robertson (Eds.), *To improve the academy: Vol. 24. Yearbook of the Professional and Organizational Development Network in higher education* (pp. 29–43). Bolton, MA: Anker.

Bogdan, R., & Biklen, S. (1992). *Qualitative research for education: An introduction to theory and methods.* Boston: Allyn and Bacon.

Brown, H. (1992). Staff development in higher education: Towards the learning organization? *Higher Education Quarterly, 46*(2), 174–190.

Chism, N. (1998). The role of education developers in institutional change: From the basement office to the front office. In M. Kaplan, & D. Lieberman (Eds.), *To improve the academy: Vol. 17. Resources for faculty, instructional and organizational development* (pp. 141–154). Stillwater, OK: New Forums Press.

Corbett, J., Dawson, J., & Firestone, W. (1984). *School context and school change.* New York: Teachers College.

Diamond, R. M. (2005). The institutional change agency: The expanding role of academic support centers. In S. Chadwick-Blossey (Ed.), *To improve the academy: Vol. 23. Yearbook of the Professional and Organizational Development Network in higher education* (pp. 24–37). Bolton, MA: Anker.

Glaser, B. G., & Strauss, A. L. (1967). *The discovery of grounded theory: Strategies for qualitative research.* New York: Aldine De Gruyer.

Huberman, A., & Miles, M. (1994). Data management and analysis methods. In N. L. Denzin (Ed.), *Handbook of qualitative research.* Thousand Oaks: Sage Publications.

Lieberman, D. A., & Guskin, A. E. (2002). The essential role of faculty development in new higher education models. In C. M. Wehlburg, & S. Chadwick-Blossey (Eds.), *To improve the academy: Vol. 21. Resources for faculty, instructional and organizational development* (pp. 257–272). Bolton, MA: Anker.

Lincoln, Y. S., & Guba, E. G. (1985).*Naturalistic inquiry.* Beverly Hills, CA: Sage.

Merriam, S. B. (1988). *Case study research in education: A qualitative approach.* San Francisco: Jossey-Bass.

Sorcinelli, M. D., Austin, A. E., Eddy, P. L., & Beach, A. L. (2006). *Creating the future of faculty development.* Bolton, MA: Anker.

Strauss, (1987). *Qualitative analysis for social scientists.* Cambridge: Cambridge University Press.

Taylor, K. L., & Schönwetter, D. J. (2002). *Faculty development as institutional leadership: A framework for meeting new challenges.* HERDSA Conference, Australia.

Yin, R. K. (1989). *Case study research: Design and methods* (Rev. Ed.). Newbury Park, CA: Sage.

Yin, R. K. (1994). *Applications of case study research.* Newbury Park, CA: Sage.

Appendix A: Online Director Survey

POD 2005–2006 Grant: Coming in From the Margins: Redefining Faculty Development's Role Within the Institution

Online Survey

Part I: Institutional and Center History and Attributes

1. What is your institutional type?
   a. _____ Research
   b. _____ Comprehensive
   c. _____ Liberal Arts
   d. _____ Two-year
   e. _____ Historically Black college or university
   f. Other: _____

2. How many years has your faculty development center existed?
   a. _____ less than 2 years
   b. _____ 2–5 years
   c. _____ 6–10 years
   d. _____ 11–20 years
   e. _____ more than 20 years

3. Was there an event or reason the center was created? If so, please describe.

4. Mission (faculty development center)
   Please submit your center's formal mission statement:
   _____ Do not have a mission statement at this time.

1. How many full-time staff are at your center and what are their titles? (check all that apply)

Titles:	# full-time	# part-time
a.___ Director	_____	_____
b.___ Assistant director	_____	_____
c.___ Associate director	_____	_____
e.___ Program assistant	_____	_____
f.___ Graduate student	_____	_____
g.___ Faculty fellows	_____	_____
h.___ Advisory board	_____	_____
i. Other_____	_____	_____

5. Length of directorship: I have been in this position for:
   a. ___ Less than 1 year
   b. ___ Less than 5 years
   c. ___ Between 5 and 10 years
   d. ___ Between 10 and 20 years
   e. ___ More than 20 years

6. Academic background and qualifications of director:

   _____

   My career path has included:
   a.___ Professorship   ___ Years full-time
   b.___ Administration   ___ Years full-time
   c.___ Years having worked in faculty development full-time elsewhere
   d.___ Years having worked in faculty development prior to this position at this institution
   e. Advanced degree(s)_____

   _____

7. Reporting line
   To what department or unit does your center report?
   a. ___ Academic affairs
   b. Other: _____
   To whom do you report?
   a. ___ Provost
   b. ___ Dean
   c. ___ Vice President/Chancellor of Academic Affairs
   d. Other: _____

Part II: Faculty Development and Institutional Priorities and Initiatives

1. As percentages, estimate the type of daily work your center does:
    a.___ Individual faculty/staff/graduate student teaching/learning work
    b.___ Departmental/unit teaching and learning work
    c.___ Institutional level involvement
    d.___ Other
2. As percentages, estimate the type of daily work you perform:
    a.___ Individual faculty/staff/graduate student teaching/learning work
    b.___ Departmental/unit teaching and learning work
    c.___ Institutional level involvement
    d.___ Other
3. In the past five years, what have been the key institutional *initiatives in general on your campus? [*initiative being a planning group/committee, task force, or implementation of an intervention or strategy]

Which initiatives do you see as being directly related to teaching and learning? (check all that apply)

Key institutional initiative	Key	Directly related to teaching and learning
a. Retention	___	___
b. Program assessment	___	___
c. Multiculturalism	___	___
d. Curriculum reform	___	___
e. Online and distance education	___	___
f. Service learning	___	___
g. Community-based research	___	___
h. General education reform	___	___
i. Peer review	___	___
j. Scholarship of teaching and learning	___	___
k. Learner-centered teaching	___	___
l. Interdisciplinary collaborations	___	___
m. Graduate student education	___	___
n. Other: _____	___	___

4. In which initiatives has the *center director* been a part of and to what degree? What was/is your role?

Initiative/Degree/Role	Level of Involvement
Degree of involvement Center Director's role: Initiative:	Mildly/Moderately/Significantly
Degree of involvement Center Director's role: Initiative:	Mildly/Moderately/Significantly
Degree of involvement Center Director's role: Initiative:	Mildly/Moderately/Significantly
Degree of involvement Center Director's role: Initiative:	Mildly/Moderately/Significantly

5. How was this involvement initiated and by whom?
6. In which institutional initiatives, if any, can you identify *the center* as being or having been integrally or centrally involved? What does this involvement entail?

Initiatives	Involvement entails
1.	
2.	
3.	
4.	
5.	
6.	

7. On a scale of involvement in institutional initiatives, from margins/not involved, to key leader, with slightly involved, occasionally/inconsistently involved, very involved to key leader and consistently involved, how would you describe the center here? (Use visual diagram of continuum—see Figure 4.1)
   a.___ Marginalized, not involved
   b.___ Slightly involved

    c.___ Occasionally involved, issue dependent
    d.___ Very involved
    e.___ Key leader, consistently involved

    Continuum of Involvement in Institutional Initiatives
    a. Marginalized/Slightly involved occasionally
    b. Very involved
    c. Key leader
    d. Involved/Not involved in institutional initiatives
    e. Issue dependent

8. What has enabled or impeded the center's existing level of involvement in institutional initiatives?

Enabled	Impeded
a. _____ Center mission	a. _____ Center mission
b. _____ Center leadership	b. _____ Center leadership
c. _____ Institutional leadership	c. _____ Institutional leadership
d. _____ Institutional priorities	d. _____ Institutional priorities
e. _____ Resources/Staffing	e. _____ Resources/Staffing
f. Other: _____	f. Other :_____

9. How would you describe the focus of the center?
    a. _____ Individual
    b. _____ Departmental
    c. _____ Institutional
    d. Other: _____

Appendix B: Case Study Interview Protocol

Individual History (Director of Faculty Development Center

- What has been your involvement in faculty development during your career—here or elsewhere?
- How is your time spent on a daily basis? What are the major aspects of your work and role?

- What has been or is your role or work outside of faculty development?
- What do you believe is the mission of faculty development at this institution?
- What is the faculty development center's current role in institutional initiatives?
- Is faculty development's involvement in institutional initiatives linked with you personally or individually?
- What expertise do you believe you bring to campus initiatives? Are you viewed as a change agent?
- What would you like to see happen or change in your center?
- What historical, structural, organizational, and leadership factors have enabled or impeded the center from becoming involved in institutional initiatives? Does involvement in institutional initiatives conflict w/other aspects of your faculty development role?

Faculty Development/Center History
(Director Perspective and (Administrative Leader Perspective)

- How would you describe the existing model for faculty development at your institution?
- How does it see itself? What is the center mission?
- Has the center mission changed since its beginning? Is it changing now? If so, how? Why or why not?
- On a scale with levels of involvement in institutional initiatives from *marginalized/not involved*, to *very involved*; *slightly involved, occasionally/inconsistently involved, very involved*, to *key leader* and *consistently involved*, how would you describe the center here? *(Use Continuum of Involvement survey diagram)*
- Are there institutional initiatives in which the faculty development staff have not been involved that you think could or should have involved them? What are they? Why do you think this occurred?
- What evidence would support this view?
- Which institutional initiatives, if any, can you identify the center as being or having been integrally involved or a key leader? Who initiates this involvement?
- What does this involvement entail?
- Who in the institution most values the center's contribution or leadership in institutional initiatives?

- Is there expertise that the staff of the center brings to matters of institutional priority?
- What has enabled or impeded the center's existing level of involvement in institutional initiatives?
- How would you describe the focus of the center: individual, departmental, organizational/institutional?

IDENTIFYING THE FACTORS THAT ENABLE AN ORGANIZATIONAL DEVELOPMENT ROLE

Connie M. Schroeder

T he survey results confirmed that a majority of the center directors are highly involved in institutional initiatives and broader-scale change processes. The survey collected data on a number of center-, director-, and institution-based factors predicted to affect involvement in institutional initiatives. Surprisingly, the results confirmed that very few of the center and director variables included in the survey were significantly related to the level of director or center involvement in broader initiatives. The organizational development role clearly was affected by other factors not identified by the survey. Through qualitative data collection, a far better understanding of how the directors intentionally developed their institutional leadership role and involvement in the institutional change was achieved.

Changes across a professional field that result in new roles and practices can be incorporated too slowly and ineffectively if unguided by models or in-depth investigation, and as a result, time is spent starting from scratch or reinventing the wheel. Realistically, a significant shift in how the work of developers is done will not take hold broadly if every center and director invents their own version, models are not provided or are ignored, and critical discussion is set aside in the hope of being handed a quick, prescriptive set of steps to take. In order to understand a redefined organizational development role in this current context and the accompanying extent of change this entails for developers and centers, it is important to examine this role as a change process by drawing from multiple study methods and comparing the results. As evidenced by the case study data, there is no quick fix. Rather, a gradual and intentional series of overlapping efforts are undertaken by the directors to bring their expertise to the table of institutional planning. How this role is created and sustained is complex. The evidence reported here requires a commitment to examine the intricacy of forming and enabling the factors that have been shown to reposition TLCs on the institutional radar screen.

The data collected through qualitative methods revealed a dynamic interaction between 37 factors largely not evident from the quantitative survey data (see part four, chapter 13). The 18 interviews with directors and their supervisors produced detailed descriptions of their center and role as directors involved in key initiatives on their campus from which the factors were identified. Among the eight cases, a variety of institutional types and sizes, center ages, years of experience, administrative versus faculty status, and center founder status were included (see chapter 4). Most importantly, the level of institutional involvement spanned from marginalized to key leader (see Table 5.1). Five of the case study directors were willing to share their identity and institutional affiliation while three chose to remain anonymous. Three of the case study directors became chapter authors for this volume in part three (see chapters 6, 7, and 10). Unfortunately, the sudden death of one case study director precluded completion of a chapter (Leora Baron-Nixon, University of Nevada, Las Vegas); however, her interview excerpts are a valuable contribution to this volume. From these rich descriptions, a list of institutional initiatives was compiled and 37 enabling and impeding factors identified.

The institutional case study center directors and their supervisors provided eight models of how they intentionally increased or initiated their involvement at an institutional level, and in some cases, clearly reduced their former level of marginalization from the core initiatives of the institution. The organizational dimension of their role emerged as quite distinct from their instructional development role in a number of ways, but also clearly demonstrated how they merged multiple roles. The case study results in the sections that follow are reported in a variety of formats including frequency analyses, cross-case factor analysis, and interview excerpts.

Case Reported Institutional Initiatives

From these rich descriptions, a list of institutional initiatives was compiled. A summary of the institutional initiatives in which the case study directors were involved is discussed first and followed by the cross-case center,

TABLE 5.1

Case study characteristics

Case	Institutional Type	Institutional Size	Center Age	Director Years	Director Status	Center Founder	Level of Involvement
A	Comprehensive	20,000+	10–20	6–10	Faculty tenured	No	Marginal–Key leader
B	Liberal arts	1,000–5,000	1–5	1–5	Administrator	Yes	Very involved
C	Research	20,000+	10–20	1–5	Administrator	No	Very involved
D	Comprehensive	1,000–5,000	10–20	1–5	Administrator	No	Occasionally
E	Comprehensive	10,000–15,000	6–10	1–5	Faculty tenured	No	Somewhat–Key leader
F	Two-year college	20,000+	1–5	1–5	Faculty tenured	Yes	Marginal–Very involved
G	Research	20,000+	20+	1–5	Administrator	No	Very involved
H	Research	10,000–15,000	6–10	6–10	Faculty tenured	Yes	Key leader

TABLE 5.2

Comparison of case study and survey institutional initiatives

Case Study Institutional Initiatives		*Survey Response Institutional Initiatives*	
(N = 8)	*Frequency*	*(N = 149)*	*Frequency*
Assessment/Accreditation	6	Program assessment	108
Undergraduate learning/General education reform	5	Retention	81
Strategic planning	4	Online/Distance education	74
Learner-centered teaching	3	General education reform	72
Faculty evaluation/ Compensation	3	Learning-centered teaching	71
Graduate student preparation	3	Service learning	60
Teacher training/New faculty orientation	2	Interdisciplinary collaboration	57
Retention	2	Curriculum reform	53
Technology	2	Scholarship of teaching and learning	53
Curriculum	2		
First-year seminars	2		
Teaching/Learning academy	1		
Service learning	1		
Student research	1		
Nontraditional students	1		
Developmental education	1		
Discipline-based initiatives: Science	1		

director, and institution-based factors that reportedly either enabled or impeded involvement in institutional change.

A summary of the institutional initiatives in which the case study directors were involved is presented by frequency analysis (see Table 5.2). Based on the interviews, the institutional initiatives discussed by at least half of the case studies were assessment/accreditation, undergraduate learning and general education reform, and strategic planning. In comparison, the initiatives reported by more than 50% of the survey participants as key initiatives in which they were involved included, retention, online/distance education, learner-centered teaching, general education reform, service-learning, interdisciplinary collaboration, curricular reform, and the SoTL. General education reform emerged as the common one institutional initiative among the two sources of data. These initiatives, described in the case study director and supervisor interviews, involved the center directors to varying degrees, from being the initiator and creator of an initiative, to providing leadership, expertise, connections to national initiatives, and membership on task forces or committees. Knowing the initiatives in which the directors were involved provides a contextual backdrop for in depth discussion of the key factors identified and confirms the type of involvement in which directors are currently engaged.

Factor Analysis

A total of 37 factors were identified from the interview data using content analysis. These factors were assigned to one of two broad categories, enabling or impeding factors, depending on how the directors described their impact on their institutional role. This resulted in identifying 27 enabling and 10 impeding factors. Within these two broad categories, the 37 factors were further analyzed as director-, center-, or institution-based factors. Among nine institution-based factors, several were identified as antecedent conditions or preexisting institutional conditions that the director simply had to accept and be aware of as his or her role developed. These antecedent conditions preceded the director's efforts to expand their organizational role and continued to affect this role change (Pettigrew, 1985). These factors were compared across cases to determine their commonality and are reported as frequencies (see Figure 5.1). Figures 5.1 and 5.2 identify the factors evident for each case study center and director and the subsequent chapters in which these factors are highlighted.

Those factors that emerged among 50% of the cases were identified as primary factors (Table 5.3). It is important to note that factors reported by less than half of the case study participants still indicate important factors to consider and investigate further. This reduced list of primary factors in common included 20 enabling and only 2 impeding factors, and included a mixture of center-, director-, and institution-based factors, although the greatest number of enabling factors were director-based, pointing toward the initiative required of the director in enabling their own role transformation. These primary factors were then compared with the most selected and significant factors identified through the survey in order to identify patterns among factors across varying sources of data.

The quantitative survey results identified not only factors that were significantly related to levels of involvement, but those that more than 50% of the directors selected as key factors. A comparison of factors from multiple sources of data and types of questions is reported in Table 5.4. Center leadership and

FIGURE 5.1
Cross-case comparison of factors that enabled institutional involvement

Enabling Factors (27)	Inst. A	Inst. B	Inst. C	Inst. D	Inst. E	Inst. F	Inst. G	Inst. H
Director-based enabling factors								
Expertise, knowledge, and skills -collaborative style -pedagogical knowledge -organizational change processes -curricular reform -broader national issues of T/L -grant writing (chapters 2, 5, 6, 7, 10, 11, 12)	✓	✓	✓	✓	✓		✓	✓
Credible and trusted (chapter 6) -high visibility -publishing	✓		✓	✓	✓	✓	✓	✓
Center founder/Involvement of center founder (chapter 8)	✓	✓		✓	✓	✓		
Institutional committee involvement; Strategic plan-involvement (chapter 12)	✓	✓	✓	✓	✓	✓	✓	✓
Regular contact/attendance with governance structures; deans council, faculty council; provost; vice president (chapters 10, 11)	✓	✓		✓	✓	✓	✓	
Strategic planning involvement (embedded) (chapter 12)		✓		✓	✓	✓		✓
Secured grant funding for initiatives (chapter 6)	✓	✓			✓	✓	✓	✓
Developed or utilized a change model and/or organizational change processes (chapters 6, 10)	✓	✓			✓	✓	✓	
Complementary relationships with institutional leadership (chapters 10, 11)					✓	✓		✓
New unique and blended title created for director (chapters 2, 3)					✓	✓		✓
Collaboration, partnerships, building close contacts with faculty and departments (chapters 6, 7, 10)		✓	✓	✓	✓	✓	✓	
Professional development on organizational change (chapter 10)		✓			✓		✓	
Center-based enabling factors								

Note: Factors identified by at least 50% of the cases (with four or more check marks) are considered primary factors.

FIGURE 5.1
(*Continued*)

Enabling Factors (27)	Inst. A	Inst. B	Inst. C	Inst. D	Inst. E	Inst. F	Inst. G	Inst. H
Center mission aligned with the institutional mission; mission changed to reflect broader focus (chapter 11)	✓	✓	✓	✓	✓	✓	✓	✓
Center supervisor served as advocate and conduit of information about institutional initiatives; supervisor's collaborations (chapter 6)		✓		✓	✓	✓	✓	✓
Aligned with national associations and initiatives; national recognition; Involved with national conversations (chapters 6, 10)	✓	✓	✓		✓	✓	✓	✓
Center had an advisory board or council (chapter 10)	✓	✓		✓	✓		✓	
Center reputation was credible; positive; trusted (chapters 6, 7, 10)				✓	✓	✓		✓
Center programing aligned with institutional initiatives, high profile events; faculty learning communities part of the change process (chapters 6, 7)	✓	✓	✓	✓	✓		✓	
Strong and sufficient center staff (chapter 10)								✓
Center grant offerings to faculty					✓		✓	✓
Center aligned with and explicit in the institutional strategic plan (chapter 12)			✓	✓	✓	✓		✓
Institution-based enabling factors								
Upper-level administrative support/advocacy (chapters 2, 3, 6, 7, 10)		✓	✓		✓	✓	✓	✓
Institution-wide dialogues (chapters 6, 7)	✓			✓	✓	✓		✓
Antecedent conditions								
New institutional leadership; new provost (chapters 6, 7)	✓				✓	✓		✓
High faculty turnover/expansion (chapter 6)				✓	✓	✓		
University reorganization/change (chapters 6, 7)	✓					✓		✓
Institutional culture -driven by faculty; grass roots -collaborative (chapter 6)	✓	✓			✓	✓		✓

Note: Factors identified by at least 50% of the cases (with four or more check marks) are considered primary factors.

FIGURE 5.2
Cross-case comparison of factors that impeded involvement

Impeding Factors (10)	Inst. A	Inst. B	Inst. C	Inst. D	Inst. E	Inst. F	Inst. G	Inst. H
Director-based impeding factors								
Director's role conflict and workload tensions (chapter 10)	✓	✓			✓			
Decrease in center director's institutional committee involvement (chapter 7)				✓		✓		
Differences with immediate supervisor over center vision (chapter 7)				✓		✓		
Center-based impeding factors								
Center staffing, resources, funding limitations (chapter 10)	✓	✓			✓		✓	✓
Director supervisor in discord with institutional leadership				✓				
Institution-based impeding factors								
Institutional culture resistant toward change				✓	✓		✓	
Institutional territorialism/infighting	✓						✓	
Institutional initiatives became marginalized					✓	✓		
Institutional leadership changes (chapter 7)	✓			✓	✓	✓	✓	
Multiple institutional changes -reduced institution-wide committees, collaboration, and pooling of resources (chapter 7)				✓	✓	✓		

Note: Factors identified by at least 50% of the cases (with four or more check marks) are considered primary factors.

institutional leadership, and center mission statements (significantly related to type of daily work) emerged as key enabling factors across all three types of data, and institutional leadership changes was the sole impeding factor across all sources of data. However, center resources and staffing were strongly identified as factors impeding involvement by two of the data collected, along with institutional priorities. Important to note, the primary factors revealed by the case study interviews had not been identified at the time of the survey as the survey preceded the interviews by several months. Similarly, the directors

TABLE 5.3
Primary factors enabling or impeding involvement

Primary Enabling Factors	*Primary Impeding Factors*
Director-based	**Director-based**
Expertise, knowledge, and skills	
Credibility	
Center founder	
Secured grants	
Committee involvement	
Governance structure contact	
Utilized change model	
Collaborative style	
Strategic-planning involvement	
Center-based	**Center-based**
Center mission	Center staffing
Center supervisor	
Aligned with national associations	
Center reputation and credibility	
Advisory board	
Institution-based	**Institution-based**
New institutional leadership	Institutional leader changes

TABLE 5.4
Comparison of factors across three types of data

Factors	Survey Selected Factors (Percentage)	Survey Factors Significant	Primary Case Study Factors (=/> 4 Cases)
Enabling factors			
Center leadership	71.4%	✓	✓
Institutional leadership	63.8%	✓	✓
(presidents, chancellors, vice presidents, deans)			
Institutional priorities	57.7%	–	–
Center mission statement	51.7%	✓	✓
(in relation to daily center work)			
Center resources/staffing	29.5%	–	–
Other	9.4%	–	–
Impeding Factors			
Center resources and staffing	75%	–	✓
(role/stress/conflict)			
Institutional priorities	30%	✓	–
Institutional leadership	18.1%	✓	✓
Other	24%	–	–
Center leadership	<5%	–	–
Center mission	<5%	–	–

and supervisors interviewed were not provided the list of factors that appeared on the online survey. Therefore, a comparison between the sources of data yielded different results.

Interview-based Evidence of Primary Factors

Rich descriptions obtained from qualitative data are often lengthy and yet provide the best insight into the actual lived experiences of the TLC directors and their involvement in broader institutional initiatives. Only the most insightful excerpts have been included to serve as maps for understanding the process of role change. All comments by case study directors and supervisors are identified by case study letter only (see Table 5.1).

Director-based Enabling Factors

Twelve director-based enabling factors emerged out of the case study interviews. Nine of the 12 director-based factors were shared by at least half of the total directors sampled, and therefore, primary factors. Evidence of five of the primary factors is provided below through interview excerpts.

Committee Involvement

Involvement in institutional committees consistently was an important factor in advancing the director and TLC from the margins of the institutional radar screen. This committee role took several forms. Directors and supervisors easily identified the value of being at the table as initiative planning committees were formed as well as being a regular member of and having contact with the established institution-wide initiative task forces and councils. Committee involvement as an enabling factor is explored extensively in chapters 2 and 7.

For example, director's involvement with institutional initiatives is clearly linked to steady and widespread involvement on multiple university-wide committees. One supervisor explained:

> I think one of the things is that [director] serves on many more university wide committees than she used to. She used to just run the center. But now, if we are building a building, she is on that committee. . . . We are looking at new honors housing which will have classrooms and things in it. She will be on that committee. She comes to the deans' council more often to make presentations about different learning initiatives that we are doing. She is much more visible and her staff than they were. (Case Study A)

The value of this director's involvement in multiple institution-wide committees was explained as advancing important institutional relationships and institutional knowledge—a type of expertise discussed later in this chapter.

> Part of it has been relationship-building. Part of it has been better understanding the institutional culture and values and ways of operating, seeing where things work well . . . seeing where there might be holes. (Case Study A)

Another core committee became a key facet of the director's leadership role:

> I was put in charge of one which is the new accreditation for the North Central Association, and Criterion 3 was student learning, and I was chair of that. (Case Study A)

This center director's supervisor concurred with the positive impact of the director's leadership on key institutional initiative committees:

> I think the last thing I attribute it to [had to do] . . . with [director] as cochair of our general education committee of this past year. Her involvement in these efforts gave her a lot of contact with faculty. . . . After a couple failed attempts [at reviving general education], the chancellor appointed two people, [the director] and this other faculty member from arts and sciences, and they led a team that went to . . . [the] AAC&U General Education Institute last summer. (Case Study E)

According to one director's supervisor, the reason for the director's involvement on committees grew out of the multiple roles the director plays.

> I think that his involvement is really because of these other roles that he plays . . . he can bring to those conversations what he knows about the process of [initiating] learning and innovations, broadly in pedagogy. (Case Study H)

Other directors mentioned attending established councils and having regular contact that contributed to broadening their role:

> I attended faculty councils. . . . I am a voting member of the faculty council, although I don't have faculty status. I am a member of the department chairs meetings. . . . I have been asked to be more involved in the assessment committee. . . . Faculty council—I just said, "Is it a place I can be?" and they said, "Sure. Why not?" . . . "Do I vote or not vote?" "Why don't you

vote?" We have a pretty inclusive governance structure. . . . I have pretty much asked to be almost everywhere just so I can understand and serve the institution best. So I sit on the general education advisory committee, which is integrative studies, and asked to do that so that I would understand it better. (Case Study B)

I meet the dean's council regularly. I am not a member of it but I meet them. . . . I meet the vice president, provost; have access to all the places that I need. There is no group of persons connected with teaching and learning that I cannot pick up the phone and get a conversation going that day. (Case Study F)

This accessibility to key institutional structures was consistent with the leadership style of the new president at one institution who created a team for learning, flattened the organization, and added a new academic vice president position. This director further explained that the process of working closely with the faculty on projects "blossoms" into departmental change initiatives. The director's smaller contacts and involvements evolved into larger investments and broader involvement.

General education reform, program assessment, and accreditation were identified as primary institutional initiatives. The committees planning these initiatives were often the committees or task forces through which directors established their broader role beyond instructional development. Being at the table and having a significant role on these particular planning committees helped move the center to become a key player in institutional change. This supervisor explained:

We have an assessment committee and advisory committee, and the director of the TLC is on that committee and so has a great deal of input into the direction that we are going with assessment on the campus. She is also on the General Education Advisory Committee because [general education] is another area we are looking [at] very hard. . . . So, [she has] been very knowledgeable about issues, such as assessment . . . she has been very helpful on those committees. Regardless of who the director is, one would continue to imagine that to be the case. (Case Study C)

According to another supervisor:

She was very involved in the original tactical planning group. . . . She actually is very involved in a lot of our curriculum committees campus-wide, the college of arts and sciences, and also the graduate college. . . . She is on the assessment steering committee. (Case Study D)

TABLE 5.5
Knowledge and skills enabling organizational development role

Knowledge	Skills
Broad-based knowledge	
Organizational change processes	Relationship building
Higher education institutional change processes	Ally cultivating
Higher education history; context; governance	Problem solving
Learning literature; issues; trends; pedagogy	Consulting on institutional planning
National initiatives	Decision-making; consensus building
	Strategic planning
	Grant writing
Institution Specific Knowledge	
Governance structure	
Institutional history and culture	
Institutional research/interpretation	

Director Skills, Knowledge, and Expertise

The skills and expertise the directors brought to bear on the important institutional issues were emphasized repeatedly by both directors and supervisors. The type of experience, skills, and knowledge described by directors and supervisors as enabling the directors' broader role were divided into two categories—broad-based and institution specific (see Table 5.5). This unique knowledge and expertise led to multiple opportunities to be seated at the table and collaborate through committee appointments, memberships, and leadership roles. D 'Andrea and Gosling (2001) agree, "The educational development office must offer something unique to the institution for its value to be recognized" (p. 72). These skill and knowledge sets are rarely articulated or emphasized in center director position descriptions because they speak to a different type of role than that required for instructional development. This list, compiled from director and supervisor interviews, makes evident the distinctive knowledge and expertise that a broader organizational role requires. The extension of who is at the institutional planning table and valuing of expertise across boundaries serves as the cornerstone for creating a collaborative leadership structure engaged in resolving large institutional concerns.

The directors involved in broad institutional initiatives often spoke of using valuable knowledge that was institution-based. Both the supervisor and director had attributed the director with being able to serve as a "forecaster" of institutional events and trends that would impact the institution because of the director's unique institutional knowledge (Case Study C). The supervisor further commented,

Again, in her case and anyone else that we hire as director, it really is the case of experience and perspective . . . because of the experience the director has had in training conferences and other kinds of experiences, the director brings a sort of broader perspective to these issues. [Among] faculty, who are really the ones who are doing the assessment, there is a tendency to look internally and maybe not externally as often as we should. I think the director brings that perspective. (Case Study C)

Part of the unique knowledge that enables the directors to function in a broader role entails knowing the relevant literature and other national institutional models to consider. One director commented, "One of our roles is to familiarize faculty with the literature on whatever issue we are talking about" (Case Study G). This director admitted that "having broader knowledge of models around the country, of the literature, as well as the campus, was critical in becoming "very involved" (Case Study G).

At times, the directors' prior experiences with broad initiatives at other institutions provided skills and insight that they tapped to enable a leadership role at their current institution. Directors cited key works that guided their involvement in institutional change. At times, directors referred to specific skills they had cultivated for enacting change processes and decision making.

I have been influenced to a great extent by the work of William J. Perry. The other book that . . . has influenced me in this instance has been *The University in Ruins* by Bill Readings. (Case Study G)

This director admitted having extensive knowledge and expertise in multiple areas including pedagogy, broader issues of teaching, learning, and curriculum reform, and national trends of where higher education is going. Directors may underestimate this expertise although the literature has referred to it as "specialist knowledge" and the ability to be a "repository of information on research and future trends" (D'Andrea & Gosling, 2001, p. 74). This director also highlighted having awareness of national trends,

I was very plugged into national conversations about teaching and learning. . . . I knew what the rest of the country was talking about and I think our expertise is around pedagogy and broader issues of teaching, learning, and curriculum reform; we also have expertise on big issues and trends of where higher education is going.

In terms of being viewed as a change agent, he admitted, "I think most people will say things publicly and politely, 'Well, [the center staff] are the experts on that.'" The director's supervisor spoke highly of this director's obvious and much-valued expertise.

> He has read all the stuff and remembers an incredible amount of what he reads, and is able to make connections later on with different theories . . . by helping to make it more transparent to people who are not immersed in the field [or] in the literature. (Case Study H)

Other directors and supervisors pointed out the importance of the wide institutional culture knowledge that the center director had and brought to initiatives and change processes. One director emphasized the need for developing "broad understanding of your governance structure and your history of the institution." (Case Study E). This director explained:

> I think I focus on pedagogy as far as the general education reform effort, without a doubt. I think that the center is one of the few places on our campus . . . that is really unifying for our campus. . . . We are much siloed into those individual schools and colleges. We have entered into a situation with a budget model that puts . . . four units in competition with one another for resources. . . . We [TLC] are a place that can think holistically. It can encourage others to do so. . . . One of my goals is to blur these lines. (Case Study E)

Several directors and supervisors noted the importance of a particular type of expertise or knowledge—knowledge of organizational change processes. The role they were enacting situated them in the process of institutional planning and change at a level that required a different type of knowledge than instructional development knowledge. Knowledge of organizational change processes is discussed at length in chapter 9.

National Initiative Involvement

Involvement in national initiatives and associations was identified as both a center- and director-based factor, primarily because both the center and director often were intricately entwined in these activities. For example, the directors repeatedly discussed their involvement in national higher education organizations and being part of an institutional team, task force, or committee that was charged with an initiative. Others made it evident that they exerted

their influence and shared their expertise by prompting the institution to connect with national initiatives and leading the institution's effort to learn about
an issue.

> Two years ago we went to the Greater Expectations Workshop [AAC&U],
> and we had a new provost, and we reaffirmed our mission to be a liberal arts
> institution with professional programs. But we were not communicating
> that very well to faculty and students. So we went to the Greater Expecta-
> tions. . . . We took a team, and when we came back we started a university-
> wide initiative called, "Claiming a Liberal Education." (Case Study A)

Another director explained the value of involving the institution in national initiatives through the center that would bring public attention to
the institution and its leaders because "every chancellor wants to make a big
splash!" She pointed out national recognition, grants, awards, and so forth
are important because "the institution values being in the news, and added,
"[Institution G] always likes anything that gets them in the news" (Case
Study G).

> They wanted me to connect this college to national and international con-
> versations about higher education, which is part of what I am called on to
> do. So our College is part of an AAC&U national project to put global
> learning at the center of general education. We were chosen as 1 of 16 insti-
> tutions. I am on the leadership team of that. So there are all kinds of ways
> that I am sort of centrally involved in things that are moving the college in
> new directions. (Case Study B)

> I have promoted faculty on the campus to go to AAC&U. In fact, I was
> the force behind why we finally joined that organization. I would say it
> has been very much an educational role and very much of getting fac-
> ulty more aware of issues, literature, and what other people are doing.
> (Case Study D)

Grant Writing and Securing External Funding

A number of the directors cited the obvious impact of having secured national
grant funding around institutional priorities. Securing grants as an enabling
factor is modeled in chapter 6. However, over a five-year period, one director
secured a series of external grants totaling more than five million dollars.
This enabled the director to give away money to seed and support work

on innovation and key initiatives (Case Study H). Other directors reported similar efforts:

> I am working on writing a grant that is part of the larger system that we are a part of—ethics in higher education, ethics across the curriculum, and becoming a more specifically engaged and ethically [considered] institution . . . so that will cut across everybody, if we are successful in that. (Case Study E)

This institution received a Title III grant that elevated the director's level of institutional involvement:

> The work happens in the grant where we incubated the ideas and notions . . . the grant provided a lot of conspiratorial time. We had 80 people a year working on them. We had two Title III grants running at the same time. (Case Study F)

Institutional Collaborations, Relationships, Outreach, and Partnerships

The importance of initiating, cultivating, and sustaining collaborative relationships with numerous institutional partners and colleagues was evident throughout the interviews. Directors intentionally sought and initiated these relationships, and recognized the impact this factor had on shifting their role beyond an instructional development focus. The directors developed relationships, performed outreach, initiated partnerships, and established working relationships long before institution-wide initiatives and committees were formed. Their supervisors more often described this aspect of the director's leadership style as collaborative.

The large constellation of collaborative relationships cited as most important by center directors included: deans and department chairs; faculty, institutional research/assessment, departments/schools, student affairs, faculty learning communities first year programs, provosts, teaching assistants, center advisory board (council), and national association leaders. For example, an outstanding factor for one director was the intensely collaborative and connected nature of her relationships across a multicampus institution. She firmly stated, "Almost everything we do now is collaborative" (Case Study F). For example,

> I work with a core consulting team which is the very biggest group which gets together to talk . . . they call it the consulting team, but what it is, is 10

people from around the college, different places, who talk to the director and the director brings big picture issues to that group. . . . Another, I work with the learning evidence team, looking at how we are going to garner real evidence of student learning . . . that is broad, but what I work in and what I am interested in, are the matters that are close to teachers, and learning, and curriculum. (Case Study F)

A collaborative leadership style was demonstrated and emphasized by another center director, who emphasized developing "real personal interactions, and real connections" (Case Study G). This director referred to these connections as cultivating "partners in innovation" and stated, "I think our relationships are very porous, or our boundaries are very porous and we have a lot of new connections with various other support units on campus." The director's supervisor concurred, explaining, "He talks a lot about the importance of having collaborators to affect change in learning." The director's supervisor continued, "I came around to understand how having a community is very important for change" (Case Study H). Another director pointed out how she sought out and initiated relationships around the campus with key leaders, "Early on I know I made appointments with certain people that I knew" (Case Study C). Another director concurred:

> the reality is, the relationships that the director forms are going to have the greatest impact. (Case Study E)

Another director's supervisor pointed out the director's approach to the learning-centered institutional initiative, "I know she went one-on-one with each department and that was initiated by her—to go to the departments" (Case Study D).

Apart from formal contacts and partnerships, informal contacts were also viewed as leading to greater involvement. One director emphasized the investment she had made in informal talk and exchange, regular outreach activities, connections through committee involvement, building relationships with associate deans, and "with the administrators who are heavily involved in undergraduate education." She emphasized building on involvement and collaboration with schools and colleges. The one-on-one work with the faculty often evolved into a work with greater visibility and broader-level initiatives or grant involvement at the department or division level. The sense of facilitating "connections" and bringing resources and people together permeated the discussion with this director. Likewise, the supervisor emphasized this aspect:

The important thing for us is to build relationships with the administrators who are heavily involved in undergraduate education. . . . One is sort of one-on-one and on an ad hoc basis, and then more strategically through the associate deans. (Case Study G)

Center-based Primary Enabling Factors

Seven of the nine center-based factors were identified by more than 50% of the case study participants. Interview data supporting five of these primary center-based factors is provided from a variety of institutional and center types. Involvement in national initiatives has been discussed in a previous section both as a director-based and as center-based primary factor.

Center Missions

The factor, center missions, was identified on the survey as significantly related to the type of work the directors perform, and emerged again in discussions with the directors and supervisors. Two types of enter mission alignment were discussed. Directors spoke of aligning the center's mission with the institutional mission through explicit reference to the institution, culture, and broad initiatives in the mission statement. Second, directors and supervisors mentioned internally aligning center programs with the center mission. This coherence, between institutional mission, center mission, and center programing, enabled the director to make decisions that seamlessly merged the instructional and organizational development aspects of their role. For example, to align with the institutional mission, one director stated that the center mission should include, "making possible institutional change" (Case Study A). Case Study G also explained, "Our mission . . . is more clearly to serve the whole faculty and initiatives that are supported by the central administration, as well as departmental initiatives, and faculty projects." The center director's supervisor pointed out:

> We were not offering them a resource that they can take or leave. We actually tried to enter the culture of the place. We became less remedial and more developmental in focus. (Case Study G)

Another director commented on the need to revise the center mission statement when she assumed the director position, "There was something there before, but I changed it . . . when I came in, I changed it. . . . I quite a bit changed the way we operate" (Case Study D). Center missions and an analysis of the critical components of exemplary center mission statements are discussed in chapter 11. The remaining enabling factors discussed here include the role of center director supervisors, center credibility, center staff, and center programing alignment with initiatives.

Directors' Supervisor Role

The directors spoke extensively about the key role of their immediate supervisors and how much they contributed to integrating this broader role into their work:

> in terms of where I was in the organizational structure . . . I was just kind of hanging out there, but I reported directly to the provost for the first three to four years, which I think was really good because he has been there a long time and was well respected . . . the fact that I reported to him helped to give the center some recognition that it might not have had otherwise. (Case Study A)

This supervisor had also supervised the center for five years previously. Both the director and supervisor shared a broader vision for the center.

> About three years ago [the director] and I were talking and we said this center is too marginalized. It is just supposed to give workshops and grants and keep out of the way. So when we came back from [AAC&U] we said we really need a culture change here. (Case Study A)

The advocacy role of the supervisor was mentioned consistently by the case study directors as a necessary support in their efforts to be involved more broadly. One director enthusiastically admitted, "He is really an advocate for our program and that is good "(Case Study G). Therefore, it is imperative that the director and supervisor share a common perspective about the director and center's role in the broader institutional change efforts.

The value of the supervisor's role was due, in part, to the supervisors' "connections" and collaborations and the length of their stay at an institution. His or her knowledge of the institutional structures and culture, and the unique positioning of his or her role in the institutional structure and reporting line, more often to academic affairs, was helpful to the center director. The supervisor often was a member of groups and attended meetings that the director was not invited to attend. Supervisors' committee membership and their access to institutional priorities and developing initiatives, is an important link for the TLC director. The supervisor shares this institutional knowledge and serves as "conduit for issues" so that directors are always aware of what is on the institutional radar screen and which issues are coming up on the horizon.

In describing how the center director created a new initiative and became very involved in leading it, the director's supervisor explained, "I think it was very much the provost in conversation with [the director]. The two of them have very complementary ways of looking at things and it was a natural output." This supervisor further pointed out, "Well, the provost is a big admirer of [the director's] work" (Case Study H).

The supervisor of one center demonstrated the ability to advance the leadership role and institutional perception of the director's expertise one and explained:

> I meet with the deans. I am sort of a regular with the deans' group. I meet independently with the vice-president for academic affairs. I also convene a group of chairs, which is actually quite unique. (Case Study D)

The highly important relationship between the center director and the director's supervisor was described as a partnership. "We are actually partners in what we do. I know we both consider ourselves partners." (Case Study D)

Center Credibility/Trust

Several directors commented on the way the center credibility played a role in having their input on initiatives valued by others:

> I think it is just simply the TLC going out and doing its job and doing it well, so that over time, people have come to trust them. (Case Study C)

Staffing/Staffing Reprioritizing

Center staffing and workload distribution required some rethinking and re-configuring in order to make room for the time invested in working on larger institutional initiatives. Center staffing could be an enabling factor, but it functioned as far more of an impediment if not carefully attended to or if the center staffing could not adapt to the new demands. The director explained how this role affected her workload and priorities: "Other things that I had been doing at the center are being relegated to a less important role." (Case Study E). This intentional shifting, delegating, and rebalancing allowed her to broaden her role.

An important key factor that enabled another director was the good, quality, smart people on his center staff. He pointed out:

> I think the people who work for the center are highly qualified, very active in one form or another, both in partnering with faculty on presentations and things like that. I think that it is very important to try to cultivate the intellectual life of the staff as much as possible. They feel like they are academics as well. (Case Study H)

Center Programing and Alignment With Core Initiatives

Important to note, the directors clearly saw center programing around initiatives as supporting their involvement in organizational development, but was not confused with the institutional involvement itself. In this way, the center programing, when aligned with the strategic priorities of the institution, brought the instructional and organizational dimensions of their role together very closely (see chapter 7). At a larger university, center programing of the "high profile events" served as an enabling factor for a center. The Scholarship of Teaching and Learning (SoTL) work stemming from the center was directly linked to institutional initiatives (Schroeder, 2007). Similarly, one director pointed out that the focus of the SoTL projects included criteria that matched the institutional initiatives, creating further alignment (Case Study G).

Faculty learning communities were mentioned several times as creating an opportunity for aligning the center with institutional priorities. This alignment occurred more easily because the director had gained early knowledge of the institutional priorities and had participated in developing the initiatives while also designing center programs that advanced the broader initiatives. This places the center in alignment with the institution's strategic plan (see chapter 12) from a proactive stance rather than in reaction to initiatives that are announced.

Institution-based Primary Enabling Factors

Finally, six primary factors were institution-based, including institutional leadership support, institution-wide dialogues, institutional culture, new institutional leadership, high faculty turnover or expansion, and institutional change. Of these six factors, institutional leadership support was selected as a factor by more than 63% of the survey directors, was significantly related to the survey director's level of involvement, and emerged as a common factor among the interviewed directors and supervisors. Three of the institution-based factors are discussed below with supporting evidence from the in-depth interviews.

Institutional Leadership Support

> The president of the university has sent in the nominations for the TLC for the Hesburgh Award for the last two to three years running. (Case Study C)

The president at one institution was not only an advocate but also founder of the director's position.

> Our president here—he is just terrific. He is the guy who took me off the grant and put me here, internally funded the position—the big order that helped us do a number of things, and I cannot say enough how important [President X] really [is]. (Case Study F)

> I felt like I had support from the highest level, which was my boss, who was the provost at the time. . . . I had a feeling of strong support for moving that agenda forward with the provost.

Regarding support from institutional leadership, a director pointed out:

> You need to have the support of the higher up. They just need to say the right things and they need to give you the resources and get out of the way. (Case Study A)

> [In] the government structure or the upper-level structure, there are five vice-presidents who form the cabinet with the president, and I know all of them and I work closely also with the vice-president of student affairs who sits on my advisory committee. He has been an equally strong advocate. I think he also has the president's ear and the team works very closely with my [vice president of academic affairs]. . . . I think those kinds of supports have been coming from many places, from key faculty leaders, and department chairs. (Case Study B)

Support and advocacy for the leadership role of the center extended beyond the supervisor and into higher levels of the administration. The director mentioned the importance of relationships with associate deans and administrators, but specifically identified upper-level advocacy for the entire program as enabling their involvement. The center clearly benefited from the being one of the dean's priorities and as a funding source (Case Study G).

> I work with him [the president]. He works with me. He makes sure I come to the board of trustees. I have written articles and he sees the articles and he publicly speaks about our program as something that the college should be proud of. (Case Study F)

Institutional Culture

The culture of the institution, as with the other case study models, played an important role in determining how well the director's broader involvement would be received. In institutional cultures with grass-roots traditions and successful faculty involvement in leadership initiatives, a widely participative approach to who sits at the table was helpful (see chapter 6).

New Institutional Leadership

One new president initiated the structure for the change process that moved the TLC from the margins to the institution's center:

> At the same time we got a new president and we started a big round of hiring, and he said to us, "I want you to take the steering committee's recommendation and fund a new program." The president generously gave us resources and . . . we had these massive summits where anyone interested could show up and sort of vote by consensus. (Case Study F)

Qualitative Evidence of Impeding Factors

Ten factors impeding the directors' institutional involvement were identified, two of which were primary—institutional leadership and center staffing. Five of the impeding factors are supported with interview excerpts below. Overwhelmingly, the factor that was cited most frequently as an impediment to being involved in organizational change was center staffing and resource limitations. Relatedly, the directors and supervisors also admitted role conflict over center priorities and balancing time spent on initiatives and traditional instructional development work. Additional impeding factors included institution or institutional leadership changes, institutional culture, differences between key institutional leaders and the center director or supervisor, and weak key institutional relationships. Several of these impeding factors are illustrated below with brief supervisor and director comments.

Center Staffing Limitations

Directors often stated that the investment of their time in a broader level of institutional involvement impacted the center staff and previous role they had performed. Very simply, one director admitted, "The center staff is stretched" (Case Study H). The supervisor at a smaller institution and center pointed out, "The problem is, it is a one person operation." (Case Study E)

One center director reported that being involved in institutional initiatives had indeed affected center workload decisions and created inner conflict with competing priorities and the need to "let go . . . to do the bigger things which do not have the [same] satisfying results." She initially wanted "to maintain the same commitment to presentations, workshops, consultations, and the typical work of the center but admitted, "I think we have maxed out the staff. . . when you move things to the center, then the demands are so much bigger" (Case Study A). The impeding factor of workload tensions and implications for staffing are discussed in depth in chapter 10.

A director's supervisor echoed the staffing limitations concern and the workload constraints creeping up on the director:

> She really needs the staff expanded in order to branch out into some of the new areas. That is very much a part of the next planning process for the center as well as the college, to figure out how to expand it, so that more needs [are] met. (Case Study B)

The lack of resources and support for the center and director to fulfill this role was apparent. "If we are going to see this center . . . as something of real value to this institution, we need to support it better . . . have more visibility, and support it financially with more human resources." This director further highlighted the staffing pressures, "I just think that we are so understaffed that . . . some other things are compromised" (Case Study E). Another case study director admitted that the center staffing size was not sufficient for the "giant initiatives" they undertook (Case Study G).

Director Role Conflict, Workload Tensions, and Conflicting Priorities

Establishing this leadership role brought some element of confusion in trying to determine in which initiatives to be involved. The director's supervisor commented:

> Which ones does she need to be involved in and which ones are going to go ahead by themselves? Which ones do we need to put some energy in so that they go in the right direction? We have not sorted that out exactly. (Case Study A)

A more in-depth series of comments from one center director provides understanding of how a director confronts opportunities for involvement while trying to integrate traditional instructional development roles and tasks:

> I am at a point where I need to prioritize and pull back from some things because I am completely over-extended. (Case Study B)

> My time in individual consulting has gone down dramatically and that is a direct result of my committee work going up dramatically.
>
> And so I do not want to get to a place where I have become essentially a stand-in associate dean. (Case Study B)

This director further described the ambivalence and conflicting feelings about her expanding leadership role when approached to be on the leadership team for a new initiative:

> I want to play a real backseat role. I am just getting really over-extended. The bigger this has gotten the more I am thinking, "Why don't faculty lead this charge—it is curricula?" I am not even sure it is a good place for me. I proposed that maybe this is a good moment for me to step back. There was tremendous resistance. I think that they like the connection with a place that is focused on pedagogy, on teaching. It is that kind of neutral safe space, not politically charged. (Case Study B)

From the supervisor's perspective, potential conflicts may resolve due to the strong reputation of the center:

> In this next phase of the center's life, because the faculty has so much confidence in the center and in the center's director now, we think there may be an opportunity to look back and link assessment more directly to the work of the center, still keeping it formative but at least introducing it into the menu of things that the center supports. I think those are going to be conversations that take more time to really know. (Case Study B)

Another director admitted to the evitable conflict in priorities that has arisen from spreading her time out between the traditional responsibilities and the call to be involved at the institutional level:

> Sometimes I have been thrown off course from what I would say my role should be by events that are happening institutionally. . . . I just think that

we are so understaffed that, without a doubt, some other things are compromised. The simple fact that I do not have as many hours in the week means that other things that I had been doing at the center are being relegated to a less important role. Ideally, I would like to continue to do everything I was doing and take on that added responsibility. (Case Study E)

The result of integrating her involvement in institutional initiatives has been a pulling back on other activities. For example:

One [result] would be the day-to-day engagement around existing programs. . . . In my first year here I was in much closer contact with the facilitators of those teaching circles on a regular basis. We have a grant fellowship program and I would be checking in and supportive of the grantees. . . . So it is that kind of management of things that has sort of gotten looser. . . . I guess where the shift is, whereas I might have assumed more responsibility for some of the planning of those events, I am taking the role of administrating how we get that done—so I wouldn't do as much of it myself. I would say, "Okay, we are going to do this series of brown bags this semester, I need descriptions by this date" as opposed to creating the descriptions for the event—delegating more. (Case Study E)

Institutional Leadership Change

As a primary impeding factor, leadership changes carried potential risk and benefits.

That person retired two years ago and the new person does not understand what I do, at all. . . . I am not a part of the strategic planning committees going on in the university now but I was before. I see it as a lower-level involvement. (Case Study D)

It is not a statement about either, but the changeover in leadership of the provost is causing everyone to step back and figure out what level of support you have in those kinds of things. Had the same provost been here, I think it might be a different story. (Case Study E)

Significant changes at another institution were positive because the new president created a team for learning, flattened the organization, and had collaborative team process. With tremendous faculty turnover, the new faculty were socialized with a new philosophy of teaching and learning, and a new academic vice president position was added (Case Study F). Five changes in the vice president of academic affairs made it challenging and difficult for this center director:

> The programs have coordinators and division deans, but no parallel structure of deans. There is a lack of interest in the development of faculty. It would be nice if more took a real interest in development of the faculty—and they are supposed to in their job description, but few . . . think it is their job. They are just not interested in that. (Case Study F)

Another director recognized the loss of the center founder and the impact this leadership change had on her committee involvement:

> I reported immediately to [associate vice president for academic affairs], the original person who had that job was the person who started the center, not in terms of being the director, but in terms of bringing it to the campus and selling the idea to the administration, and making sure there was funding for it. So that person was a big supporter of the center as well as thinking that the center had [to have] a lot of leadership. That person retired two years ago. . . . So I have been asked to be on less task forces, less asked to be part of large university initiatives. (Case Study D)

Institutional Culture

Multiple aspects of the institutional context were cited as having some impeding influence on the director being able to actualize the broader role he or she envisioned. The challenges of enacting this role at research institutions revolved around the cultural norm of individual pursuits versus the collegial, collaborative culture described at other institutions. However, Case Study H provided a model for research university centers and directors. Institutional culture further impacted centers and directors.

According to one center supervisor, the institution has undergone significant structural and academic program changes recently. As a result, the professional schools since added have "less buy-in" with the TCLT than the rest of the original academic program areas of the college. Therefore, he reported, there is resistance to moving toward a full time director (Case Study E).

> people still think that research is the most important issue. I have to say, a university is the only organization . . . in which people are rewarded for following their own interests almost entirely. That being the case, people do not see themselves as members of the team or some sort of overarching enterprise. (Case Study G)

Major institutional leadership changes frequently generated a series of political adjustments. Large initiatives were redistributed to units not structurally related to the center and several initiatives became marginalized at one institution. Turnover in administration also created the perplexing challenge of how to get onto the radar screen of the new leadership. As reported, institutional infighting and territorial barriers hampered both the initiatives as well as the center's involvement in them:

> In my opinion, that [initiative] has been given to a particular line of the administration and is therefore marginalized. So it is not a campus-wide initiative anymore. It is ongoing, but I have no idea what is ongoing. (Case Study G)

Institutional Changes/Growth: Limited Resources

According to the supervisors and directors, the resources and money are limited due to significant institutional growth:

> We have had phenomenal growth here, and as a result of that, there is always a shortage of resources. (Case Study C)

Conclusion

The issues in higher education surrounding teaching and learning beckon for a collaborative team of experts across disciplinary and administrative boundaries. Center directors are positioned to play a critical role in the shaping of key teaching and learning issues as institutions struggle to change. Being leaders, change agents, and experts at the institutional level, while functioning in an instructional development role at department and individual levels, is not only possible and taking place but necessary.

The content analysis and rich descriptions of the case study interview data revealed 27 primary factors among 37 that enabled or impeded the involvement of centers and directors in institutional initiatives. Analyzed further, the factors were divided into the categories center-, director-, and institution-based and illustrate the process involved in carving out a substantial organizational dimension to this work, and how to sustain what amounts to a paradigmatic shift in what had become largely an instructional development role.

Identifying the common factors among the center directors and their supervisors from centers already involved in broader institutional change provides what is likely, the first research-based map for directors to use in moving toward the center of their institutional radar screens. The detailed models of specific primary factors in part three bring into focus the way this role develops over time.

Three sources of data—significance testing of survey variables, selection of factors on the survey, and interview data—brought much needed insight into the organizational role that centers and directors are performing both in and outside of the United States. The survey confirmed a significant relationship between seven enabling or impeding factors and the level of involvement in institutional initiatives. Six of the seven significant enabling and impeding factors on the survey also were selected by more than 50% of the directors listed elsewhere on the survey. Comparison between these two types of survey results and case study evidence identified common factors that surfaced from all three sources of data and several types of questions. Through cross-case analysis of 18 interviews with directors and supervisors, 21 primary (of four or more cases) enabling and impeding factors were identified. A comparison across all sources of data provides a well-grounded and initial understanding of how to create this role (see Table 5.3).

Part three presents a series of chapters that integrate relevant literature from inside and outside higher education, further detailed evidence, and center models, three of which were authored by case study participants. The third section of this book makes evident how the data—the factors that were carefully brought to light—play out in the lives of the center directors and their roles as institutional change agents. Each chapter in part three concludes with concrete recommendations for enacting the enabling factors in order to further develop the role of institutional change agent.

References

D'Andrea, V., & Gosling, D. (2001). Joining the dots: Reconceptualizing educational development. *The Institute for Learning and Teaching in Higher Education and SAGE Publications, 2*(1), 64–81. Retrieved October 26, 2009, from http://alh.safepub.com

Pettigrew, A. (1985). *The awakening giant.* Oxford: Basil Blackwell, Ltd.

Schroeder, C. M. (2007). Countering SoTL marginalization: A model for integrating SoTL with institutional initiatives. *International Journal for the Scholarship of Teaching and Learning, 1*(1). Retrieved December 31, 2009, from http://www.georgiasouthern.edu/ijsotl

PART THREE

REPOSITIONING CENTERS AND DIRECTORS ON THE INSTITUTIONAL RADAR SCREEN

I n part three, chapters 6 through 12, the 27 primary case study factors that enabled directors from across a variety of institutional missions and teaching and learning centers (TLCs) to function as institutional-level change agents are described in greater detail. Although several primary factors are the focus of each chapter, multiple primary center, director, and institutional factors are modeled in each chapter as factors function in dynamic relationship to one another, each factor triggering additional factors that further enable and support their organizational development role. The case study chapter authors have carefully selected key action and events that make transparent how they built broad-level institutional involvement into their center and role as directors. The recommended strategies at the end of each chapter recap the steps entailed in integrating this role alongside the instructional development dimension of the developer's role. As change agents, their common and unique experiences serve as successful models of initiators, leaders, and collaborators of institutional change. These models may help prompt the field to recognize a second significant paradigm shift taking hold in this field, much as it did in the 1960s and the decades that followed, bringing instructional development to the foreground of a very different looking carry role of developers. Chapter 13 concludes this book with a nod to an emerging grounded theory of this role change and an effort to convey a sense of urgency in higher education behind this call to investing in and reinterpreting organizational development—reframed as the work of change agents through collaborative work between developers and colleagues within institutions.

6

LEADING FROM THE MIDDLE

A Faculty Development Center at the Heart of Institutional Change

Catherine E. Frerichs, Diana G. Pace, and Tamara Rosier

S orcinelli, Austin, Eddy, and Beach chapter 4, (2006) examined and identified current practices and future issues in faculty development based on responses from 494 faculty developers across the United States and Canada (a 50% response rate). As developers, they argue that we are now in the "Age of the Network," where "the challenges and opportunities appear more intensified and complex" (p. 160), and point out that we face challenges that no single part of a university can address alone. These "forces of change" include the changing professoriate; the changing student body; and the changing nature of teaching, learning, and scholarship. Even though it is paramount for faculty developers to recognize these changes, "support of institutional change priorities" (Sorcinelli et al., 2006, p. 160) was only sixth in a list of new issues addressed by faculty developers. While faculty developers as a group recognize the necessity to focus on student learning, they have not seen *organizational* change as a high priority for centers or the role of directors. Sorcinelli et al. (2006) document the extent to which developers continue to focus on individual faculty while also recognizing that they must work collaboratively within their institutions if complex issues such as general education reform, matters of race, class, and gender, and assessing learning outcomes are to be addressed.

From Marginalized to Key Leader

The 2002 five-year self-study of the Pew Faculty Teaching and Learning Center (Pew FTLC) at Grand Valley State University (GVSU) showed a center true to its mission. It was indeed "enhancing student learning by supporting faculty members in their efforts to teach effectively." The center had strong faculty support, a high level of satisfaction with programing, an extensive grants program, and an award-winning mentoring program for new faculty. The center was thriving; why make any significant changes? However, an outside consultant who visited in early 2003 challenged the Pew FTLC to "play a more central role in deliberations about teaching and learning at GVSU." Chism (1998) outlines the features of such a teaching and learning center (TLC) role change. The center focus she describes is less on individual consultations and more on organizational development, less on providing answers than asking questions, and less on service than on leadership. In short, it is a shift "from the basement office to the front office" (Chism, 1998, p. 141). The dean of the College of Interdisciplinary Studies concurred: the director had completed six successful years at GVSU, why not do more?

Although a significant departure from the director's existing level of institutional involvement, her role shifted from the successful but narrower focus solely on faculty and instructional development. At GVSU, the *Claiming a Liberal Education* (CLE) initiative was collaboratively envisioned, initiated, and led by a team that included the director of the Pew FTLC. Through the process of bringing about broad institutional change through the CLE initiative, the director and center's roles underwent a dramatic transformation. As a case study participant in the study underlying this book, the director described the center's level of institutional involvement as having moved from "marginalized to key leader" (see chapter 4). What events and actions on the part of the institution, the center, and the director would explain this significant transformation of the center? A brief summary of the institutional context precedes an outline of the change process, the director's role as a codirector of the initiative, and the outcomes of a significant institutional change process.

Institutional Context

Institutional Growth Sets the Stage for Institutional Change

In 2003, GVSU, a comprehensive, regional university, then 40-years old, had grown quickly to 21,500 students, 17,800 of whom were undergraduates. At that time, GVSU was the fastest growing university in Michigan. For each of the previous five years of self study the university had added between 80 and 110 new faculty. As the 2003 data for freshmen from the Cooperative

Institutional Research Project (CIRP) indicated, more students than at comparable institutions were unlikely to have come with an understanding of what a university education entails. More than half had at least one parent without a college degree. One-quarter of the 2003 students attending college for the first time came from homes with an estimated family income of below $50,000. Two-thirds indicated that they would be working to help pay college expenses. Students of color were disproportionately represented in these groups (Henderson-King, 2004a).

Despite this growth, GVSU had also recently completed a process of redefining the university's purpose. It had grappled with answering how it was going to define itself for the early years of the twenty-first century. As a result, the newly revised statements of mission, vision, and values *reaffirmed* the orientation with which the university had been founded; *excellence in teaching* was to continue to be the primary focus for faculty, and the university was to remain grounded in the *ideals of liberal education*, which one sees today in the lead statement on the GVSU website:

> A strong liberal education serves as the foundation for Grand Valley's wide array of undergraduate and graduate homepage programs, fostering critical thinking, creative problem solving, and cultural understanding. Through personalized learning enhanced by active scholarship, we accomplish our mission of educating students to shape their lives, their professions, and their societies. (www.gvsu.edu)

Investigating and Cultivating the Need for Change

Claiming a Liberal Education (CLE), the broader institutional initiative described in this chapter, had quiet beginnings. As one of the early documents in the CLE initiative noted, "This degree of growth and change has led to questions about the content, goals, and standards of a university education" (Henderson-King, 2004a, p. 1). Through informal conversations in spring 2003, faculty had reported frustration in their teaching role, stating that student consumerist views of their role put pressure on them to lower their expectations. Two events at GVSU occurred simultaneously but independently to bring to light the growing frustration and dissonance with current expectations about teaching and learning. If the institution undertook wide-scale change that affected teaching and learning around these issues, the opportunity to expand the director's role and shift the center to the core matters of the institution would be possible, although not guaranteed.

Acting on this reported frustration in collaboration with the vice provost for student affairs became the first critical juncture in what was to grow into a full-scale institutional initiative. As a result, the director's role expanded to include broader institutional involvement.

Initiating Dialogue and Collaboration

First, as a response to these informal conversations, the center's director and the vice provost for student affairs *brought together* members of the center's advisory committee, student affairs staff, representatives from faculty governance and student senate, as well as other students and faculty for a discussion. This step clearly entailed not only collaboration but also *initiating* collaboration.

The initial topic was the reported faculty frustration in their teaching role, given the consumerist views of many students. Some faculty believed that easier classes would get them higher ratings and acted accordingly. Faculty cited the personnel practices that compounded this problem; the only evidence required by the faculty handbook for effective teaching was student ratings of faculty. Some of the students participating in the discussions saw themselves primarily as consumers whereas others said that they cared first about their learning. Faculty could expect more from them and they would meet those expectations. The result was a mixed range of expressed frustration. It was ironic that these opinions emerged so strongly after the university had just reaffirmed to remain grounded in the *ideals of liberal education.*

The second event highlighting the current attitudes toward teaching and learning came from the Seidman College of Business at GVSU. A group of Seidman faculty were conducting research on teaching and learning taking place in its own college, funded by the Pew FTLC. Using faculty and graduating seniors as subjects, they reported that 81% of their students attend college primarily to obtain a credential, and that "The faculty dramatically underestimated the amount of course-related outside work students are doing" (McKendall, Bhagwat, Giedeman, Klein, & Levenburg, 2006, p. 47). Just as with the discussion themes, these research results were consistent with the literature on faculty and student views of their roles (Levine & Cureton, 1998; Schilling & Schilling, 1999; Skorupa, 2002).

The McKendall et al. (2006) study and the collaborative, informal discussions had reported the strong utilitarian motivation of most students (and some faculty). Thus, the initial threads of motivation for institutional change derived from a growing recognition that the teaching and learning currently characteristic of GVSU conflicted with the liberal education expectations embedded in its institutional mission—expectations still supported by faculty, administrators, and some students. Increasingly, they felt a discrepancy between ideals and actual practice.

The institutional change initiative that emerged out of this growing dissonance at GVSU had the same source of leadership as is frequently described in the literature on faculty development. The director and her supervisor recognized that *the center could be both a source and a catalyst for change.* They were also eager to continue the collaboration that had begun with student affairs, convinced that academic affairs and student affairs must cooperate if the initiative were to be successful. At GVSU, both divisions report to the provost, thus facilitating cooperation. For its part, student affairs leaders recognized that, by participating, they were following recommendations set forth in *Learning Reconsidered* (American College Personnel Association & National Association of Student Personnel Administrators, 2004), a widely disseminated publication by two national Student Affairs organizations. It urged student affairs personnel to focus their efforts on the whole student with an emphasis on student learning and connecting out-of-class and in-class learning.

Diana G. Pace, associate dean of students, and Catherine E. Frerichs, director of the Pew FTLC, became co-directors of what was later called the CLE initiative. The key steps we and our colleagues took, the key conditions occurring at GVSU, and the institutional research efforts undertaken that informed this change process are captured in Table 6.1.

Leading Through Expertise, Vision, and Institutional Alignment

The leadership skills we had developed and alignment of our efforts with the institutional mission were key factors in advancing this initiative to the next step. Already familiar with the higher education literature that explains that the college or university's mission is the necessary starting point (e.g., Kezar, 2006; Legorreta, Kelley, & Sablynski, 2006; Lieberman, 2005; Taylor & Schönwetter, 2002), we framed the initiative funding proposal to the provost in those terms. *Our goal was to align student and faculty expectations with the goals of a liberal education.* We envisioned that this initiative would address the disparity in expectations between utilitarian and liberal education. We, as change agents, defined the problem in terms of the institutional mission, outlined the goals of the initiative, and requested funds for a part-time faculty researcher who had qualitative and quantitative research skills beyond those possessed by either CLE initiative director. We estimated that we were undertaking a four-to-five–year project. The changes we were seeking could not happen quickly.

TABLE 6.1
Chronological sequence of leadership efforts and institutional factors

Date	Pew FTLC and Initiative Leaders[a]	Relevant Data	Institutional Factors
2002	Carried out Pew FTLC self-study	—	Intensive growth, positive culture; mission, vision, and values revised
2003	Outside consultant	CIRP	—
Spring	Pew FTLC/Student affairs began discussions	Seidman College of Business research	Growing frustration
Fall	Defined problem and envisioned initiative. Prepared proposal for the provost, aligning initiative with institutional mission; enlisted researcher and identified research questions.	—	Support of the provost and president
2004	Conducted focus groups, surveys	—	—
Spring	Adopted Gladwell's change model	—	—
Summer	Attended AAC&U Institute	—	
Fall	Organized three intergroup dialogues; sent recommendations to chairs, deans, provost; prepared CLA application to Lumina Foundation	—	161 participants; strategic planning cycle
2005	—	—	Advisory committee formed
Spring	—	—	—
Fall	—	First CLA cycle	Faculty senate supported resolution. Increased emphasis on assessment to prepare for NCA accreditation
2006/2007	CLE activities continued	—	—
2008	Conducted follow-up faculty focus groups	—	NCA accreditation visit
2009	Conducted follow-up student focus groups	—	—

Note. AAC&U = Association of American Colleges and Universities; CIRP = Cooperative Institutional Research Project; CLA = Collegiate Learning Assessment; FTLC = Faculty Teaching and Learning Center; NCA = *North Central Association.*
[a]The codirectors and leaders of the CLE initiative at GVSU are listed in the appendix.

Upper-Level Support and Credibility

This alignment between the initiative and the institutional mission cinched the financial support and enabled the center director's involvement to continue. The provost has since stated that the director "gave [us] the reins for developing the project" because our proposal fit the university's mission "so well" and was consistent with her own values and experiences when she developed a TLC at her previous institution. Fundamentally, she said, she trusted the leaders (G. Davis, personal communication, September 12, 2008). In giving the codirectors this freedom and, later, becoming one of the initiative's cosponsors, the director was enabling them to "lead from the middle," "to influenc[e] from among, rather than from above, below, or in front of one's group" (Robinson, 2002, p. 19; see also Pearce, 2003; Raelin, 2003). The provost approved the proposal as she has approved all subsequent requests of this initiative.

Collaborators in Change

As change initiators and leaders, we recognized the need to further galvanize and motivate change. The need for change is a key element in advancing the process of change. To do so required institutional research to make a strong enough case for initiating the scale of broad institutional and cultural change we were discussing and to guide it as it progressed. If both qualitative and quantitative research with a broad group of faculty and students confirmed our hunches from the informal discussions and research of McKendall et al. (2006) from the Seidman College of Business, we would have the kind of evidence-based message we needed. We wanted this research to answer the big questions that brought together the institution's reaffirmed liberal arts mission with the growing disparity in expectations between students and faculty that we had been able to capture in part. As the initiative's codirectors, we selected a social psychologist as the faculty researcher, forming the collaborative leadership core of the initiative. We decided to collect evidence to answer the following questions:

1. Are students and faculty able to articulate, and do they endorse, the value of liberal education?
2. Do students and faculty recognize the high expectations implicit in teaching and learning within the context of liberal education? (Henderson-King, 2004b)

The project's researcher, assisted by the codirectors, organized focus groups in early 2004 with 45 faculty who teach undergraduate students and, separately, 14 undergraduate students. (It proved extremely difficult to recruit students, even with incentives.) Online surveys conducted with undergraduates and their faculty had response rates of 27% and 33%, respectively.

These data confirmed our expectations. Both students and faculty had much to say that was positive about teaching and learning at GVSU. At the same time, the faculty frustration with students who saw themselves primarily as consumers was palpable. Faculty agreed unanimously that students do not do the best work they are capable of. They do what they need to in order to get by. When students were asked in focus groups how often they did their best work, their responses were mixed. Some faculty, the researcher found, may actually be encouraging low expectations, a finding confirmed as well in the McKendall et al. (2006) study, where one-third of the faculty admitted that fear of negative evaluations affected their teaching actions.

When faculty were asked in focus groups whether students were well educated when they left GVSU, most hesitated, then said they were unsure. The researcher summarized what they were sure of: "Many faculty and some students would like to see a change in the Grand Valley culture. They would like to see a richer intellectual environment that would foster liberal education and all that it entails" (Henderson-King, 2004c, p. 2). Faculty also recognized the need for a major structural change—less emphasis on student ratings of faculty during personnel reviews—if they were not to be penalized for expecting more of their students.

The focus group data also corroborated broader research for this initiative from other focus groups of faculty and students conducted by students in the introductory research classes in advertising and public relations, 2004–2006. The research in itself furthered our goals—students carrying it out learned about liberal education and student/faculty expectations, as did the participants in their groups.

Another source of data provided helpful evidence that strengthened the case for institutional change. Prior to the CLE initiative, the National Survey of Student Engagement (NSSE), a measure of the level of engagement of undergraduate freshmen and seniors in educationally effective practices, had not been used at GVSU. It was administered for the first time in early 2005 as a means of gathering additional information about GVSU freshmen and seniors and their perception of their education at GVSU. The results confirmed to us that while we, and many faculty, were not satisfied with the level of expectations at GVSU, our students were not so different from those at peer institutions where students had taken the survey. Our students, both freshmen and seniors, responded similarly to questions about their engagement in an academically rigorous curriculum. GVSU seniors reported lower gains than their peers in several areas of concern to us, such as "learning effectively on your own" and "solving complex real-world problems," whereas GVSU freshmen reported similar gains in those same categories (Office of Institutional Analysis, NSSE 2005).

Institutional Leadership Support

Neither our surveys and focus groups nor the NSSE results gave us direct measures of student learning outcomes or enough evidence on actual outcomes to reinforce and unite the institution toward making a significant change. We looked to a new instrument—the Collegiate Learning Assessment (CLA)—to provide us this information. The CLA, developed by the Council for Aid to Education, assesses critical thinking, problem solving, written communication skills, and the ability to construct and evaluate arguments—all skills at the heart of liberal education. With the support of the provost and president, we prepared a successful application to participate in a longitudinal study of the CLA, funded by the Lumina Foundation. A random sample of freshmen and seniors took the test in fall 2005. The longitudinal study would enable GVSU to document the difference that a GVSU education makes, for the first time ever. The freshmen "did not demonstrate particular writing skill beyond that expected based on their SAT scores"; the seniors, however, "perform[ed] well on writing tasks relative to other seniors with similar SAT scores" (Guevara, 2006)—evidence for value added from a GVSU education.

A Model for Change

The results of data gathering from these multiple sources made explicit to us and our supervisors that in attempting to align student and faculty expectations within the context of liberal education, the institution's original and reaffirmed mission, we were undertaking nothing less than changing GVSU's current culture. We had a consistent philosophy in our foundational documents, had even recently reaffirmed our mission, and the institution was still living out a conflicting experience in the daily lives and classrooms of teachers and students.

Leading from the middle as we were, we needed an egalitarian model to guide our next steps in the change process. It also required a systemic approach to change: literally, all parts of the university were going to be affected and therefore must be involved in the change. Finally, it required leaders who had the respect of the university community and who were actively supported by administrators at higher levels.

Expertise and Organizational Change Model

We found our model in Malcolm Gladwell's *The Tipping Point: How Little Things Can Make a Big Difference* (2000). Gladwell begins with the premise that the best way to understand certain kinds of change is to think of them as epidemics: "Ideas and products and messages and behaviors spread just like viruses do" (p. 7). Why did Hush Puppies shoes become fashionable so quickly, and why did a dramatic fall in murder rates occur in New York City over a five-year period in the early 1990s? Even though we knew we could not use the language of epidemics and viruses when we discussed the initiative with broader university audiences, we wanted a change in student and faculty expectations to spread like a virus. We envisioned an epidemic of liberal education overtaking the campus. The actual metaphor we often used in our discussions came from our proximity to Lake Michigan. We imagined the university as one of the giant, ocean-going freighters we often saw far out on the lake. What did it take to get one of them to shift course?

There are three parts to Gladwell's model for change framed as conditions: the three groups people who *initiate* the change, the message itself, and the larger group that *embraces and spreads* the change.

Gladwell's condition 1: Change initiators

Gladwell argues that three types of people must be involved in initiating the change: connectors, mavens, and persuaders.

Connectors: Connectors know many people. Because we as co-directors had extensive experience at GVSU and, between us, knew most of the faculty and all of the Student Affairs staff, we believed we qualified well as Connectors, as did our supervisors, who, combined, had even more history at GVSU than we did and provided upper-level support throughout.

Mavens: Mavens are people with the relevant knowledge. We needed Mavens. We directors had unique and broad expertise and knowledge of the institution, of the literature of faculty and student expectations. We had also read widely in the literature on liberal education, as well as engaged in years of discussion about it with colleagues at several institutions. Our researcher provided us with the specific knowledge that we needed for this initiative through focus groups and survey data. NSSE and CLA results enabled us to put the institutional data in a national perspective.

Persuaders: Knowing how to apply the results of the research would have to come from other people in various positions throughout the university. They would become Gladwell's Persuaders, who embodied Senge's (2006) idea of systems thinking.

Gladwell's condition 2: Change message

All entities in the organization needed to be a part of this initiative, from the secretaries who saw students on a daily basis to the president and Board of Trustees. When it came to actually making changes, we knew that GVSU's generally positive culture, optimistic tone, and can-do attitude would work to our advantage. Almost anyone at the university would carry our message well. The message itself also mattered—Gladwell's second condition for change. Gladwell claims that a message needs to be "sticky . . . so memorable, in fact, that it can create change, that it can spur someone to action" (Gladwell, 2000, p. 92). We believed that the results of our on-campus research, combined with data from national sources, had created a "sticky message." The lively discussions that resulted when we presented these data to faculty confirmed this conclusion.

Gladwell's condition 3: Spreading a contagious message through groups

We decided how we would apply Gladwell's third major condition for change, the function of groups in spreading a contagious message, during the summer of 2004. An expanded group of us—the two directors and the faculty researcher, and in addition, a faculty member, an administrator, a student affairs member, and a student—spent a week in Snowbird, Utah, as part of the Greater Expectations Institute, a program of the Association of American Colleges and Universities (AAC&U). As with the other case studies in this book, the Pew FTLC director's involvement with the AAC&U Snowbird team greatly enabled her involvement with the core planning and implementation of this large initiative. For a century, the AAC&U has championed liberal education, and in recent years, has put a particular emphasis on new research and language to make its ideals continually relevant.

Before leaving Snowbird, the team had to determine how we would bring the plan that we had developed for the initiative back to GVSU. We wanted to think that our message and plan would immediately appeal to our various constituents. The freighter might even turn itself. Our administrative leader drew us back to the reality of our university's culture. We were not selling Hush Puppies. We were bringing a complicated set of ideas to colleagues with multiple, legitimate, and sometimes conflicting agendas. Reminding ourselves of Gladwell's use of multiple groups became the starting point for rethinking our approach. Even though we were leaving Snowbird with a plan, we would first educate the university community about the issues and invite them to tell us what should happen next.

Gladwell cites a number of studies to show that groups of 150 or less are optimal for getting the word out, whether one is selling a book or deciding how to reorganize a company (pp. 175–192). We determined that we would recruit 150 people from across the university who understood and supported what we were doing. The mechanism for achieving this goal came from a technique, Intergroup Dialogues (IGDs), which had been presented at Snowbird (Schoem & Hurtado, 2001; Zuniga, 1998). Groups are organized to discuss a particular issue, consisting of representatives from larger interest groups and the results are then analyzed. Through this informal qualitative research, we would be moving the CLE initiative forward by inviting others to assist in defining it (Kemmis & McTaggart, 2000).

From our work in Snowbird, we could see that the IGDs would also allow us to introduce issues of diversity into the discussion of liberal education and expectations and to move beyond simply considering who our students were. Now we had the vocabulary and perspective to consider diversity in another way by incorporating it more explicitly into our definition of liberal education through the lens of "inclusive excellence" to "comprehensively link diversity and quality and place them at the center of campus planning and practice" (AAC&U, 2008).

Facilitating and Initiating Dialogues

During fall 2004, we organized a series of three IGDs among our three constituency groups: faculty, staff, and students. The number who participated, 161, enabled us to meet Gladwell's third criterion for significant change. The meetings were organized around readings related to liberal education, student/faculty expectations, the results of the focus group discussions the previous spring, diversity, and inclusive excellence. As a result, further plans developed as part of the CLE initiative. For example, the groups strongly recommended clear, consistent communication regarding liberal education and expectations and the necessity for continuing dialogue on these issues. The recommendations, and means to implement them, were sent to department chairs, deans, and provost's office administrators, since the university was in the midst of a round of strategic planning (Pace, Henderson-King, & Frerichs, 2005).

Two years after the first informal conversations about conflicting expectations among students and faculty, in the spring of 2005, even before we had the results from NSSE and the CLA, we felt confident enough in our message and the supporting research to form a university-wide advisory committee. Along with the IGD participants, they were to become Gladwell's

Persuaders. The positions of the CLE advisory committee members enabled the institution-wide change we were seeking as well as indicated the broad and deep support we already had from university leaders.

We secured cosponsorships from the provost, the vice provost for student affairs, the Pew FTLC, and the Colleges of Interdisciplinary Studies and Liberal Arts and Sciences. Any public statement about the initiative included its goal—aligning student and faculty expectations with the goals of a liberal education—and its sponsors. Later that year, the faculty senate recognized the advisory committee and passed a resolution supporting the CLE initiative. We could not have continued our work without the support of the faculty senate.

Table 6.2, which summarizes the changes that occurred over the life of the CLE initiative, also makes evident the range of representation from across the university. We gathered together in the advisory committee the people who could either set the change process in motion or actually make the needed changes that would permeate the institutional culture and structures. During the committee's two meetings in 2005–2006, and again in 2006–2007, members reported on change in their areas. The CLE initiative cannot claim credit for all of the changes reported in Table 6.2, but most would not have occurred without the heightened university-wide awareness of liberal education and an emphasis on higher expectations for both students and faculty.

Space limitations do not permit a detailed discussion of other changes that may be at least indirectly linked to the CLE initiative—the results of the second cycles of NSSE and CLA and a second round of focus groups, in 2008 with 73 faculty and in 2009 with 95 students. The 2007 NSSE scores increased significantly in areas related to high expectations and connecting learning inside and outside the classroom (Office of Institutional Analysis, NSSE 2007). The CLA results demonstrated that rising juniors scored as expected on the basis of their performance as freshmen (Guevara, 2007).

Understanding of and support for liberal education remained strong among faculty. Our analysis of the faculty focus group discussions provided evidence for significant shifts in faculty's view of themselves as teachers and of their students as learners, due in part not only to the initiative but also, surely, to a greatly increased emphasis on assessing student learning outcomes during the years of the initiative to prepare for a North Central Association accreditation visit in 2008. Unlike in 2004, faculty could now articulate what they did to encourage high expectations in their students. Again, unlike in 2004, they had a basis for determining whether GVSU students were well educated (Frerichs, 2008).

TABLE 6.2
Claiming a Liberal Education (CLE) initiative direct or indirect institutional changes 2004–2008

Provost

Instituted and funded initiatives that directly support CLE goals: assessing and strengthening advising program, developing model for student success. Funded four years of discussion on liberal education with faculty, staff, and students. Revised new faculty orientation for greater focus on liberal education. Established task force to study feasibility of university-wide student rating form.

Institutional Marketing

Focus groups of faculty and students to develop brief, direct messages about liberal education. Current university tagline is a result. Previous themes of convenience and affordability no longer foregrounded.

Academic Services

Summer orientations for first-year students revised to emphasize liberal education and academic challenge.

College of Interdisciplinary Studies

More than doubled sections of Introduction to Liberal Education; about one-third of freshmen take course, continued the IGDs with focus on diversity, organized provost's liberal education discussions, instituted Community Reading, now in fourth year, and organized team for second Greater Expectations Institute with focus on engaging students by integrating the curricular and cocurricular.

College of Liberal Arts and Sciences

Liberal education expectations now in all position descriptions; faculty statements on liberal education in their courses now on CLAS website; unsuccessful attempt to develop college-wide student ratings form, with research funded by Pew FTLC.

Seidman College of Business

Included liberal education in strategic planning.

Faculty Governance

Passed resolution supporting the CLE initiative, recognized the CLE advisory committee as provost's committee.

Pew Faculty Teaching and Learning Center

Aligned programs with initiative. Set aside grant funds for CLE-related projects; continued to make liberal education a priority in grant funding; offered programming designed to publicize and discuss CLE research and principles; CLE codirectors discussed liberal education with secretarial staff, plant services, and public safety personnel; Liberal Education Academy established to enhance practice of liberal education for faculty.

Student Affairs

Reorganized welcome-week activities for greater academic focus, including emphasis on liberal education; staff discussed readings on liberal education; developed diversity action plan, including goal of 25% people of color on staff; Housing staff planned programing designed to encourage students' critical thinking and appreciation for diversity, new programing communicated to faculty; working with faculty, established learning communities for first-year women in science and engineering, also for prelaw men and women.

Note. CLE = Claiming a Liberal Education; CLAS = College of Liberal Arts and Sciences; IGD = Intergroup Dialogues.

Students in the 2009 focus groups showed clear differences from the 2003 groups in their views of learning and a liberal education. They indicated greater positive personal change since arriving on campus and were more willing to take responsibility for their learning. There were far fewer comments that indicated a consumerist perspective. All of the students could define liberal education whereas none could in 2003 (Pace, Frerichs, Rosier, & Ellenberger, 2010).

In Hindsight: Factors Enabling Broader Involvement

Over the past six years, the Pew FTLC at GVSU has demonstrated that it can fulfill its original mission *as well as* take on a much broader role in the university as a whole. A number of key factors worked together in accomplishing the transformational change in the role of the center and director *as well as* in the institution. Together, this constellation of factors enabled redefinition of the director and center's role into a highly visible leadership role that collaborated through all aspects of initiating broader scale institutional change. The *Coming in From the Margins* study by Connie Schroeder, the center- and institution-based factors that enable involvement in the liberal education institutional initiative at GVSU, included:

GVSU Center director-based factors

- Skills
  - leadership
  - facilitation
  - initiative
  - envisioning
  - proposal/grant writing
  - collaboration
- Expertise and knowledge
  - organizational change processes and models
  - culture
  - governance system
  - institutional data
  - research; interpreting research results; institutional research studies
  - national resources; instruments (NSSE; CLA)
  - literature on liberal education, increasing expectations

- National professional association involvement (AAC&U)

GVSU Center-based factors

- Center alignment with institutional mission
- Center advocates

GVSU Institution-based factors

- Supervisory and upper-level support
- Institutional leadership
- Institutional culture

Lessons for Faculty Developers in Leading From the Middle

Not only did GVSU successfully enact institutional-level change but the Pew FTLC also transformed itself, as Chism (1998) suggested, from an already successful center to the front office or "front lines," collaborating and cultivating a tipping point as initiators of change. The center's initiatives are examples of what Senge (2006) calls a "learning organization." The members of a learning organization use systems thinking, "a discipline for seeing the 'structures' that underlie complex situations, and for discerning high from low leverage change" (2006, p. 69). If members can look beyond individual parts to see the whole, they can help to create the reality of their organization and not simply react to particular events. The following recommendations are key for any center that is undertaking a similar large-scale initiative:

1. Cultivate a bird's-eye view of the institution, understanding its mission and major obstacles to achieving the mission. Align with the institutional mission.
2. When a problem is identified that is within the purview of the center, identify others who care about the problem, who may work with you, as Gladwell's model suggests. Raise awareness of the need for change.
3. Select a model to guide your change, preferably one that carries with it emotional weight, such as Gladwell's tipping point. The model in itself can help to recruit allies.
4. Communicate with appropriate administrators, seek their support, and keep them informed.
5. Gather and publicize baseline data, keep accurate records during the initiative, and gather and publicize follow-up data.

6. Educate a broad selection of the community about the problem and modify your definition of the problem based on their responses; invite their assistance and do not second-guess their efforts.
7. Be involved in the change yourself. The Pew FTLC director taught a freshman-only section of Introduction to Liberal Education for four years of the project; the associate dean of students also teaches every year.

Note

The authors thank Donna Henderson-king, associate professor of psychology, and faculty researcher for this project, for her comments on the manuscript.

References

American College Personnel Association & National Association of Student Personnel Administrators (2004). *Learning reconsidered: A campus-wide focus on the student learning experience.* Washington, DC: ACPA.

Association of American Colleges and Universities. (2008). *Making excellence inclusive.* Retrieved September 23, 2008, from http://www.aacu.org/inclusive_excellence/index.cfm

Chism, N. V. N. (1998). The role of educational developers in institutional change: From the basement office to the front office. In M. Kaplan (Ed.), *To improve the academy: Vol. 17. Resources for faculty, instructional, and organizational development* (pp. 141–154). Stillwater, OK: New Forums Press.

Frerichs, C. (2008). *Expectations and engagement in the context of liberal education: What do faculty say about the Grand Valley experience?* A report on faculty focus groups, Winter 2008. Retrieved October 5, 2008, from http://www.gvsu.edu/cms3/assets/B78A66C2-A774-13A2-78CDCF13A1345FC3/Microsoft%20Word%20-%20CLE%2008.focus%20group%20summary.pdf

Gladwell, M. (2000). *The tipping point: How little things can make a big difference.* New York: Little, Brown.

Guevara, J. (2006). *Collegiate Learning Assessment: Comparison of Freshmen and Seniors.* Institutional report—September 2006, Collegiate Learning Assessment, comparison of freshman and seniors, Grand Valley State University. Retrieved September 23, 2008, from http://reports.ia.gvsu.edu/cla/CLA_Institutional_Report_Seniors_and_Freshman.doc

Guevara, J. (2007). *Collegiate Learning Assessment: Comparison of Freshmen and Rising Juniors.* Institutional Report—October 2007, Collegiate Learning Assessment, comparison of freshmen and rising juniors, Grand Valley State University. Retrieved September 23, 2008, from http://reports.ia.gvsu.edu/cla/CLA_rising_juniors.doc

Henderson-King, D. (2004a, 21 February). *The 2004 greater expectations institute: Narrative*. Grand Valley State University. Retrieved October 5, 2008, from http://www.gvsu.edu/forms/ftlc/Microsoft%20Word%20-%20AAC&UN.pdf

Henderson-King, D. (2004b, 10 March). *Aligning student and faculty expectations*. Grand Valley State University. Retrieved September 23, 2008, from http://www.gvsu.edu/cms3/assets/B78A66C2-A774-13A2–78CDCF13A1345FC3/Microsoft%20Word%20-%20Report%20on%20Faculty%20Focus%20Groups.pdf

Henderson-King, D. (2004c, Fall). *Expectations and engagement: What do student and faculty say about the Grand Valley experience?* Pew Faculty Teaching and Learning Center, Grand Valley State University, Allendale, Michigan.

Kemmis, S., & McTaggart, R. (2000). Participatory action research. In N. K. Denzin, & Y. S. Lincoln (Eds.), *Handbook of qualitative research* (pp. 567–605). Thousand Oaks, CA: Sage.

Kezar, A. (2006). Redesigning for collaboration in learning initiatives: An examination of four highly collaborative campuses [Electronic version]. *The Journal of Higher Education, 77*(5), 804–838.

Legorreta, L., Kelley, C. A., & Sablynski, C. J. (2006). Linking faculty development to the business school's mission [Electronic version]. *Journal of Education for Business, 82*(1), 3–11.

Levine, A., & Cureton, J. S. (1998). *When hope and fear collide: A portrait of today's college student*. San Francisco: Jossey-Bass.

Lieberman, D. (2005). Beyond faculty development: How centers for teaching and learning can be laboratories for learning [Electronic version]. *New Directions for Higher Education, 131*, 87–98.

McKendall, M., Bhagwat, Y., Giedeman, D. C., Klein, H. A., & Levenburg, N. M. (2006, Spring). Identifying the gap between student and faculty expectations: Report from a business school [Electronic version]. *Journal of the Academy of Business Education, 6*, 44–51.

Office of Institutional Analysis. NSSE 2005. Addendum, April 18, 2006. Grand Valley State University. Retrieved September 23, 2008, from http://reports.ia.gvsu.edu/nsse_041806.php

Office of Institutional Analysis. NSSE 2007. Grand Valley State University. Retrieved September 12, 2008, from http://reports.ia.gvsu.edu/nsse_082107a.php

Pace, D., Frerichs, C., Rosier, T., & Ellenberger, K. (in press) (2010). *What students say about their liberal education experience at Grand Valley: A replication study*. Liberal Education.

Pace, D., Henderson-King, D., & Frerichs, C. (2005, Winter). *Claiming a liberal education initiative, intergroup dialogue report*. Grand Valley State University. Retrieved October 5, 2008, from http://www.gvsu.edu/forms/ftlc/Microsoft%20Word%20-%20Deans22.IGD.12.04.pdf

Pearce, T. (2003). *Leading out loud: Inspiring change through authentic communication* (Rev. ed.). San Francisco: Jossey-Bass.

Raelin, J. A. (2003). *Creating leaderful organizations: How to bring out leadership in everyone*. San Francisco: Berrett-Koehler.

Robinson, W. P. (2002). *Leading people from the middle: The universal mission of heart and mind*. Provo, UT: Executive Excellence.

Schilling, K. M., & Schilling, K. L. (1999, May–June). Increasing expectations for student effort. *About Campus, 4/2*, 4–10.

Schoem, D., & Hurtado, S. (Eds.). (2001). *Intergroup dialogue: Deliberative democracy in school, college, community, and workplace*. Ann Arbor: University of Michigan Press.

Senge, P. M. (2006). *The fifth discipline: The art and practice of the learning organization* (Rev. ed.). New York: Doubleday.

Skorupa, K. (2002, December). *Adult learners as consumers*. Retrieved February 29, 2004, from http://www.nacada.ksu.edu/Clearinghouse/Advising_Issues/adultlearners.htm

Sorcinelli, M., Austin, A. E., Eddy, P. L., & Beach, A. L. (2006). *Creating the future of faculty development: Learning from the past, understanding the present*. Bolton, MA: Anker.

Taylor, K. L., & Schönwetter, D. J. (2002). Faculty development as institutional leadership: A framework for meeting new challenges. Quality conversations, Proceedings of the 25th HERDSA annual conference. *HERDSA, 647–654*. Milperra, NSW, Australia: Higher Education Research and Development Society of Australasia.

Zuniga, X. (1998). *Fostering intergroup dialogue on campus: Essential ingredients*. Retrieved October 25, 2004, from http://www.diversityweb.org/Digest/W98/fostering.html

Appendix: Claiming a Liberal Education Leaders

Frederick Antczak, dean, College of Liberal Arts and Sciences, co-sponsor.

Gayle Davis, provost and vice president for academic affairs, co-sponsor.

Catherine Frerichs, director of the Pew Faculty Teaching and Learning Center, 1997–2009; currently, professor of writing; codirector.

Donna Henderson-King, associate professor of psychology, faculty researcher.

Bart Merkle, vice provost and dean of students, co-sponsor.

Diana Pace, associate dean of students, co-director.

Tamara Rosier, assistant director, Pew Faculty Teaching and Learning Center, assisted in follow-up research.

Wendy Wenner, dean, College of Interdisciplinary Studies, CLE co-sponsor.

7

INFORMING AND DIRECTING THE PLANNING OF INSTITUTIONAL PRIORITIES AND INITIATIVES

Phyllis Blumberg

C ommittees and task forces are the seat of much power in academia and are catalysts for altering the culture, policies, and practices of an institution. They can influence teaching and learning at multiple levels of the institution, from decision-making to planning the directives and implementation of large-scale initiatives. Committee involvement in a variety of ways, I have learned, is essential to expand the role of developers to include involvement with broader institutional issues of teaching and learning. As reported in chapters 4 and 5, committee involvement is a key factor in enabling director involvement. A number of other institution-, center-, and director-based factors worked together before, during, and after my committee involvement to raise my level of leadership and visibility. The primary factors that enabled my involvement in addition to committee involvement included leadership, collaborative relationships, institutional strategic plan alignment, institutional mission alignment, and knowledge and expertise in a number of areas (see chapter 5). To begin this discussion, a brief exploration of types of committee involvement is necessary.

Levels and Types of Committee Involvement

Shared governance and institutional leadership between administrators and faculty typically occurs through institutional committees, and it is where change agents gather (Marshall, 1999). After the highest level of administration determines and sets new initiatives, more campus leaders become involved in planning how to make the initiatives become operational. Committee involvement in institutional initiative planning can mean a wide range of formal and informal commitments. At one end of the spectrum, formal committee representation may be by appointment and may happen directly, or it may be initiated and communicated through the director's supervisor. If administrators do not invite or appoint staff from the TLC directly, center directors can seek representation when committees or task forces are organizing. Center directors can also volunteer themselves or their center staff as informal consultants for individual colleagues or teams by sharing their expertise and skills with individual leaders charged with implementing institutional initiatives. Directors may need to reach out to these leaders and describe the unique skills and knowledge that they can bring to an initiative. People who are responsible for implementation of institutional priorities are often happy to have skillful volunteers assisting them. In this capacity, faculty developers may take on real tasks, provide leadership, and collaborate on the development of products, and other times may offer key advice and consultation. Depending on the skill sets of the faculty developer, work load, center staffing, and the number of other involvements, the roles provided and the level of involvement are likely to vary with each initiative.

Unique Knowledge and Expertise

To advance this role, it is critical for top administrators to realize that developers have unique expertise and knowledge to share during the planning of initiatives. Institutional leaders and top administrators may not know the breadth and depth of knowledge the developer can bring. The developer must contribute this knowledge as is relevant, and seize opportunities to inform accordingly. Awareness of this expertise may come from a variety of sources, including directly from center supervisors, colleagues, or ideally, direct dialogue with top administration. This dialogue may take place within committees, but most likely it takes place in one-on-one meetings with top administrators, although this may be more realistic at smaller institutions.

This unique knowledge and skill set can be divided into common knowledge areas and skills for *all* faculty developers. In addition, individual developers or directors will bring unique expertise depending on their particular experiences and background. The common and traditional domains of expertise for *instructional development* have often included knowledge about pedagogy, technology, and student learning and development.

Broader-scale involvement is likely to require expertise in additional areas, such as curriculum development, program assessment, higher education, literature and current trends, and emerging national initiatives and controversies in higher education. Generally, when administrators ask faculty developers to serve on committees or work with implementation teams, they are seeking these knowledge and skill sets.

As one of the case study participants in the *Coming in From the Margins* study, I have been a director of the TLC at the University of the Sciences for 11 years. Established in 1821, the University of the Sciences in Philadelphia (USP) was the first pharmacy school in the country. It is a specialized institution with about 175 faculty and approximately 3,000 students, many of whom are right out of high school. Many will graduate as health professionals with advanced degrees. The following section provides three different examples of my involvement in planning and implementing institutional initiatives and a discussion of the roles I provided in each (see Table 7.1). The common and specific skills and expertise that I brought to these institutional initiatives are also made evident. In all three examples, the highest level of administration announced these institutional priorities as goals without concrete plans for their operation. Two of these examples came out of different cycles (I and II) of our institution's strategic planning.

My leadership role in these three initiatives included serving on a tactical planning committee to plan strategic imperatives, working with teams to develop new educational programs, and serving on several planning committees to design and implement a new general education program for our undergraduates. This leadership role merged well with my other TLC directorship responsibilities as I determined key center programing efforts and activities that helped advance the *Example 1*, the student-centered learning and living initiative. My role and the TLC became aligned with the institutional strategic plan. This alignment enabled me and the center to become highly visible on the institutional radar screen and function as anything but marginalized from the key institutional priorities and initiatives.

Planning and Implementing Institutional Initiatives

Example 1: Student-Centered Learning Strategic Initiative

During the 2001–2002 academic year, administrators identified six strategic imperatives, including the development of a culture of student-centered learning and living, to direct the university's planning (USP, 2002). The Tactical

TABLE 7.1
Overview of three institutional involvement examples

Source	Committee Involvement	My Role in Initiative
Example 1—Initiative: Student-centered learning strategic initiative		
Strategic planning cycle I	Tactical Planning Group	member, educator, facilitator informant, resource, convener center alignment with strategic planning
Example 2—Initiative: Revising general education curriculum.		
Mandated university-wide goal	Committee involvement: curriculum committees	expert, educator, resource, consultant, organization and instructional developer, center alignment with university goal
Example 3—Initiative: Educational program expansion.		
Strategic planning cycle II	Tactical Task Force	expertise, national association and initiatives knowledge, pedagogical/assessment expertise, consultant, center alignment with strategic planning

Planning Group on Student-Centered Learning and Living defined objectives, developed future action steps, and outlined outcome indicators. As the director of the TLC, I was an *appointed member* of this tactical planning group, and I served as the key educator/ informant and resource for this planning group throughout their work.

Roles as Change Agent: Educator/Informant/Facilitator

By scheduling discussions with faculty, I learned of faculty concerns about the phrase "student-centered learning." Student-centered learning, from their perspective, seemed to focus on consumer satisfaction (Weimer, 2002). Because of information disseminated by the TLC, the faculty recommended a change to "learning-centered teaching," which places the emphasis on student learning while giving faculty an important role in this learning. I, along with the other faculty members of the task force, successfully informed and facilitated discussion around the change in nomenclature. While this phrase change may seem minor, leveraging this change was an important move that preempted significant resistance later that would have countered the ultimate change sought after in the institutional culture. I used my leadership and facilitation skills and my knowledge of higher education and learning-centered teaching during these discussions to ensure a receptive climate for this initiative. Many more faculty accepted this strategic imperative because they agreed with the terminology chosen and agreed with its purpose (Blumberg, 2004). The Tactical Task Force Group identified educating faculty, staff, and administrators about learning-centered teaching and implementing more learner-centered teaching approaches as the key action steps.

Integrating Instructional and Organizational Development Roles

My role with the Task Force and my typical center director responsibilities merged seamlessly as I played a leadership role through committee level involvement in this initiative. In fact, these roles often blurred. My knowledge of culture and organizational change strategies informed my decisions and efforts as the director. This type of knowledge and expertise also was frequently reported among the case study directors in the study (see chapters 5 and 9).

For example, in 2002–2003 the TLC was charged by the Tactical Planning Committee with directing the efforts needed to educate faculty, staff, and administrators on learning-centered teaching and received an additional $8,000 to achieve this purpose. The TLC planned and implemented yearlong *instructional development* activities that focused on learning-centered teaching. This included 4 day-long workshops given by outside experts in learning-centered teaching, 16 discussions, and a day-long event held for faculty and staff at the end of the year. With the additional $8,000, I invited four internationally known experts on learning-centered teaching to give workshops to the faculty. Each of their days on the campus ended with a special session where the expert met with deans, department chairs, and program directors to help them explore how to support necessary changes. These experts, together with the readings I provided the faculty and administrators, helped the university to define what was meant by learning-centered teaching. With the combined recruiting efforts of administrators, chairs, and my heavy promotion of the workshops, about 70% of the faculty attended at least one of these workshops and the majority of these faculty attended at least two. While our TLC might have been asked to initiate these programs even if I had not been on the Tactical Task Force, my broader role with planning the learner-centered initiative ensured the center's leadership role at the front end of the initiative planning. I was able to align the center events in ways that were better timed with the initiative's growth and development. I was able to perform my instructional development role with greater insight into the broader university goals and the specific challenges of this initiative. The generous amount of additional money the center received for educational purposes allowed the TLC to continue to advance this institutional initiative by further educating the faculty with the best national speakers on this topic. In this way, my organizational and instructional development roles fit together toward advancing the institutional priority to change the culture of the university.

At the end of the 2002–2003 academic year, as the director I led the TLC to organize and sponsor a consensus conference to cultivate agreement on a definition of learning-centered teaching and how to practice it. From the conference, I developed a consensus statement of the faculty's and staff's views of learning-centered teaching, which was used in planning for future educational efforts and implementing this initiative (Blumberg & Everett, 2005).

Implementing Institutional Initiative Planning

The following year, 2004, I implemented an intentional change strategy that aimed to further advance this institutional cultural transformation toward learning-centered teaching. I coordinated a faculty learning community for 10 faculties from across the university to learn in depth how to implement learning-centered teaching and to design learning-centered courses. This model of training the faculty was an intentional, grassroots or diffusion model of change aimed to further institutional cultural transformation (Schroeder, 2001). The faculty became trainers in their departments for helping other faculty to transform their courses.

Over the last five years, I have been further defining and elaborating on learning-centered teaching. For example, I developed a series of rubrics to help faculty transition from their current methods of teaching to more learning-centered approaches in an incremental way (Blumberg, 2009) and made presentations at all departmental meetings to explain the rubrics.

In summary, since 2001, I was at the center of one of the institution's core initiatives, from its inception through all phases of its implementation, both as a *key leader* of the initiative as well as director of the TLC. My leadership role on the Task Force was vital in shaping the initiative itself by informing the language and process of institutional culture change. I was able to lead by drawing on the knowledge and perspective I have of the institution and literature in the field. I was able to align strategically our center with this core institutional initiative, not as a reactive measure, but from an insider's view within the Tactical Task Force. Finally, as the TLC director, I acquired additional resources and funding to further advance the initiative. My work with the initiative from its inception made the center work more effectively and in sync with the implementation stages of the initiative. My knowledge of the campus, faculty, and learning enabled, not only my role to be viewed as essential, but also the initiative to modify its strategies and assumptions.

My institutional level role affected the center and my role. Department chairs continually asked me to help them address issues that arose in the implementation of this approach to teaching. All of my efforts and involvement with the learning-centered teaching strategic initiative have given the center more visibility on campus both with faculty and administrators. We are clearly on the institutional radar screen versus hidden on the margins. And now, whenever learning-centered teaching is mentioned, it is always associated with the TLC.

Example 2: Revising General Education Curriculum

Faculty developers are often involved in general education initiatives (Sorcinelli, Austin, Eddy, & Beach, 2006). Most likely, they are part of these initiatives because of their expertise and knowledge of pedagogy, curriculum development skills, the change process, and higher education trends and resources. However, association with any large curriculum reform can be controversial. It is possible to make enemies over changes in the curriculum, especially if instructors perceive the faculty developer as part of a movement to take away current requirements in specific departments. Developers should be more neutral in the turf battles that often take place when curricular change is proposed. In this type of initiative, developers may be staff on or members of the curriculum revision committee rather than chair it.

At my institution, the liberal arts curriculum in place from the 1980s through the early 2000s specified the number of courses students were required to take in specific disciplines. In 2003, the chief academic officer mandated faculty to change this curriculum. She did not mandate the nature of the change except to specify that it had to be compliant with current accreditation standards, including learning outcomes assessment. She requested a task force, with representatives from each college within the university, to develop a proposal for a new liberal arts curriculum. I *volunteered* to be on this task force because I knew that my expertise in learning outcomes, assessment, and knowledge of national dialogues about education would add value. Seated at this planning table, I contributed expertise in a number of areas. For example, I was immediately able to help task force members understand what learning outcomes are and how they are measured. I made it a point to investigate what national organizations were discussing general education and convinced the chief academic officer that we need to join the American Association of Colleges and Universities (AAC&U), an organization that often discusses liberal arts. This knowledge of national organizations and trends was identified by other case-study center directors as a primary factor enabling their involvement as well, and should not be underestimated. Although initially the TLC director may be asked to serve on a task force because of the expected instructional development skills and knowledge, the broader set of skills and knowledge developers can provide, may become evident immediately.

Another area of my expertise was tapped for this initiative. Most faculty were unfamiliar with outcomes assessment. The TLC gave many workshops on outcomes assessment. In collaboration with others, I developed a template for faculty to use to document learning outcomes in their courses. Some departments use this template.

The TLC has been a vehicle for educating faculty about learning outcomes and the current national thinking of general education. In alignment with the initiative, I direct the center to disseminate relevant articles and bring outside experts to campus, and serve as a venue for discussion and debate among the faculty. For example, during the first two years of the task force, I financially sponsored a few task force members to attend national conferences on the general education reform. In addition, using my center's honorarium money for outside speakers, I hosted a consultant from the AAC&U. He gave a presentation to the faculty, and spoke to the general education task force and administrators. As is usually the case, changing general education programs is an emotional turf battle. Periodically during the four years, this task force developed or revised proposals on the general education. The TLC hosted dialogues and presentations on the general education to guide the current thinking of the task force. Because of these open forums with faculty and the outside speaker, we educated faculty on national trends in the general education, learned about the faculty's concerns, revised our proposals, and learned how to prepare our arguments better.

Initiative Success

The new general education program that was finally approved has both discipline-specific requirements, such as six credits in the humanities, and the achievement of specific learning outcome skills, such as information literacy and technological competency. Students mastering these skills are assessed within the context of courses from across the university. The Task Force defined appropriate teaching/learning and assessment methods for each of these learning outcomes and developed examples of how students could master these skills in a variety of disciplines.

Collaborating with governing bodies proved essential to the implementation of the new curriculum. Not surprising, collaborative partnerships are also essential for the developer to shift primarily from an individual level or instructional development focused role, as reported by nearly all the case study directors (see chapter 5). Specifically, in my case, once the faculty governing body accepted the proposal for the new general education curriculum, the TLC cohosted, together with the Faculty Council, educational sessions on the new curriculum. These sessions discussed requirements and how courses would get approval to be part of the new curriculum and enabled the general educational reform to advance. The TLC is seen as the logical place for educational forums for the faculty. Collaborative partnering with a formal governing structure came about partly because I was aware of the issues that the faculty were struggling with, and through my good relationships with the leaders of the Faculty Council. Relationships with governing bodies and their members are critical factors in assuming a broader leadership role.

I also serve on the university-wide curriculum committee, which is responsible for approving courses for the general education program. I came onto this committee in several ways. For a few years, I was elected as a representative from the college where I had my academic appointment. More recently, I have been appointed by the President of the Faculty Council as an ex officio member. This places me at the table where curricular decisions and institutional initiatives intersect.

Using my knowledge of curriculum development and learning-centered teaching, I persuaded the university curriculum committee to require instructors to show that their courses are internally consistent in terms of objectives, teaching, and learning activities and assessment (Diamond, 1988; Fink, 2003). My knowledge and influence on the committee-led members to recognize the need for alignment and coherence in course design. All instructors who wanted their courses to be approved for the general education curriculum needed to demonstrate this alignment (Biggs, 1999) by completing a table that lists the objectives, teaching-learning activities in the course, and how the students will be assessed on each objective. Ultimately, I developed a tool for the curriculum committee that enables faculty to show how the three-course components are aligned and congruent with each other in writing and in practice (Blumberg, 2009). My role combines *instructional development*, in the sense that course designs are improved, but even more important, I impacted the values and beliefs, practice and behavior, and policy at a much broader level.

The multiple dimensions of my role and contributions I provided throughout this process illustrate what developers actually can do through their involvement in key initiatives and what they can contribute. The combined role of *instructional* and *organizational development* enhanced the success of both roles. Rather than one path or strategy, this *organizational development role* is a mixture of opportunities seized, cultivated, and maximized.

Example 3: Educational Program Expansion

This university, like many others, has set an aggressive goal for expansion as part of the latest strategic plan. Currently, a key goal is to develop many new educational programs at all levels—from short certificate programs to degree programs at the undergraduate, graduate, and professional levels. Some of these programs are new doctoral programs where we already have undergraduate or master's degree programs. Other undergraduate and graduate programs are in new disciplines for us (Fink, 2002). This is a major institutional initiative and priority.

With the expansion into new academic areas, the university needed to hire new faculty who were experts in these areas. Some hired experts who have not been educators in the past and most of them have not developed a new program. I *volunteered* to serve on search committees for the new program director or to assist in the recruitment process in less formal ways. Through my proactive working with search committees and candidates for positions, I have helped to steer the direction of the search and the selection of the new program directors. Once hired, I work with them intensively to develop the new programs. Specifically, I often direct them toward best pedagogical practices, as discussed in the next paragraphs.

I have developed various paths for working with the faculty charged with developing new programs. I often volunteer to serve on the planning and implementation committees by calling the chair of the team. Sometimes, my supervisor volunteers me to work with these planning teams. In a few cases, the chairs of these program development teams have asked me to work with them. Regardless of my entry point onto the program planning team, my expertise and skills are called upon in several ways.

As developers, we need to demonstrate a number of expertise areas when helping planners think about creating an environment for learning both for classroom and online courses. Many new program directors think that deciding on the list of topics or contents and their sequence within the program are all that are necessary to plan new academic programs. To broaden their planning, I expose planning teams to alternative ways of disseminating information to students, different experiential activities, and ideas of authentic assessment. I often ask the faculty to consider a capstone course that connects out-of-the-classroom experiences with the course work. I continually expand my own expertise by calling upon faculty developers at institutions with similar programs to find out how their programs operate. To further help move the institution toward attaining one of its priorities, I assist in the completion of the required proposal forms to get courses and educational programs accepted. Since I have served on the curriculum committees that approve these proposals, I have a good idea of how to write them successfully.

Recently I have been on the planning team for the development of a masters in public health degree and several masters in business administration programs. Because these are applied or professional programs, their new program directors came from industry (in the case of the business program), community or clinical settings (in the case of the public health program). The administrators and instructors charged with the development of these programs were new to academia in general. I work with these individuals one on one outside the formal meetings to educate them about curriculum development, teaching methods, and how the academy operates. As a noncontent expert in these fields, I can ask questions about concerns that those in the field may not think about and help the program planning team to think outside of the box and create a more unique program. I can ask devil's advocate inquiries to help the planning team question familiar but unsuccessful methods. I often help program directors translate what they want to say so that new students who are novices in the field understand what the curriculum is.

Faculty developers are essential to the team that plans and develops these new academic programs. Being on the new program planning team from the ground up may affect the actual program, the learning and instruction, or the overall success of the initiative. As developers, we might need to convince the chairs of these planning teams that we can bring unique expertise to the table in addition to pedagogical expertise, such as knowledge of how programs are organized and how to collaborate on the development of the curriculum and courses. Faculty developers can educate these teams about best practices in higher education. We can show them different teaching and learning approaches that have worked in other programs or in other disciplines. TLC professional staff can discuss curricular approaches with the content experts and give them relevant literature to read both within their disciplinary fields and in the wider context of learning.

Essential Roles as Change Agent

To be effective in planning and implementing institutional priorities and initiatives, developers need to assume additional aspects of their role beyond expert teacher and workshop leader. I expanded my instructional development role as TLC director to assume multiple leadership roles in directing or advancing key initiatives through strategies that integrated faculty, instructional, and organizational development. These aspects of my role blended extremely well.

The focus of most faculty developers' efforts is on improving the quality of instruction. *Instructional development* focuses on impacting learning by improving courses or curriculum. *Organizational development* looks at the structure and process of the organization. When faculty developers engage in these larger roles and responsibilities, they can balance their focus on improving the quality of instruction at the same time they are working on the institutional initiatives. By expanding the narrower instructional development role to include leadership and organizational development at a broader level, developers can be *more* effective in improving the quality of instruction and student learning through the traditional instructional development programing and services. The list below identifies the roles performed and the impact achieved because of my leadership on these initiatives. My major roles were that of the informer/disseminator, facilitator, collaborator, and change agent.

My Roles in Informing and Directing Institutional Initiatives

1. Informer/disseminator of ideas, language, and methods:
   (a) *Who:* Constituents including administrators, faculty charged with specific tasks, and the faculty at large
   (b) *What:* Understanding about
      • National conversations and resources on topics
      • Conceptual understanding of:
         Philosophy of learning and teaching
         Teaching-learning dynamic
         Learning-centered teaching
         Learning outcomes
         Outcomes assessment; course assessment

Course alignment

Trends in higher education

Organizational change strategies

- Curricular development process and skills

Course design

Pedagogy: active learning

Student assessment methods

2. Facilitator of
   (a) *Who*: Faculty's notions of a general education program
   (b) *What:* Consensus on learning-centered teaching;
   How to implement learning- centered teaching

3. Collaborator
   (a) *Who:* Faculty council; new program planning teams
   (b) *What*:
   - Template document on learning outcomes
   - Planning process for implementing the learning-centered teaching
   - Approval process for general education courses
   - Documentation to show that courses are aligned
   - Policies on general education requirements
   - Tactical planning document

4. Change agent
   (a) *How:*
   - Identify resistance; informing language
   - Acquire resources for implementation
   - Align center initiatives with larger institutional initiatives
   - Host and organize forums, discussions
   - Follow-up with individual consultations
   - Disseminate information coming from the literature and from campus committees
   - Convene discussions
   (b) *What:*
   - Educational program reform
   - Development of new educational programs
   - How courses are taught
   - Course approval policy
   - Involvement in national initiatives (AAC&U)

(c) *Impacted What:*

- Course design
- Instruction using more active learning and learning-centered approaches
- Assessment of student learning
- Policies of course approval
- Program assessment

Because I was able to integrate both organizational and instructional development dimensions, I was able to have an impact on course design, instruction, student assessment of learning, and policies and program assessments at individual, departmental, and institutional levels. The end of the chapter lists key strategies that were successful for informing and directing institutional initiatives and should apply to a variety of contexts. Of course, developers will find that some of these strategies apply better in some situations than others. Faculty developers should have the expertise and leverage to be able to use all of these strategies.

Conclusion

Faculty developers need to be present when administrators and faculty plan important initiatives such as curriculum revision. Faculty developers often have unique expertise and knowledge that they bring to these committees and task forces. Informing and directing institutional priorities is an essential aspect of the work of individuals in faculty development centers. In fact, presence on key committees or collaborative and consultative work with colleagues and leaders on initiatives may have a greater influence on learning than all of our workshops and learning communities combined. As this chapter illustrates, faculty developers' presence can include serving on institutional initiative strategic planning or implementation committees as well as working individually as a consultant for the leaders charged to carry out the institutional initiatives. Faculty developers may find themselves seated at the table of these initiatives through volunteering or being appointed to important committees, and by working with key individuals who are charged with implementing new initiatives. It is our task to make sure that we are able to fulfill these key influential roles by being present when institutional initiatives are planned or implemented and that we are prepared with the knowledge and skills to perform an organizational development role (see Table 7.2).

TABLE 7.2
Proactive strategies

Educate
- Acquaint top administrators with the strengths and expertise of the faculty developers
- Educate faculty and administrators on current thinking by inviting outside speakers to campus
- Share current literature with administrators, faculty
- Share examples of successful implementation across campus through public forums that are widely promoted
- Work one on one outside of the formal meetings to educate leaders as needed
- Share expertise on national higher education developments:
  - Topics being discussed
  - Trends in higher education
  - Issues in instruction, student assessment and faculty roles and responsibilities
  - Controversies over relevant issues

Learn/Investigate
- Research how other similar programs run and bring appropriate resources to the team members
- Contact faculty developers at other institutions that have similar programs to determine how their programs operate
- Investigate national organizations for relevant initiatives and resources

Initiate
- Send faculty to relevant meetings or conferences by helping to pay their expenses or getting the administrators to pay their expenses to attend
- If necessary, convince the chief academic officer of the need to join national associations that are relevant to these topics
- Encourage administrators' attendance at these meeting

Seek representation on key committees and task forces
- Volunteer to serve on the tactical, planning, or implementation committees
- Discuss opportunities with supervisor

Communicate
- Be neutral in the turf battles that take place
- Be staff on or members of the controversial committees and do not chair them
- Communicate trust and reliability by doing the actual work within committees such as gathering and analyzing data, writing reports
- Help leaders to translate their ideas about their programs or policies so that novices or those outside the discipline or program understand what they are trying to say

Promote Dialogue
- Convene or host town meetings, debates, etc.
- Discuss different approaches and help people to think out of the box
- Describe different teaching and learning approaches that work in other programs or in other disciplines
- Carefully frame devil's advocate inquiries to help others question the status
- Provide support for innovation and risk taking

References

Biggs, J. (1999). *Teaching for quality learning at university*. Buckingham, England: Open University Press.

Blumberg, P. (2004). Beginning journey toward a culture of learning centered teaching. *Journal of Student Centered Learning*, 2(1), 68–80.

Blumberg, P. (2009). *Developing learner-centered teaching: A practical guide for faculty*. San Francisco: Jossey-Bass Publishers.

Blumberg, P. (2009). Maximizing learning through course alignment and using different types of knowledge. *Innovative Higher Education*, 34(2), 93–103.

Blumberg, P., & Everett, J. (2005). Achieving a campus consensus on learning-centered teaching: Process and outcomes. *To Improve the Academy*, 23, 191–210.

Diamond, R. M. (1988). Faculty development, instructional development, and organizational development: Options and choices. In E. C. Wadsworth (Ed.), *Professional and organizational development in higher education: A handbook for new practitioners* (pp. 9–12). Stillwater, OK: The Professional and Organizational Development Network in Higher Education.

Fink, L. D. (2003). *Creating significant learning experiences*. San Francisco: Jossey-Bass. *Legacy, Vision and Value*. (2007). Unpublished document, University of the Sciences in Philadelphia.

Marshall, W. J. (1999). University service. In V. Bianco-Mathis, & N. Chalofsky (Eds.), *The full-time faculty handbook* (pp. 113–128). Thousand Oaks, CA: Sage.

Schroeder, C. M. (2001). Faculty change agents: Individual and organizational factors that enable or impede faculty involvement in organizational change (Doctoral dissertation, University of Wisconsin-Madison, 2001) *Dissertations & Theses*: A&I. (Publication No. AAT 3020629).

Sorcinelli, M. D., Austin, A. E., Eddy, P. L., & Beach, A. L. (2006). *Creating the future of faculty development*. Bolton, MA: Anker.

University of the Sciences in Philadelphia (USP). (2002). *Tactical Planning Group Report on Creating a Culture of Student-Centered Learning and Living*. Unpublished document.

Weimer, M. (2002). *Learner-centered teaching*. San Francisco: Jossey-Bass.

8

DEVELOPING AND ACTING ON A CENTER VISION

Connie M. Schroeder

W hen the case study center directors were asked how their role came to include involvement in broader institutional change initiatives, they spoke with clarity about first envisioning a broader role for the center and as the director. These directors intentionally brought *to the center* an agenda that would involve playing a key role in institutional change initiatives. Although center vision had not been predicted as one of the factors enabling institutional involvement, and thus did not appear on the center director survey, the qualitative interviews with both the center directors and their supervisors consistently traced the director's vision of the center as the beginning point of creating a broader role. The purpose of this chapter limits this discussion of organizational vision as a director-based factor enabling this role change. However, a brief review of the somewhat unfamiliar language and definitions of organizational vision frames this discussion.

All types of institutions and centers conceptualized an organizational role that departed from the current instructional focused practice of the center. Each of the interviews with new, well-established, or founding center directors discussed "their vision" as directors and efforts to formulate an organizational dimension to their center. Although the initial conceptualization and vision of this broader role had originated with the directors, each director initiated a collaborative process for introducing or revising the center vision. Center vision is discussed here as a director-based factor rather than a center-based factor because the directors initially conceptualized a center vision that was strongly influenced by the director's attributes, interests, skills, and expertise (as well as institutional and center attributes), and then devised a collaborative process for enacting their vision. Several questions come to mind regarding vision as a mediating factor. Why is center vision important to advance a broader role for faculty developers and center directors? How do the directors formulate a center vision that articulates broader institutional involvement? Whose ideas should contribute to formulating the vision? What is the role of the center founder in the visioning process? What specifically needs to be embedded in the center vision in order to facilitate an *organizational development* role? How does the director communicate and enact the vision to impact their level of institutional involvement and expand their leadership role? What is the difference between the director's vision of the center and the center's mission?

The directors set about to develop a center mission that would merge an instructional development mission and role with broader leadership and involvement in institutional change. To be successful, this required enacting a strategic process that included formulating, communicating, and implementing their vision. These three components of the envisioning process serve as the framework for this chapter. This discussion is preceded by a brief review of the organizational literature regarding the function of organizational visions in bringing about change.

Organizational Vision

Most organizational leaders inside and outside of higher education are familiar with the notion of having a vision for the organization or the unit under their direction. The role of an organizational vision has been discussed in business and management literature for some time. Higher education leaders and administrators are often unaware of or dismiss this organizational literature and may assume that business and organizational research have little to contribute to the nonprofit context or the unique blend of values in an educational organization. Higher education does differ significantly from other kinds of organizations. As an organization, it has been called "one of the most complex structures in modern society" (Alpert, 1985, p. 241) and more complex than similar sized businesses (Ford, 1993, p. 449). Despite the differences in organizational cultures, much has been learned about vision, leadership, and organizational change that can inform the center director who is initiating or changing a center vision.

The wide array of disciplines from which education and faculty developers originate predisposes some to have significant knowledge of organizational theory and processes while others rely on experience as a guide. As higher education tries to become more agile and adept to frequent and wide-scale change, expertise in the application of organizational knowledge is essential across all major units in the institution.

Organizational change has stepped up in priority across nearly all types of organizations, resulting in increased attention to organizational vision, mission, and planning. However, the organizational literature has not carved out a consistent definition of vision, nor has it been systematically studied beyond case study descriptions (Larwood, Falbe, Miesing, & Kriger, 1995). Large studies of vision statements are few, with the exceptions of factor and content analysis of vision statements, and analysis of variables affecting vision and organizational size (Larwood et al., 1995).

Despite the gaps in literature, organizational vision has been attributed with several functions. Zaccaro and Banks (2004) describe the purpose and function of an organizational vision as creating an idealized future state of the organization. Vision provides guidance about the past and future directions (Collins & Porras, 1996) and can be viewed as the organization's conceptualizations. In addition, organizational vision is attributed with providing structure and meaning (Larwood et al., 1995), and is often discussed in the context of leadership. As a component of leadership, effective visionary skills are positively valued and highly sought. The ability to manage change is closely linked to skill in developing a vision (Ready & Conger, 2008). An organizational vision is also considered as a task that a leader is expected to accomplish (Larwood et al., 1995).

Organizational Vision as a Change Strategy

Although the concept of organizational vision is not new, in recent years it is heard more often in tandem with discussions of organizational change and as a prerequisite to transform or motivate an organization to change (Cummings & Worley, 2005; Senge, 1990; Zacarro & Banks, 2004). One of the most important functions of an organizational vision is to impact the status quo and take the organization in new or improved directions. Organizational vision often functions as a tool for changing an entire organization. Most often, the scale of change intended is larger than that of a unit, such as the center director envisioning a new role for the center that entails broader organizational development. However, such a significant role change requires a center vision and a process of enacting the vision effectively. The process of changing an organizational vision is described similarly throughout the literature (Collins & Porras, 1996; Foster, 2007; Levin, 2000; Lucas, 1998). For example, the five components of the Vision Change Model (Ready &

Conger, 2008, p. 671) confirm the intentional and time consuming nature of the envisioning process (see Table 8.1). This model of changing a vision reflects the center visioning steps reported by the case study directors. A three-part process—formulating, communicating, and enacting—was common among the directors interviewed and is compared with the five-step model for organizational vision change (see Table 8.1). The center vision process is examined in a greater detail in the interview excerpts and in-depth narrative that follow later in the chapter.

TABLE 8.1
Vision change model comparison with case study director visioning processes

Vision Change Model Components	Case Study Director Visioning Process
Frame the agenda • "create an urgent agenda for action" utilizing internal and external concerns (p. 71)	Formulate the vision • align vision with supervisor's priorities • align vision with institutional mission • investigate culture, context, expectations, prior center founder, and visions (see chapters 5, 6, 8, and 11)
Engage the organization • invite differing views and perspectives and listen carefully to those who contribute legitimate concerns about the tensions created by the newly framed enterprise agenda. • "distribute ownership of the vision."	• collaborate with center advisory board, allies, and all constituents who served across the broader purposes and functions (see chapters 6 and 10)
Build mission-critical capabilities	Enact the vision • modify staffing capacities; provide opportunity for professional development of staff; expand director knowledge and expertise (see chapters 8 and 10)
Connect the dots and create alignment • encourage cross unit collaboration	• align center activities with initiatives • create partnerships, foster connections around teaching and learning, and institutional priorities • serve and volunteer for institution level committees and initiatives (see chapters 2, 6, 7, 8, and 10)
Energize the organization	Communicate the vision • report outcomes of involvement to supervisor, center staff, and partnerships

Center Vision as a Role Change Strategy

The director and supervisor interviews indicated that center vision was a key beginning point for shifting the traditional director and center role to include the role of change agent and leader in broader institutional initiatives. The director's center vision served as a change tool—a strategy for initiating and advancing a change in the scope and mission of the center. In some cases, the director was the sole person who envisioned this broader role.

Directors who considered their center institutionally too peripheral were able to shift the center and their own role to become significantly involved at the broader institutional level using their vision as the starting point. The directors who successfully integrated an organizational change and development agenda into their center vision enacted a higher level of institutional involvement. Given the multiple demands upon the center and director's time, a well thought-out and articulated center vision anchored this involvement as an integral and sustained dimension of the directors' work that might not have found its way onto the *director's* crowded radar screen. Their vision was translated into the daily work of the center and the many strategic choices and decisions they made about staffing, mission, time, committee involvement, and how they used and broadened their expert knowledge and skills. A compilation of excerpts from the directors' recorded and transcribed interviews are followed by an in-depth narrative of one director's envisioning process. Analysis of this data revealed a visioning process that entailed formulating, enacting, and communicating their broader center vision.

Formulating a Center Vision

Investigating and Expanding Existing Center Visions

A director hired into an established center likely will inherit a center mission statement that indicates in center's vision. In one case study, the director of a new center reported that considerable research had been done across campus prior to the hiring process to determine the center vision and mission. At an established center, more investigation may be required to uncover the original center vision, but it is important to understand the origins of the center, how its current mission statement was developed, and how closely the current mission reflects the founder's vision for the center. With a bit of inquiry, the current director can determine whose vision prompted the establishment of the center and how this vision may still influence the center. This original vision may be very much alive in the center mission statement, the advisory board or council, among longstanding center staff and levels of supervisory leadership, and in some original documents. Additionally, the first center founder may be the immediate supervisor, still in close proximity for consultation, or serve as a challenging influence. This history is important to gather before introducing a new or modifying an existing center vision.

The initial vision of a center can originate from a number of sources including the administration, faculty, advisory boards, significant institutional events prompting center formation, and grant funding. Center visions that emerge out of specific events sometimes can be conceived narrowly but may provide critical information to guide new center visioning. A specific agenda or issue that prompted its origin may still confine the role of the center and director. When a particular issue frames the creation of a center, it is often translated into the founding mission statement and may require expansion further down the road. The vision and mission statement of the center should be revisited and discussed over time to ensure that both are congruent with one another and speak to the current needs of both the center and the broader institutional context.

Investigating Center Founders

The organization's founder can play a pivotal role in the success of the new leader's vision. According to Boeker (1989), "The length of time that a founder remains with a firm can influence the extent to which an initial strategic direction becomes well-defined" (p. 509). This literature frequently describes the founder's influence as an obstacle to future change if they have remained aboard the organization as part of the management (Landau, Drori, & Porras, 2006). This "imprinting influence" has been noted in numerous studies (Boeker, 1989, p. 492). Therefore, if the center founder's vision did not entail an organizational development role, this literature suggests that the influence of the center founder's vision will be difficult to change.

At some of the case study centers, the original champion of the center now sat higher up in the administrative or faculty line after appointing the first director, or initially gathering the resources and support for establishing the center and guiding the subsequent director search. Four of the case study institutions had center founders still present who supported expanding the current director role to include involvement in institutional level initiatives (see chapters 5 and 9). For example,

> The outgoing provost—the former provost, was the person who instituted the center, and she was approaching her retirement. She had always felt strongly about the center, so structurally the center had a direct reporting line with the provost's office. . . . I think she was doing something in setting it up to try to elevate the importance . . . and has kept it there. (Case Study E)

The following directors' interview excerpts discuss the role that the center founders and institutional mission played in formulating the vision for the center.

Directors as Center Founders

In some cases, the first center director is considered the founding director. In other contexts, the leader whose efforts led to the founding of the center may be attributed the title of the founder even if they did not direct the center. Three of the case study participants provided further insight into either being the center founder or the first center director. For example, one newly hired director reported being expected to articulate an initial vision during the interview. In another case, the director was expected to engage in lengthy campus research and discussion once hired in order to devise a mission statement that reflected the shared vision of multiple stakeholders at the institution. The collaborative culture of that institution dictated an inclusive process by which the new director and institutional stakeholders would be able to articulate a consensus-driven vision. In the following case study, the director was able to enact his vision rather quickly as the founding director.

Randy Bass, one of the case study directors and executive director of Georgetown University's Center for New Designs in Learning and Scholarship (CNDLS), and assistant provost for Teaching and Learning Initiatives, founded and established a center that was a *key leader* in institutional initiatives from the start. The rapid and broad-based success of this center was attributed to a number of factors, including his initial vision as the founding director. Five years after its founding, he described the center as "a visible mass of activity . . . a kind of innovation entity" and his continuing vision for CNDLS: "I want [the center] to be an important strategic and intellectual dimension." His vision, now enacted, was evident to his supervisor who attributed much of the successful involvement of the center and director in institutional initiatives to the director's vision, skills, and leadership style: "I think a lot of CNDLS's success, not all of it, but a lot of it [was] his vision . . . his ability . . . and collaborating was an interesting tool" (Case Study H).

Revising Established Center Visions

Although several of the case study participants were the founding center directors and were able to develop the original center vision and mission statements, most of the directors assumed their roles at an established center. One thing was clear—directors at established centers are able to reroute the role and level of involvement of the center to include an *organizational development* role. This occurred by both newly hired directors who set about to create expand and the reach of the center with their vision, and among established directors who came to re-envision the center and their role in broader institutional change. In fact, on the surveys, 71.4% of the directors identified their own leadership role as a key factor that enabled their broader involvement, and this factor was then found to be significantly related to the level of involvement reported. The leadership role consistently entailed redefining the center vision.

The case study directors described how they used very strategic and incremental measures to translate their vision and broader role. For example, one director dramatically shifted the function and view of the center from being "remedial" to being involved with broader issues as well. "I think it is a catalyst also . . . and I think that [if] it is done right . . . [it is] an organizational development center as well as a teaching and learning center" (Case study C).

Alignment With Institutional Mission

Several examples illustrate the way the directors intentionally considered alignment with the institution's mission in their visioning process. For example, one director wrestled with initiating the first center mission and chose to situate the center within the big picture of the university, and its cultural values, and existing rewards.

> I came in with an agenda to make some organizational change in how the center was used within the larger institution—in the alignment of values with rewards around issues of teaching and faculty development. (Case Study E)

> When I first came here 22 years ago, it was essentially a state-teaching institution, and there was very little research expected of people. It is now both a teaching and research institution. The ambition is to become what used to be called a Research One institution, and along the way we decided that we did not want to lose our teaching focus. I think that the importance of the TLC actually became more significant for us during that [mission] change. (Case Study C)

> [In] my actual interview presentation piece . . . I connected the TLC to the university mission and in it I already articulated a lot of those connections . . . every one of the mission's goals have a very direct tie-in to teaching and learning—even if teaching and learning is not stated there. (Case Study C)

Case Study A center director recalled having had discussed the marginalization of the TLC in 2003 and saying, "This center is just too marginalized! We can't stay at the margins. This is just too peripheral." The director's supervisor concurred that the movement from the margins of the institution had begun with the director's vision and the initiation of a culture change.

> We consciously said this is too peripheral. If we are a teaching institution, which is what we say, then we really need to get this more in the center.

At the time of interview, the director described the center as having become very centrally located within the institution.

> So I had the chance to build . . . from really a place that gave workshops on various topics and had a little bit of money to give away. We have now an endowment of $1.9 million. I think it is accurate to say I think we are in the center of the universe. (Case study A)

> The director assumed the position and changed the mission statement of the center. There was something before but I changed it . . . when I came in and I changed it, and I quite a bit changed the way we operate. (Case Study D)

Similarly, this director's vision and realignment of the center to that of including broader issues around teaching and learning is evidenced in the supervisor's description:

> If you looked at the website four years ago, it would have been very much just about individuals. If you look at . . . the annual report in recent years, you will see that the director has been more involved in larger scale projects like strategic planning, like general education reform. Secondly, the nature of the programing has been expanded to focus on what I would say are larger scale issues . . . more emphasis has been placed on what I would describe as interdisciplinary, understanding processes, changes in the institution . . . those kinds of things. (Case Study D)

> I guess first and foremost, prior to my taking on this role, the center was primarily focused at servicing individual faculty. It continues to do that and has expanded those services in the time that I have been here . . . so I describe what I have done as both bottom up but also top down work over the last several years . . . People view the center differently in terms of its importance. It used to be, "Oh, that is a nice thing, if you would like to do

that" and increasingly, "We should be talking to the center about that. That is an issue that the center can help with."

An agenda item when I arrived was to say, if we are going to see this center for learning and teaching as something of real value in this institution, we need to support it better and we need to have more visibility at the center, support it financially with human resources—whatever it [takes], to get it out there and to have people know where it was and to be involved with it. So we are a part time center—even now, in the sense that the director is only two-thirds time in administration and still teaching. When I came in, there was no permanent administrative support and we now have a half-time administrative assistant . . . I have worked really hard with the students through our work study program to keep the doors open 40–45 hours a week so that we are no longer just this ancillary thing, because you can't be taken seriously when you are open seven hours a week. So [that] kind of change happened.

An important aspect of expanding the center vision of one center was the transformation from being viewed as servicing primarily individual faculty. This center mission was revised in 2006, following the institution's mission statement revision in 2005. The chancellor appointed the director as cochair of the general education team two years after becoming the director. That same year, the director and a team attended the AAC&U General Education Institute. The center director's involvement in institutional initiatives was very visible and intentional. (Case Study E)

As the founding director and hired from outside the institution, one center director discussed the lack of a clear center vision within the institutional context.

[The center] . . . was originated as part of the strategic planning process and it was built around major components of the college. When I first came, people wanted me to do everything including finding them extra chairs and classroom space, so they really didn't know what it was. (Case Study B)

The center director's supervisor explained,

I think we had a number of conversations in gearing up for the whole strategic planning initiative that kept bringing us back to this cluster of issues that pointed to a TLC, and it was one of those happy moments where administrative perception of needs and faculty perception of needs coincided . . . wasn't a hard sell either way. (Case Study B)

Future Envisioning—Ongoing Reenvisioning

The process of envisioning an organization is never really over. The notion that visions need to be revisited is prevalent in the literature (Ready & Conger, 2008).

> Just a few decades ago, organizations could stay the course with a strategy for a period of years. The idea that a new vision would be needed, perhaps with some frequency, would have been treated with mild amusement, if not outright derision (Ready & Conger, 2008).

The directors reported the process of formulating, enacting, and communicating this new vision as continuous. As the vision of an institutional leadership role assumes prominence among more institutions and their TLCs, other institutional structures and positions may be impacted. One director's supervisor discussed the director's ongoing vision for the center that would build further upon having established a broader role for the center:

> For the future, the director sees a gathering together of teaching- and learning-related units under one area and the creation of a new title to lead this wheel or hub of units and services: So right now we have a separate office having to do with assessment. We have separate offices for technology in the classroom. We have separate offices for online learning . . . right now we are separate and disparate in ways that I think are not necessarily beneficial to the institution. . . . So we are suggesting an associate provost for teaching who would be over all of those disparate services right now [and] interests—all of those things sort of coming together. (Case study E)

Whether the center has a vision or the director is expected to create one, the director is faced with the choice of overtly bringing a broader organizational development role to the center vision and translating that vision into the center mission.

Communicating the Center Vision

Communicating Vision Through Words

The director's center vision, if well formulated through a collaborative and investigative process, requires careful planning for communicating the vision and enacting the change it conveys (Holpp & Kelly, 1988; Westley & Mintzberg, 2005). In a recent survey among organizational leaders, 73% claimed they had a clear vision but only 44% claimed they had communicated it well (Kinicki & Williams, 2006). A broader center vision, as the directors discuss in this volume, entails communicating a change in the center and director's roles, even if both are already functioning in this role. Some directors changed the center vision after they had begun working in a broader capacity and others began communicating the vision before they enacted the role change.

To ensure the new vision is effectively incorporated into the core of the center, this new vision must translate coherently downward toward the center mission, staffing, and budgeting as well as upward, to the institutional radar screen and strategic planning (see chapter 12). Center reporting lines, existing structures, and institutional leadership changes can challenge newly carved roles that have not been institutionalized and are not in existence anywhere but the director's imagination. Zaccaro and Banks (2004) claim, "As a strategy for change, the vision must be "translated into a cascading strategic plan" (p. 367). The new vision must also be communicated in institutional documents that specifically name who is at the table (including the center director) and how strategic objectives will be met in ways that name the TLC. It is easy for the work of the center in broader initiatives to be invisible or silently assumed. Therefore, it is important to ensure that the center vision and mission statement are reflected in the institution's strategic plan and the planning documents of task forces to which the center the director contributes. Over time, and yet quickly, as a number of directors reported, their role became expected, valued, and sought to the point that they needed to reassess in which initiatives and to what level in each they could participate.

Communicating Vision Through Vivid Images

An organizational vision is often expressed in words and at times recorded in documents. Collins & Porras (1996) explain that a visionary leader must be able to communicate a description that conjures up lasting imagery and needs, in other words:

> a vivid description—that is, a vibrant, engaging, and specific description of what it will be like to achieve . . . an image that people can carry around in their heads. It is a question of painting a picture with your words. (p. 74)

They argue that this "picture painting is essential" as it functions to make the vision tangible in people's minds (Collins & Porras, 1996, p.74). Kouzes and Posner (2007) explain:

> The word vision itself has at its root the verb "to see." Statements of vision, then, should not be statements at all. They should be pictures—word pictures. They're more image than words. For a vision to be shared it needs to be seen in the mind's eye. (p. 145)

Metaphors are a common organizational management tool (Berg, 1985; Morgan, 1986; Pondy, 1983; Tsoukas, 1991). Rather than hide a new vision for the center, the new center vision needs strong images when they are introduced. The center director, in consultation with the supervisor, need "to make conscious use of metaphorical expressions to give vividness or tangibility to abstract ideas" (Kouzes & Posner, 1995, p. 134) and manage the metaphors they create to signal change (Marshak, 1993).

The directors and their supervisors were asked to translate their center vision into a metaphor or image that captured or highlighted the *organizational* involvement and leadership dimension they had imagined and enacted in their vision. Would the selected center metaphors differ in important ways from the metaphors commonly imagined for the work of developers and the typical instructional or the faculty development focus? Often heard metaphors for the faculty developer's work include coach, guide, gardener, "candle-bearer" and "Sherpa guide" and even virus like (Sorcinelli, Austin, Eddy, & Beach, 2006, p. 175). However, the following set of metaphors and images captured the director's center vision as being intricately connected to and involved with the larger institutional picture (see Table 8.2) and did not reflect the typical images associated with a focus on level of individual change or solely programing activities and the role of instructional development. These images far from portrayed a marginalized entity, but instead, portrayed a well-integrated and connected unit.

Enacting a New Center Vision

The center vision of an institutional leadership role was described by images of wheels, hubs, catalysts, seeds, gardeners, porous entities, bridges, and webs. These metaphors evoke a sense of multidimensional connection and dynamic involvement, and a sense of innovation and change. Additionally, these images reflect the role of change agent and represent different ways of functioning than that of instructional development. However disparate, both types of metaphors need to find harmony and integration within centers of teaching and learning.

The concept of a multidimensional role is not new in higher education. Faculty are called upon to fulfill the traditional three-leggeds tool of research, service, and teaching. Tension occurs and achieving balance is hard. The knowledge, skills, and roles of each are distinct and yet related. Sorcinelli et al. (2006) pose critical questions for this discussion, "Will faculty development be a useful but marginal resource, or will it be conceptualized and organized in ways that make it central to institutional quality, health, and

TABLE 8.2
Case study directors' center organizational vision metaphors

Case A	percolator, things can bubble up, a bridge, catalyst, web-of-webs, petri dishes, sustainer, spark, gardener "I serve as the *bridge* between administration and faculty. So there are desires from both sides and I help them meet in the middle."
Case B	"Ripples." "Rays of light." "It is the spreading out of things." "I see the center at the center, sort of metaphorically, and operating out of that center, but always in relationship in a web to all kinds of other things, never in isolation. . . . I think people see it as a catalyst."
Case C	"A 'forecaster' of institutional events and trends that would impact the institution." "A catalyst."
Case D	"Building bridges." "I am a spoke . . . the wheel . . . certainly not one spoke. . . . I think that I do a lot of connecting."
Case E	"A wheel or hub of units and services."
Case F	"A hub of community and intellectual inquiry." "A shepherd of redesign." "A connecting wheel." "A think tank."
Case G	"A teaching commons." "Our doors are open now." "An underground change agent." "A moderated change agent." "We're holding up a mirror." "Organic gardeners—planting seeds." "One of the interesting things that happened here is a kind of migration or almost . . . an influenza outbreak, a diffusion of innovation model."
Case H	"A kind of innovation entity." "An intellectual home." "An engine of innovation." "Very porous boundaries." "A visible mass of activity." "One of the ways I am trying to get staff to think about this is, what is sort of a pyramid model, [a] kind of base of support. The middle part of the pyramid is kind of improving current practices, but then the top of the pyramid is what I call new practices, and I think that it is our job—to lead the way around new practices, and that should be part of what we do." "One of the ways that I have thought of it for a long time was more as a kind of network organization or a major organization and not just a unit."

excellence, and essential to individual faculty members' growth?" (p. 175). They point out:

> While there will always be a creative and dynamic tension between individual and institutional needs, faculty developers will be well served by attending not only to the interests of the individual faculty member or special interest groups . . . but also to larger institutional concerns. (p. 169)

Perhaps never before has envisioning the role of centers and faculty development entailed *integrating* the three original prongs for this field–faculty, instructional, and organizational development. Very likely and over time, new structures, titles, and position descriptions will evolve to advance innovation and excellence in teaching and learning at all levels, while developers continue to incorporate technology, assessment, and partnerships across campus. Several of the case study directors have unique titles and already work within new structural designs. Reenvisioning centers may entail short and long range changes that evolve along with other parts of the university as it shifts toward a learner-centered mission and collaborative leadership models.

A well-established center vision that incorporates a multidimensional role for developers and that is translated into the center mission statement provides important scaffolding for the future of the center. These efforts may help secure its survival should institutional leadership change. Translation of the vision through the center mission may become the basis for appointing or recruiting the director to institutional level committees and integrating the center into the objectives of the strategic plan, large-scale initiatives, and institutional grants. Enacting the center vision by connecting the center vision and mission to the institutional strategic plan has the advantage of making the center's role known across administrative units. Folded within the strategic plan, the center becomes linked to budget decisions and clearly aligned with institutional priorities. It would make sense to begin with a center vision, devise a center mission, and embed the center within the strategic planning process. However, in reality, a director inherits a center, the existing mission partially alludes to broader involvement, and the vision for the center seems firmly entrenched in instructional development efforts.

The following case narrative provides an in-depth map of how the formulation, communication, and enactment of a center vision served as a tool that aided the director to change the director's and center's role.

Narrative 1: Case Study Susan Gano-Phillips, University of Michigan–Flint

Formulating a Center Vision for Institutional Involvement

As a newly appointed director of a TLC at the University of Michigan–Flint, I found myself challenged to develop and define a vision for the future of the center. Not unlike many new faculty developers, I delayed defining a vision for the center for quite a while, citing my "newness" to the position and my level of frenzied activity, managing many existing and new programs as explanations. It was not as if I did not have a vision—I had to articulate ideas about the future of the center when I interviewed for the position. However, my initial vision for the center was void of broader institutional consultation and full knowledge of the center's historical context. Ultimately, over the course of my first three years in the position, I engaged in a process to define more fully, communicate, and act on a center vision.

While acknowledging that the personal vision of the director is insufficient to define a center's vision, it is important to note that the personal interests and skills of the director typically do play a significant role in the development of a center vision.

For my part, I had been introduced to the organizational development approach to educational development at the beginning of my tenure as director, and this approach resonated with my interests and past experiences. I valued how an organizational development approach focuses on the organization's structure as well as processes that optimize the organization's effectiveness. Enacted in centers of teaching and learning, this approach often entailed engaging campus-wide issues including such tasks as redefining faculty evaluation processes or curricular matters, such as campus learning communities or general education reform.

Investigating: Performing an Environmental Scan

To complement my interests and skills, I had to consider a wide variety of contextual factors and consult broadly to develop a vision for which there was campus-wide support. These factors included the institution's culture, human and financial resources, the history of the past educational development on campus, and the level of support from the administrative and faculty leadership. I learned about the institution's context by reading the center's policy documents, advisory board meeting minutes and annual reports, carefully analyzing the center's financial records, and engaging in extensive consultation with the provost, deans, department chairs, students, and faculty colleagues.

Despite the anticipated inconsistency of feedback regarding the center, its primary mission, and its activities, this environmental scan provided me with data that I analyzed and translated into my recommendations for a future vision and mission. My vision ultimately boiled down to wanting to change the way in which the center was viewed and utilized within the larger institution. It was my aim to move it from a position on the periphery, where it had been for many years, into a position of more central prominence and focus, which could elevate the importance and value associated with institutional teaching. I wanted the center to be engaged in decision-making in many areas of university functioning because of its centrality to the university mission.

Collaborative Envisioning: Center Advisory Board Involvement

I then took the outline of the center vision and mission to the center's advisory board. Over a series of meetings, the advisory board and I discussed various options for the center, the advantages and disadvantages of various courses of action, and ultimately revised the center's mission statement and vision for the future. I solicited the faculty advisory board members to engage actively in prioritizing goals as well as a long-term plan for the center. I shared my concerns, as well as my personal interests and vision for the center, while listening carefully to the concerns raised by the board members.

Simultaneous to my work with the advisory board, I initiated consultations with key administrators and faculty. My consultations with the Provost (to whom I directly reported) resulted in an invitation to present a report detailing a vision for the future of the center. Because of the work that the advisory board and I had been engaged in, the advisory board was able to produce this report in approximately one month's time. Once this report was circulated, the work of enacting the vision became my central challenge.

Enacting and Communicating the Center Vision

In reality, I had begun working to align the center's activities with an organizational development vision from almost the moment I began my work there. For example, I began to act on this vision by increasing business hours from approximately 15 to 45 per week by utilizing trained work-study students to demonstrate a more thorough "presence" on campus. I welcomed invitations for collaborative opportunities with other offices on campus, and after agreement on the center vision, began to actively seek out these collaborations. I made it known that I was willing, in fact, desired, to sit on some large-scale ad-hoc university committees who were tackling institution-wide issues. Sometimes my appointment to these committees was noted as representative of my academic background (as a College of Arts and Sciences representative), rather than as the center director. However, I used these committee appointments to speak broadly in support of the teaching mission of our institution and as a representative of the center. With time, I started to be appointed to these committees, and even to chair them, because of my position as the center director (i.e., Task Force to Evaluate Teaching Among Lecturers, General Education Reform Committee). The center was no longer at the periphery of the institution, but rather it was frequently being consulted and engaged to move the institution forward!

The biggest challenges in enacting the broader vision of the center were center staffing and human resource limitations. A wise, and more senior advisory board member warned me that some current activities and programing may need to be eliminated in order to achieve other long-term systematic goals. At the time when we revised the center mission and vision, I was an ambitious and overachieving new director. I wanted to prove the board member wrong, but the workload proved unmanageable. I ultimately relented, giving less time and attention to some current programing in order to devote more time to institution-wide committees and projects. Simultaneously, I began to build systematically a case for increased financial support for the center, ultimately increasing (fractionally) the appointment of the administrative assistant and bringing the director's position to full time.

Regardless of resources available to the center, it will be important annually to continue to set and communicate center goals, and to measure progress against these goals at the year-end. Furthermore, directors need to engage in evaluation of daily/weekly activities against goals on an ongoing basis to avoid burnout and to increase alignment of day-to-day activities with long-term goals.

Strategies for Formulating, Communicating and Enacting/Implementing a Center Vision for Institutional Involvement

Formulate the Center Vision

(a) Perform a thorough environmental scan
(b) Carve an initial center vision
(c) Translate vision into a draft of the center mission (see chapters 2, 5, and 8)
(d) Seek advisory board consultation on the vision, mission, and future direction of the center

Enact the Center Vision

(a) Welcome invitations for collaborative opportunities with other offices on the campus
(b) Initiate consultations with key administrators, faculty, and the provost
(c) Make it known that you are willing to sit on some large-scale ad-hoc university committees who are tackling institution-wide issues

(d) Systematically build a case for increased financial support for the center

(e) Consider if current activities and programing need to be eliminated in order to achieve other long-term systematic goals

(f) Evaluate daily/weekly activities against goals on an ongoing basis to avoid burnout and to increase alignment of day to day activities with long-term goals

Communicate the Center Vision

(a) Develop and circulate a document or report detailing the new vision and mission for the future of the center

Conclusion

The center vision differs from the other enabling factors identified by the study in that the center visioning process functions as a strategy not only to *enable* involvement but also as a key strategy in *changing* the role of the director and center. The current literature describes organizational vision as a change strategy and provides relevant insight regarding the function of visions and the task of envisioning, skills for envisioning, the role of founders, and models for changing vision. Will the professional development of directors expand to include the necessary expertise and skills required for this broader role? What is preventing a broad-based commitment to developing faculty, educational, or academic developers in their knowledge and skills as leaders and change agents? In order to broaden the already articulated instructional development role, directors need to be successful as visionary leaders for their centers. Ready and Conger (2008) attributed the lack of successful visions as failure to:

- focus—too many competing priorities
- engage a partner
- develop the new skills the people needed to actualize the vision
- clarify mixed messages—the old patterns and behaviors are clearly more recognized and valued, subtly reinforced
- navigate clashing powers and cultural dynamics—is the old guard threatened by the new vision?
- recognize existing talent layers of change agents who "embody the behaviors and values of the new call to action" (p. 71)

Because the context of higher education differs from a business context, special attention needs to be paid to the unique obstacles encountered by center directors as they prepare to transform the center's vision. As the earlier narrative case example illustrated, center staffing and resources were the strongest impediments in enacting a new center vision. These obstacles were a common source of constraint and frustration as each of the directors implemented their broader role in institutional initiatives alongside their existing instructional development efforts. This issue should be discussed at the very beginning of the envisioning process with the supervisor, advisory board, and center staff. With careful planning for implementation of the new center vision, priorities can to be assessed carefully and work load changes anticipated and handled proactively.

The case study models, from large and established centers to smaller institutions or centers with part-time directors, and new centers, provide assurance that the center re-envisioning process can be done successfully.

References

Alpert, D. (1985). Performance and paralysis: The organizational context of the American research university. *Journal of Higher Education, 56*(3), 241–281.

Berg, P. (1985). Organizational change as a symbolic transformation process. In P. J. Frost, L. F. Moore, M. R. Louis, C. C. Lundberg, & J. Martin (Eds.), *Organizational culture* (pp. 291–299). Beverly Hills, CA: Sage.

Boeker, W. (1989). Strategic change: The effects of founding and history. *Academy of Management Journal, 32*(3), 489–515.

Collins, J. C., & Porras, J. I. (1996). Building your company's vision. *Harvard Business Review, 74*(5), 65–77. Retrieved March 20, 2010, from http://www.intenz.dk/fileadmin/user_upload/Danske/Downloads/built_to_last_sammendrag_paa_engelsk.pdf

Cummings, T. G., & Worley, C. G. (2005). *Organization development and change* (8th ed.). Madison, WI: South-Western.

Ford, F. R. (1993). Business, financial, and administrative functions. In D. W. Breneman, L. L., Leslie, & R. E. Anderson (Eds.). *ASHE Reader on finance in higher education* (pp. 449–460). Needham Heights, MA: Ginn Press.

Foster, R. D. (2007). Effective organizational vision: Implications for human resource management. *Journal of European Industrial Training, 31*(2), 100–111.

Holpp, L., & Kelly, M. (1988). Realizing the possibilities. *Training and Development, 42*(9), 48–55.

Kinicki, A., & Williams, B. (2006). *Management: A practical investigation.* Burr Ridge, IL: McGraw-Hill/Irwin.

Kouzes, J., & Posner, B. (1995, June). *The leadership challenge.* San Francisco: Wiley and Sons.

Landau, D., Drori, I., & Porras, J. (2006). Vision change in a government R & D organization. *The Journal of Applied Behavioral Science, 42*(2), 145–171.

Larwood, L., Falbe, C. M., Miesing, P., & Kriger, M. P. (1995). Structure and meaning of organizational vision. *The Academy of Management Journal, 38*(3), 740–769.

Levin, I. M. (2000). Vision revisited. *The Journal of Applied Behavioral Science, 36*(1), 91–107.

Lucas, J. R. (1998). Anatomy of a vision statement. *Management Review, 7*(2), 22.

Marshak, R. J. (1993). Managing the metaphors of change. *Organizational Dynamics, 2*(1), 44–56.

Morgan, G. (1986). *Images of organizations.* Beverly Hills, CA: Sage.

Pondy, L. R. (1983). The role of metaphors and myths in organization and in the facilitation of change. In L. R. Pondy, P. J. Frost, G. Mornga, & T. C. Dandridge, (Eds.), *Organizational symbolism.* Greenwich, CT: JAI Press.

Ready, D. A., & Conger, J. A. (2008, Winter). Enabling bold visions. *MIT Sloan Management Review, 49*(2), 670–676.

Senge, P. M. (1990). *The fifth discipline: The art and practice of the learning organization.* New York: Doubleday.

Sorcinelli, M., Austin, A. E., Eddy, P. L., & Beach, A. L. (2006). *Creating the future of faculty development: Learning from the past, understanding the present.* Bolton, MA: Anker.

Tsoukas, J. (1991). The missing link: A transformational view of metaphors in organizational science. *Academy of Management Review, 16*(3), 566–585.

Westley, F., & Mintzberg, H. (2005). Visionary leadership and strategic management. *Strategic Management Journal, 10,* 17–32.

Zaccaro, S., & Banks, D. (2004, Winter). Leader visioning and adaptability: Bridging the gap between research and practice on developing the ability to manage change. *Human Resource Management, 43*(4), 367–380.

9

KNOWING AND FACILITATING ORGANIZATIONAL CHANGE PROCESSES

Connie M. Schroeder

I f one was to ask educational or faculty developers if they are involved in *organizational change*, the likely answer would be "yes." If asked to describe what they do in that capacity or to define it, the most common response would be that *everything* they do is aimed toward changing and improving the institutional culture through developing the practices of teaching and learning, and some would cite specific programs and resources and offer changed courses and pedagogy as evidence of culture change. From this perspective, as individuals change their beliefs and practices as a result of a wide range of traditional instructional faculty development efforts, the institution and culture ultimately change, although indirectly.

The link between individual change and organizational change, particularly in higher education and teaching practices, has been investigated for several decades. Research efforts have reported that the changes in individual teaching practices do result from conceptual changes (Cranton, 1994; Gravett, 1996; Ho, 1998; Ramsden, 1992; Trigwell & Prosser, 1996). Going beyond the idea of individual learning as a basis for individual change, further research investigated "individual learning and transformation as a mechanism for organizational change and organizational learning" (Schroeder, 2001). Argyris and Schon (1978) and Senge (1990) explored the manner in which individual and organizational learning are related. Argyris and Schon (1978) concluded that "there is no organizational learning without individual learning... individuals restructure the continually changing artifact called organizational theories-in-use" (p. 20). In this sense, all development aimed to shift individual concepts may contribute to organizational change processes.

Ultimately and implicitly, the idea behind supporting instructors through workshops and individual development efforts is to improve or change the individual instructors' practices and enable affective student learning. Because higher education became concerned somewhat recently with broader institutional change, developers naturally look for the potential of their work to impact the institution as a whole. Facilitating the adoption and implementation of new learning paradigms that will modify individual teaching and learning practices—for example, active learning, assessment, distance learning, and learning-centered teaching—became the focus of the instructional development role. One workshop, instructor, and scholarship of teaching and learning (SoTL) scholar at a time would surely add up to affect overall institutional improvement and contribute to organizational development and change.

The impact of these efforts can be substantial over time even though the field struggles with measuring and validating their institutional impact. Institutional change through typical instructional development programs, such as these and other individually focused efforts, rely on a particular set of organizational change models and strategies, including social cognition models and diffusion strategies well suited to individual learning and change. These efforts must and should continue as *one dimension* of the developer's and center's work. However, models often used for broader, institutional initiative change rely less on these models and more on planned change strategies. Could there be more than one organizational change basket?

When pressed, most developers will not be able to identify an organizational change theory or model they or institutional leaders use. Instead, developers will often claim that their institution invents its own unique change process tailored to the institutional culture and climate, and deny that institutional initiatives use any general change theory or model. Such statements dismiss the overarching models of change into which even the most custom-designed institutional change processes fit. Despite the fact that developers need to demonstrate a wide array of skills and knowledge just to meet the instructional development needs, there is no formal preparation for this field. Therefore, there exists no vehicle for collectively shifting the preparation of developers to include *knowledge and skills in organizational change*. Yet, over half of the directors surveyed are involved in institutional initiatives that lead to change (see chapter 4). Those who come from an organizational behavior background, higher education administration, or adult leadership often have acquired significant relevant knowledge that is helpful for working with institutional change. Others have been around academia long enough to learn what works and what does not, based on intuition, experience, and consulting with colleagues. Professional development opportunities in organizational change should be readily available for new and seasoned developer professionals in order to learn to plan, implement, and assess large-scale projects. With the widespread attention to curricular reform, assessment, and technology, the developer's professional development needs are considerable and require intentional planning on the part of each developer, the center director, and supervisors of center directors, and particularly, professional organizations.

Value of Organizational Change Knowledge

This chapter's purpose is to provide evidence of the director-based factor that enabled involvement in broad-scale change initiatives, *knowing and facilitating organizational change processes* that emerged from the qualitative data, and describe how directors acquired and used this knowledge. It is not to provide a primer on organizational change in higher education. Resources that address this knowledge are easily accessed and appear throughout this chapter. Based on the evidence from directors and their supervisors, developers *are* involved in broader change initiatives and need to give serious attention to acquiring and utilizing knowledge and skill in organizational change processes in higher education. The following reasons argue for the developer to acquire organizational change knowledge and skills.

1. Change is complex; it is not a quick study.
2. Change is here to stay on the landscape of higher education (and all organizations).
3. Higher education institutions are unique organizations in value, culture, structure, etc.
4. Higher education institutions are particularly resistant to change.
5. Developers are uniquely situated between administration and faculty with significant institutional knowledge and institutional connections, relationships, and partnerships.
6. Developers are connected to national trends and initiatives in higher education.
7. Developers are knowledgeable about unique literature and research on teaching and learning.
8. Centers are often marginalized at the fringes of the institution, undervalued and underfunded.

9. The role of developers internationally is misunderstood and lacking in definition.
10. Evidence points toward organizational change process knowledge being a factor in enabling broader involvement.
11. The complex issues confronting higher education and institutions require multiple teams of cross-unit expertise in order to make progress.
12. The majority of directors are involved to some degree in institutional change initiatives.

Knowledge of institutional change strategies and organizational dynamics are listed as two of the necessary knowledge areas for change agents (Lindquist, 1978). More recently, Robert Diamond, the late and noted leader in faculty development, described the need for developers' organizational change knowledge as "an understanding of the literature and research on . . . organizational theory as it applies to colleges and universities" (2005, p. 34). In his discussion of institutional change agency, Diamond further listed essential director knowledge and skills in mission and vision development, leadership (motivation and change), and management and governing. By becoming competent in at least a foundational knowledge of change processes in higher education, the developer may be able to identify gaps in an initiative's planned change process and recommend combining strategies and approaches or accurately predict faculty resistance. Knowing organizational change processes will help the developer to understand the considerable differences between the change models used with institutional level change and how they differ from those used for achieving individual change through instructional development. In addition, knowledge of higher education change processes can prepare the developer to situate institutional change processes and plans into larger frameworks and identify hidden assumptions that accompany each type of approach (Kezar, 2001). A brief overview of the major models of organizational change provides a foundation for analyzing the case study directors' use of organizational change processes later in the chapter.

Organizational Change Models

The categories of organizational change models and strategies have shifted and been reconfigured over time (Lindquist, 1978; Nordvall, 1982). Kezar (2001) summarizes the literature on change and offers six categories of change models—evolutionary (dialectical), teleological, life cycle, political, social cognition, and cultural (p. 5). She defines important distinctions between innovation, adaptation, diffusion, and reform that are useful for fostering a common language among developers for this broader role. The literature further divides first order change from second order change (Kezar, 2001). Most higher education change is first order change—change that fits within rather than modifies the underlying values and structures. First order change, she points out, is associated with organizational development. According to Kezar (2001), each change model discussed below makes assumptions about the following dimensions of organizational change: sources, level, timing, focus, structure, process, attitude, intentionality, and response time.

Evolutionary change, or adaptive change, models reflect systems thinking in which change in one part impacts the rest of the organization as it evolves over time. This model emphasizes incremental change strategies and reaction to circumstances, variables, and the environment. Change is unplanned and adaptive to the environment.

Teleological models, or planned change, include rational models with goals, step-by-step processes, and assessment, along with a leader or change agent. This change is prompted by the need for change and is intentional, structured, and linear, relying on the internal organization and collaboration and involvement of many. Change through institutional initiatives is planned change, often called strategic planning, and there is often "a table" at which the change leaders are seated to research the problem and formulate the initiative plan. Lindquist (1978) points out that this model relies on "developing a great message" much the same way Gladwell's (2000) model was used to create a "sticky message" (see chapter 6).

Life cycle models emphasize the stages of an organization as it matures and the adaptation of individuals to the organization for change to occur. Training and development enable this adaptation so that the organization can grow. People are central to this change process.

Political (dialectical) change models rely on people mobilizing for change and this change results from opposition, despite sometimes pervasive inactivity. Informal groups, alliances, and coalitions form as interest groups and continue to build alliances through engaging influential people, negotiating deals, and persuasion. Oftentimes, this may entail resistance-building and efforts to subvert change. These groups are not structurally positioned and are temporary, often utilizing hallway conversation and informal contacts to grow.

Social cognition change models are the bread and butter of typical instructional development programs. This model emphasizes discussion and learning and might use such strategies as seminars, reading groups, or resources. Cognitive dissonance is used to foster learning, and learning is coupled with change (Argyris, 1994). In this model, it is important to uncover assumptions, develop mental models, and reframe meaning while cultivating a common language (Kezar, 2001). It makes sense that institutions of higher education, and particularly efforts with autonomous faculty, would utilize ways to make change based on individual learning (Argyris & Schon, 1978). Profit-driven companies may not have time for everyone to construct new meaning or to discuss mental models since their change happens very rapidly in a fast-paced, market-driven environment.

Cultural change models view fostering organizational change as altering its cultural elements, including its history, symbols, values, beliefs or myths, mission and vision, or traditions—such as organizational rituals. In response to natural shifts within the human environment, the process of change therefore, is collective, long-term and often slow.

Organization Change Expertise

If involvement in institutional change occupies an important aspect of a developer's time, where does a developer, already immersed in numerous responsibilities, acquire this knowledge?

The center directors interviewed acquired the knowledge and skills needed to facilitate organizational change through a variety of sources, and conveyed an intentional effort to improve their knowledge of organizational models and processes. For example, as one director explained:

> I read a lot. I read, read, read, read. . . . I don't know this for sure but the wisdom I have gotten from POD has a lot to do not only with helping people think about pedagogy in their classrooms but with culture change, with thinking about what could be on a very broad level. So when I envision my work . . . I am also thinking culture change. . . . I think I have already wandered into culture change. (Case Study B, see chapter 5)

An important professional development resource, the National Institute for New Faculty Developers sponsored by POD, served this purpose as well.

> I want to, first of all, give credit to a training or development activity that I participated in on my first day on the job or a couple days before I was to start the job. I attended the National Institute for New Faculty Developers. . . . I read all the materials, and the organizational change stuff became clearer to me. (Case Study E)

Another director emphasized the importance of theoretical knowledge combined with institutional knowledge.

> It is hard to separate that because I have a background in the organizational behavior and change, and so I am trying to think of what would it be like

not to have that. . . . You still need the knowledge of the specific institution, some of the history, the players, the personalities, and the processes that the institution goes through to make change. So the theoretical [knowledge] can be guiding but the specifics are essential. (Case study E)

Organizational Change Knowledge Narratives

The four narratives below describe either the process of changing the role of the center from marginalized to become repositioned within the core of institutions priorities, or a process of institutional change, or both simultaneously. In each narrative, aspects of organizational change processes and strategies are bold-faced to highlight their use. The narratives are followed by an analysis of these change processes in terms of the four most frequently utilized change models—planned, social cognition, political, and social interaction. The value of knowing and applying organizational change models to understand, lead, or influence change lies in becoming skilled in strategically and intentionally taking actions to effectively move change initiatives forward.

Narrative 1 : Case Study E

Susan Gano-Phillips, University of Michigan, Flint

Example a. Providing the Groundwork for Changing the Center's Mission

I entered faculty development work after nine years as a faculty member, without formal training in educational theory or higher education administration. I guess you could say, I "learned the job while I did it." Despite the lack of formal preparation for work as a faculty or organizational developer, my training as a clinical and community psychologist included both knowledge bases and skills that were invaluable in promoting organizational change processes. These included:

- communication skills
- theory in learning, motivation, and change behaviors
- problem-solving skills
- sensitivity to diversity and diverse attitudes/opinions
- recognition of the complexity of group interactions and the slow evolution of institutional culture

When I applied for the directorship of the faculty development center at UM-Flint, I had a goal of organizational change, though I had not identified it [clearly] as such. Instead, I had identified a **discrepancy** between our stated campus values and some of our practices related to learning and teaching. I listened carefully to what faculty told me about the challenges they faced as teachers and scholars, both within and outside the tenure process. For example, some faculty noted that despite the fact that the institution is seen as a "teaching institution" (the old Carnegie "comprehensive" classification), relatively little attention was paid to the assessment and evaluation of teaching in promotion and tenure cases. Similarly, **the data** [I had collected] suggested that funding for faculty [teaching] development was substantially less than for research, institutionally. It was these types of misalignments of values and resources that I hoped to address.

Our teaching and learning center had operated for five years prior to my assuming the directorship and was servicing many faculty with workshops, consultations, a resource collection, and pedagogical funding competitions. I wanted to continue these services . . . and to expand beyond these individually focused services to change the role of the faculty development center on our campus. The center had been servicing a relatively select group of faculty who were already highly motivated to engage in the best practices to facilitate student learning. *I felt we needed to embed the center within the culture of the institution more centrally, to raise its visibility,* and to engage a much broader array of faculty and staff if we were to achieve our stated mission of "advancing excellence in teaching throughout campus."

[Although] the center was viewed as a "nice" addition to the university, it was not viewed as an integral office to the functioning of the university—*it was not at the center of any important decision-making or institutional change.* I felt the campus needed to develop a **"positive restlessness"** about teaching and learning that would lead to continuous improvements over time.

But given the limited financial and human resources available to the center (a two-thirds time director and a half-time administrative assistant), how was I to make these significant changes to the center and its role on campus? Unless I was to abandon much of the individually focused programing of the center, I would need to garner new resources. I decided to use both a "top-down" and "bottom up" [change] **strategy** to raise consciousness about the center, its changing role within the institution, and the need for new resources. The "top-down" approach focused on building support among the administration while "bottom-up" approaches focused on the faculty and staff needs of the institution.

Administratively, I spoke to deans and other high-level administrators **about the need** for *alignment* of goals, priorities, and values with the day-to-day practices of the institution, gently **demonstrating our [institutional] misalignments.** *I met regularly with deans* and other administrators to both share the work of the center and to assess their unit's needs. I also made efforts to help nonacademic affairs administrators see the connections between their areas of responsibility and the values and goals of faculty development (i.e., retention services, academic advising). Finally, I **collected and presented data** to the administration, which showed increased demand for center services from their respective faculties/staff and high levels of satisfaction with the services that had been provided. These conditions set the stage for future funding requests.

From a **grassroots perspective, I sought to learn** about and meet the unmet departmental and individual needs for faculty development among the faculty. As examples, department chairs wanted programing to support the teaching development of their untenured faculty, and many faculty wanted to know more about the practical and logistical application of new technologies in teaching. Thus, a First Year Faculty program and a Technology Brown Bag program were developed.

I was able to meet many of these faculty needs by **building formal collaborations** with other units that were better resourced than the center. . . . I had successfully engaged nonacademic units in **partnerships** with academic affairs to support student learning and faculty teaching at an institutional level. *I had begun to broaden the campus's definition of faculty development.*

Over time, my open-mindedness, my willingness to collaborate with others (including the assessment office, technology services, and student services), and my sense of "positive restlessness" about improving learning and teaching brought new opportunities for programing and increased awareness of the centrality of the TLC to the institution as a whole. The **center was invited to the table** and played significant roles in *institutional strategic planning and general education reform* in the two years that followed.

Example b. At the Table of General Education Program Change

The existing general education program that we have on campus has been here since 1982. It is a distribution model that had just grown out of control. . . . The last committee that had been formed in [the] 2004–2005 academic year worked for about half the year and could not even come up with a plan that they could agree to. . . . They consulted with me as director of the center. The provost that commissioned [this] committee said, "They are at an impasse. Can you meet with them?"

My role in what I did was consultative. That was my role in how we moved that process forward in a productive way. And then [we] got hooked up with ACC&U. . . . We came back and we [developed] a process that **involved the faculty in the development of the plan**. So we didn't have a plan in mind that the administration was pushing at us. . . . [W]e, in affect, came back saying "this really has to come from the faculty if we ever hope to get it approved."

On a personal level, I had high ambitions and what seemed like limitless energy for my new position. Over time, however, it became increasingly apparent that hard work alone would not allow me to accomplish quickly all of the organizational change goals that I had set. Perhaps the most valuable lesson that I learned in my early years is that, like everything else, organizational change work and collaboration take valuable time. Resources (both human and financial) must be diverted from short-term to more long term goals if organizational change goals are to be achieved. Listening intently, modeling "positive restlessness" about continuous improvement, and building collaborations and credibility with all center constituencies proved to be a winning combination.

Narrative 2: Case Study D

Phyllis Blumberg, University of the Sciences, Philadelphia

Example a. Tactical Planning Group Member: Learning-centered Teaching

During the 2001–2002 academic year, administrators identified six strategic imperatives, including the development of a culture of student-centered learning and living, to direct the university's planning. The Tactical Planning Group on Student-centered Learning and Living **defined objectives, developed future action steps, and outlined outcome indicators.** As the director of the TLC, I was an *appointed member* of this tactical planning group, and I served as the key educator/ informant and resource for this planning group throughout their work.

By **scheduling discussions with faculty** in 2002, **I learned of faculty** concerns about the phrase "student-centered learning." Student-centered learning, from their perspective, seemed to focus on consumer satisfaction (Weimer, 2002). Because of **information disseminated** by the TLC, the faculty recommended changing this imperative to "learning-centered teaching," which places the emphasis on student learning while giving faculty an important role in this learning. I, along with the other faculty members of the task force, successfully **informed and facilitated** discussion around the **change in nomenclature.** While this change may seem minor, leveraging this change was an important move that preempted significant resistance later that would have countered the ultimate change sought after in the institutional culture.

Example b. Learning-centered Teaching Initiative and Center Programing

In the following year—2004—I implemented an intentional change strategy aimed at further advancing this institutional cultural transformation toward learning-centered teaching. I coordinated a faculty learning community for ten faculty from across the university **to learn in depth** how to implement learning-centered teaching and to design learning-centered courses. This model of training the other faculty was an **intentional, grass roots, or diffusion model of change** aimed at further institutional cultural transformation (Schroeder, 2001). The faculty became trainers in their departments for other faculty to transform their courses.

Narrative 3: Case Study F

(Anonymous)

Redesigning Core Competencies for Students

In those days, we did not have a terribly collaborative structure. So she [grants writer] knew to look for challenges at the college that could get funded. . . . We had about $450,000 a year for five years. . . . We got a one-third Title III grant for our west campus . . . so they **created the position** of a college-wide faculty development coordinator. . . . We had a leader at that time who really believed that the strategies would be more effective if they came from the faculty. . . . So it was the **faculty who were doing the reading** and looking at their own practices and planning changes, and then implementing them and studying them. So it was a real **grassroots** effort. It still was somewhat on the periphery of college operations . . . and I would say that since that time . . . when we got an academic vice-president and then with our new president, all of that really lives now in our Strategic Learning place.

One of the interesting things that happened here is a kind of migration or almost like an **influenza outbreak—a diffusion of innovation** model. **The work** [that happened within] **the grant** [was] **where we incubated the ideas and notions**, and it was adopted by the College of Administration. . . . So we have worked on this grant work for **two, three, and four years** [and] they significantly rewrote our mission statement of the college, . . . **so it was not driven by a sense that we were really in dire shape.** In fact . . . one of our challenges is that the old guard of faculty, people who had been here for 15–20 years, was really **very complacent, very happy with the way things** were, with their reputation, and especially with their salary. The president had given a 10% raise three years running. So there was a division in the faculty [between those] very complacent—who had been here for 15–20 years and the faculty who had been here for only five years. . . . They were the people who were the more driven faculty—the people who were interested in student learning. . . . We had two Title III grants running at the same time. So with the generous funding, we were **able not just to expose faculty but [to] work with them** and release them for two courses to really get involved in the course redesign work. Then **they had the pilot** and had to **collect data** and . . . we redesigned the core competencies for students. First, we had to bring that out to the whole faculty. So we had about one-**third of the faculty involved** in the rewriting of that. People who worked with us deeply on the grant, I think maybe half of them, are now in some other position at the college in a leadership position. . . . They were all "graduates" of the work on the grant . . . what **the grant provided was a lot of conspiratorial time**.

At the same time we got a new president, and we started a big round of hiring and he said to us, "I want you to take the steering committee's recommendation and find a new program." That was one of the transitions felt, really . . . from the margins to the center. The president generously gave us resources, and we worked 15–20 hours in workshops on what should be in the tenure program . . . and then we had these **massive summits where anyone interested could show up and sort of vote by consensus**. It was really an interesting time. In getting us to move on this, the whole learning center became exciting to enough people that it led to some pretty big changes.

So six of us took a retreat to Tampa led by AAHE and we came home with a draft. Then the president edited it, approved it, and launched it. Out of that grant work, the college stepped up and named some **college positions**, including an academic vice-president, that we had not had before. Eventually, it has evolved now into an academic vice-president and chief learning officer.

Narrative 4: Case Study A (see chapter 6)

Catherine E. Frerichs, Diana G. Pace, and Tamara Rosier, Grand Valley State University

Initiating and Claiming a Liberal Education Initiative

About three years ago [the director] and I were talking, and we said this center is too marginalized. It is just supposed to give workshops and grants and keep out of the way. We said we really need a culture change here. The results of **data gathering** from multiple sources made explicit to us and our supervisors that, in attempting to align student and faculty expectations within the context of liberal education—the institution's original and reaffirmed mission—we were undertaking nothing less than changing Grand Valley's current culture. We had a consistent [institutional] philosophy in our foundational documents, had even recently reaffirmed our mission, and the institution was still living out a conflicting experience in the daily lives and classrooms of teachers and students.

Leading from the middle as we were, we needed an egalitarian model to guide our next steps in the change process. [This] also required a **systemic approach to change**: literally, all parts of the university were going to be affected, and therefore must be involved in the change. Finally, it required leaders who had the respect of the university community and who were actively supported by administrators at higher levels.

We found our model in Malcolm Gladwell's *The Tipping Point: How Little Things Can Make a Big Difference* (2000). Gladwell begins with the premise that the best way to understand certain kinds of **change is to think of them as epidemics**: "Ideas and products and messages and behaviors spread just like viruses do" (p. 7). Even though we knew we could not use the language of epidemics and viruses when we discussed the initiative with broader university audiences, we wanted a change in student and faculty expectations **to spread like a virus. We envisioned an epidemic of liberal education overtaking the campus.**

Thus, the initial threads of motivation for institutional change derived from a growing recognition that the teaching and learning currently characteristic of Grand Valley conflicted with the liberal education expectations embedded in its institutional mission, expectations still supported by faculty, administrators, and some students. Increasingly, **they [faculty] felt a discrepancy between ideals and actual practice.**

The institutional change initiative that emerged out of this **growing dissonance** at Grand Valley had the same source of leadership as is frequently described in the literature on faculty development. The director and her supervisor recognized that *the center could be both a source and a catalyst for change.*

We, as change agents, defined the problem in terms of the institutional mission, outlined the goals of the initiative, and requested funds for a half-time faculty researcher who had qualitative and quantitative research skills beyond those possessed by either *Claiming a Liberal Education* (CLE) initiative director.

As change initiators and leaders, we recognized the need to further galvanize and motivate change. **The need for change** is a key element in advancing the process of change. To do so, it required institutional research to make a **strong enough case** for initiating the scale of broad institutional and cultural change that we were discussing, and to guide it as it progressed. . . . **The changes we were seeking could not happen so quickly.**

Analysis of Case Study Director Change Processes

These directors demonstrated their use of organizational change strategies and models perhaps without knowing they were applying specific principles and concepts (see chapters 6, 7, and 10). Each director utilized strategies from more than one change model category; however, one model—planned change—seemed to dominate their approaches. Interestingly, the director with the strongest disciplinary background in organizational behavior utilized the most diverse change models and strategies (see Figure 9.1).

Change Strategies

Although change models share may be directed toward both first and the second order change, the assumptions and strategies of each model help identify their distinctions. Nevertheless, change strategies can overlap between models (Kezar, 2001). A basic knowledge of organizational change models and how common strategies are applied within each model can be of great help when functioning as a multilevel change agent. Several of the directors mentioned grassroots change and the spreading of innovation. Their involvement needs to be analyzed for evidence of political, social interaction, or social cognition strategies as well. For example, Kezar (2001) clarified that diffusion is a change strategy, not a model, and can be used in several models.

For example, Eckel, Hill, Green, & Mallon (2001) identified eight intentional strategies and eight pitfalls in making successful institutional change, and three contributing contextual factors in a study of 26 participating institutions. The eight strategies included:

- being congruent with the purposes and values of the institution
- developing connections—new connections among individuals from different parts of the institution
- developing connections to other institutions, funding agencies, and national efforts
- cultivating senior-level support
- recognizing windows of opportunity created by everyday events and capitalizing on serendipity
- finding small levers for change
- using consistent language
- changing a culture in ways congruent with the existing culture

FIGURE 9.1
Narrative change strategy analysis

Narrative/ Model	Planned Change Lewin (1947); Unfreezing the organization: Need for change	Social Cognition (cognitive dissonance)	Social Interaction	Political Model
Narrative 1 *Case study E* Knowledge Source: Background org. behavior; training and experience as community psychologist	**Leader vision; identified discrepancy; collected/ presented institutional data; raised awareness of need for alignment;**	**Built admin. support; met regularly; presented data; exposed gaps/ discrepancies; cultivated positive restlessness**	**Built formal collaborations with units across institution**	**Regular meetings— deans and admin.**
Narrative 2a & *b Case study D*	Objectives, action steps **Expertise in institutional data and research; funded and collected institutional data to raise awareness of need for change**	Disseminated information on language of learner-centered; faculty learning communities	Scheduled discussions with faculty; faculty learning communities	
Narrative 3 *Case study F* Knowledge Source: Professional reading; POD	Not in dire shape; many inactive or complacent; pilot effort to raise need	Faculty did the reading in depth course redesign work with course releases; workshops	Incubated ideas, influenza outbreak, virus spreading; 1/3 of faculty involved; grant provided "conspiratorial time"	Grant provided "conspiratorial time"; a division in the faculty . . .
Narrative 4 *Case study A* Knowledge Source: National Institute for New Faculty Developers- POD Network	Data gathering; systemic approach to change; translated need for change into making a case based on multiple sources of research and data	**Created awareness of cognitive dissonance; discrepancy between ideals and practice**	Thought of change as epidemic; change would take time	

Each strategy could be implemented using specific change models. Not surprising, a number of these strategies were identified by the case study center directors and later determined to be among the primary factors that enabled their involvement in change. They frequently mentioned making a clear case for change and collecting the right data. These models and the strategies discussed are the very minimal knowledge and skills that developers should be familiar with as they shift toward greater involvement in institutional change. This general understanding and expertise can spare the developer from the common assumption among colleagues that their institutional change process is completely unique or that it defies adherence to any organizational change model.

Conclusion

The vast amount of literature on organizational change, particularly in higher education, offers relevant knowledge to the developer, whether they are changing the role of the center and bringing it in from the margin, or contributing to or leading an institutional change process. It is hoped, and perhaps likely, that knowledge and skill in organizational change processes *will* eventually become part of the lens with which developers approach their work much the same way learning-centered paradigms and assessment frameworks came to be embedded in the mindset of developers. Aspects of the role of developers in institutional change continue to be discussed more directly among colleagues in the United Kingdom, Australia, and beyond (Bath & Smith, 2004; D'Andrea & Gosling, 2001; Eggins & MacDonald, 2003; Fraser, 2001; Hartland & Staniforth, 2003). If this field in the United States and abroad collectively embraces the work of developers in institutional change, position descriptions should begin to reflect the organizational skills and knowledge that the directors identified as critical for this aspect of their role (see chapter 5). Bath and Smith (2004) urge:

> If academic developers are to succeed in claiming and deserving the right to respect and credibility, they must make explicit the research underlying both the theories of their discipline and their pragmatic engagement with the day-to-day teaching problems that they help discipline academics to research and resolve. (p. 24)

Strategies and Recommendations

1. Develop an organizational change knowledge base.
   (a) Search literature within educational/faculty development.
   (b) Search literature within higher education.

    (c) Take a course in organizational studies (business school or school of education).

    (d) Attend POD's Organizational Development Institute.

    (e) Search literature in disciplines beyond higher education.

    (f) Analyze change processes close at hand and those in which you are involved.

2. Develop expertise and skill in organizational change processes in higher education.

    (a) Analyze a current or prior institutional change process using the dimensions of organizational change (see p. 203). Create a timeline of the process and map the dimensions of change onto the timeline.

    (b) While serving on a committee or task force, identify the types of change strategies being employed. Predict what will happen as decisions and strategies are considered and chosen. Compare actual events to your predictions.

    (c) Study several key leaders at your institution and identify the change strategies they use.

    (d) Imagine changing the developer's role and the role of the center using each of the change models. What strategies would you use to apply each model to the change you have identified? Which models best fit your style, the culture of the institution, and the TLC? Why? Which models would be challenging or impossible to utilize? Why?

    (e) Evaluate a change effort at your institution that failed or is not making progress. Which change models are being applied and which strategies you would use to re-energize the stalled change process?

    (f) Interview key leaders at your institution regarding successful and failed change efforts. Take notes, analyze obstacles, and look for patterns. Identify change models in action.

    (g) Consider how the institution can be led to recognize an urgency to change. What data can you gather or become familiar with, institutionally or nationally, that would contribute to solidifying this particular need? How is this need being communicated to the institution (see chapter 6)?

    (h) Practice identifying the best people to be at the planning table of an institutional initiative. Who would you select and why? Who is not at the table that should be? How might they change the process? Would you select yourself? Why or why not?

    (i) Analyze the culture of your institution based on Schein's (1985) organizational culture model: beliefs and values, norms and practices, and structures and policies. Which of these specific cultural components are related to the change being considered? Which components are addressed by a current institutional initiative and change process? Which are not being addressed? How might each component facilitate the change and how might each hamper the change process?

(j) In the initiatives in which you are involved, how will the team measure the progress of change? What will be the indicators that the change is successful?

References

Argyris, C. (1994). *On organizational learning*. Oxford: Blackwell.

Argyris, C., & Schon, D. (1978). *Organizational learning: A theory of action perspective*. Reading, MA: Addision-Wesley.

Bath, D., & Smith, C. (2004). Academic developers: An academic tribe claiming their territory in higher education. *International Journal for Academic Development*, *9*(1), 9–27.

Cranton, P. (1994, November, December). *Self-directed and transformative instructional development*. Hoboken, NJ: Jossey-Bass.

D'Andrea, V., & Gosling, D. (2001). Joining the dots: Reconceptualizing educational development. *The Institute for Learning and Teaching in Higher Education and SAGE Publications*, *2*(1), 64–81. Retrieved October 26, 2009 from http://alh.safepub.com

Diamond, R. M. (2005). The institutional change agency: The expanding role of academic support centers. In S. Chadwick-Blossey, & D. R. Robertson (Eds.), *To improve the academy: Resources for faculty, instructional and organizational development* (Vol. 23, pp. 24–37). Bolton, MA: Anker.

Eckel, P., Green, M., Hill, B., Mallon, B. (2001). *On change—Riding the waves of change: Insights from transforming institutions*. Washington, DC: American Council on Education.

Eggins, H., & MacDonald, R. (Eds.). (2003). *The scholarship of academic development*. Philadelphia: The Society for Research into Higher Education and Open University Press.

Fraser, K. (2001). Australasian academic developers' conceptions of the profession. *International Journal for Academic Development*, *6*, 54–64.

Gladwell, M. (2000). *The tipping point: How little things can make a big difference*. New York: Little, Brown and Company.

Gravett, S. (1996). Conceptual change regarding instruction: The professional enhancement of faculty. *Journal of Staff, Programs, and Organizational Development*, *13*(3), 207–214.

Hartland, T., & Staniforth, D. (2003, May/November). Academic development as academic work. *International Journal for Academic Development*, *8*(1/2), 25–35.

Ho, A. S. P. (1998). A conceptual change staff development programme: Effects as perceived by the participants. *International Journal for Academic Development*, *3*(1), 25–38.

Kezar, A. (2001). Understanding and facilitating organizational change in the 21st century. *ASHE-ERIC Higher Education Report*, *28*(4).

Lewin, K. (1947). *Group decision and social change*. Troy, NY: Rinehard & Winston.

Lindquist, J. (1978). *Strategies for planned change*. Berkeley, CA: Pacific Sounding Press.

Nordvall, R. (1982). *The process of change in higher education institutions*. (*ERIC/AAHE*, *7*). Washington, DC: American Association for Higher Education.

Ramsden, P. (1992). *Learning to teach in higher education*. London: Routledge.

Schein, D. (1985). *Organizational culture and leadership: A dynamic view*. San Francisco: Jossey-Bass.

Schroeder, C. M. (2001). Faculty change agents: Individual and organizational factors that enable or impede faculty involvement in organizational change (Doctoral dissertation, University of Wisconsin–Madison). Retrieved December 30, 2009, from *Dissertations & Theses*: A & I. (Publication No. AAT 3020629).

Senge, P. (1990). *The fifth discipline*. New York: Doubleday.

Smith, K. (1998). Adopting a strategic approach to managing change in learning and teaching. *To Improve the Academy: Resources for faculty, instructional and organizational development*, (Vol. 17, pp. 225–242). Bolton, MA: Anker.

Trigwell, K., & Prosser, M. (1996). Congruence between intention and strategy in university science teachers' approaches to teaching. *Studies in Higher Education*, *32*, 77–87.

Weimer, M. (2002). *Learner-centered teaching*. San Francisco: Jossey-Bass.

10

OPTIMIZING CENTER STAFFING AND ADVISORY BOARDS TO PROMOTE INVOLVEMENT IN INSTITUTIONAL CHANGE

Susan Gano-Phillips

F aculty development takes many different forms and structures in higher education as it has continued to evolve over time. More recently, the roles and responsibilities of some faculty developers have expanded to include a broad array of strategic planning, organizational development, and institution-wide activities to meet the changing needs of institutions and need for improvement of outcomes. Increasingly, faculty developers are becoming involved in activities that support either the central mission of the university (i.e., assessment and improvement of student learning) or in envisioning the future of the institution (i.e., shaping and supporting institutional culture, program development, general education curriculum reform, revision of tenure, and promotion processes). This expanded role affects all aspects of the teaching and learning center (TLC) and the staff, no matter how large or small.

These additional roles and responsibilities raise important questions for staffing of units and structures charged with faculty development activities. As one of the case study directors in the study underlying this book, I had served for nine years as a faculty member before becoming the two-thirds time director of our Center for Learning and Teaching. From the outset, I had a vision for broadening the scope of the center's activities from supporting individual faculty members to include an organizational development and organizational change perspective. This focus meant taking on some campus-wide issues as primary work activities including such tasks as redefining faculty evaluation processes, curricular matters, general education curricular reform, or the development of campus learning communities (Chism, 1998; Cook, 2001; Diamond, 2002).

While energized by the opportunities this organizational development work provided, I quickly began to question how I might accomplish even a fraction of my goals given the resource and staffing constraints that came with my new position. I was not unlike the other directors in the case study interviews that cited workload concerns or difficulty with folding this role into a small operation (see chapter 5). Staffing and resource limitations were the most frequently reported factors that *impeded* a center director's involvement in institutional initiatives (see chapter 5). As stated earlier, 75% of the directors surveyed cited center staffing, resources, and subsequent stress over workload, as factors impeding their level of institutional involvement (see chapter 4). This result indicates that these matters are important to examine, regardless of whether the staff consists of a single part-time director or an entire cadre of professionals with varying expertise. Given these common constraints, a practical array of strategies to counter staffing impediments is needed. This chapter examines how to optimize center staffing and advisory boards in order to promote involvement with institutional change. A number of interrelated and additional primary *enabling* factors, consistent across the other case studies (see chapter 5), facilitated my involvement in institutional change and are discussed, including:

- Strong center support/advocates
- Review/evaluation—advisory board
- Multiple and strong collaborations
- Center alignment with institutional strategic plan
- Center and institutional involvement in national initiatives
- Director's knowledge/expertise
- Director's center vision

In this more expansive role, a constellation of staff and resource-related decisions can lead to reconfiguring aspects of the center that better support and integrate this broader role. I propose that a series of actions involving center staff—center capacity building, center strategic planning, initiating collaborative ventures, and formulating an attitude of letting go—all work together to align center staffing with this broader role. In addition, the center advisory board, a structure situated between the center, faculty, staff, and administration, further plays an important role in expanding the work of the center and advocating for its institutional development role. Taken together, the reconceptualization of faculty development center staffing and the advocacy of center advisory boards can help to position centers more firmly on the institutional radar screen and can facilitate a more expansive role as institutional change agents.

How would center staff be reconceptualized in order to effectively integrate institutional level involvement into this role? Who should serve in these roles? What knowledge or skills should developers possess in order to be effective in this role? A brief review of what is known about TLCs, their directors, and other staff that support campus faculty development, provides an important backdrop against which to consider efforts to optimize staffing for effective involvement in institutional change.

Staff Configurations

The variety of ways in which TLCs are staffed is almost as diverse as the centers themselves. Erickson (1986) surveyed institutions in the mid-1980s and found that for the majority of institutions, faculty development was organized by an individual dean or administrator while only 14% of institutions had dedicated faculty development (teaching and learning) centers. Two decades later, a similar survey found that 54% of participating institutions had a centralized unit coordinating faculty development (a TLC), while 19% utilized individual faculty members or administrators to coordinate activities, and 12% had a committee that supported faculty development (Sorcinelli, Austin, Eddy, & Beach, 2006). Varying from part-time, single-person operations to complex units with many staff, the range of TLC professionals and paraprofessionals may include associate or assistant directors, faculty fellows (on a rotating, nonpermanent basis), administrative staff or program associates, graduate student assistants, or even undergraduate work-study student assistants. Many TLCs around the United States remain relatively small, however, with the exception of a few large centers associated with research-intensive universities (Sorcinelli et al., 2006). The majority of center directors who responded to the *Coming in From the Margins* survey did not have a large staff with which to work: Only 19% reported having an assistant or associate director for their TLC, 26% had a graduate student employed by the center (typically on a part-time basis), and 35% had a program associate or administrative staff member supporting their centers (see chapter 4). Given these staffing patterns, it is no small wonder that expanding the role of developers to engage in institutional change initiatives raises legitimate concerns about center staff time, configurations, competencies, and strategic plans.

As directors strive to become further engaged with priorities for promoting and facilitating institutional change, they are conscious of also needing to accomplish the instructional and faculty development goals of the center. Staffing to promote involvement in institutional change is neither simply nor solely a question of the *number* of staff members serving in TLCs. Rather, in addition, it entails asking *how* to develop the competencies and knowledge base of all staff inhabiting these positions. At least two staffing related issues may inform campuses regarding how to organize and develop their center staffing to optimize engagement in large-scale institution-wide initiatives. These include capacity-building through competencies, professional development, staff evaluation, collaboration, and strategic planning. Each has been described in turn.

Capacity-Building for Institutional Involvement

Capacity-building refers to the development of new skills in staff members to allow achievement of program or center goals that may now incorporate organizational development responsibilities. As the director as well as other center staff members may be involved in the planning and informing of institutional initiatives, the entire unit needs to work together toward fulfilling this and all aspects of the center mission (see chapter 11). Therefore, all members of the staff will benefit from an analysis of their knowledge and skill competencies in terms of an organizational development role. Furthermore, the capacity of TLCs to engage in *institutional change projects* can be enhanced through a program of planned and ongoing professional development for center directors as well as other center staff members. Additionally, collaborative relationships are an important way in which to extend the reach of faculty developers and build the capacity of university staff more generally as institutional change agents (see chapters 5–9).

Center Director Competencies

Because of the growth of faculty development nationally in the United States and internationally over the past quarter century, many center directors have had relatively little prior experience in faculty development, often being pulled from within the faculty ranks to serve in leadership roles (Brinko, Atkins, & Miller, 2005; Sorcinelli et al., 2006). Additional *Coming in From the Margins* survey data reported 64% of the directors had no work experience in faculty development prior to their current position. Twenty-two percent of directors reported having had less than one-year experience in their current faculty development position, with an additional 49% having had only one to five years of experience (see chapter 4). Sixty-eight percent of center directors had served in faculty ranks prior to assuming their director responsibilities.

When a faculty (or staff) member moves into a faculty development position or as a center director, as is often the case, that person frequently undergoes a significant transition that includes the development of different skills, areas of knowledge expertise, and competencies. Examples of the competencies needed for the more traditional *instructional* development work include specific pedagogical knowledge, individual consultation skills, technology integration in teaching, communication skills, event planning, marketing, financial management, program assessment skills, the ability to build partnerships/collaborations, fundraising or grant-writing skills, the ability to delegate, and potentially, the supervision and evaluation of staff. These skills, knowledge areas, and competencies will be present to varying degrees among faculty members and staff who assume faculty development roles and center directorships, based on their prior experiences, but they should not be assumed to be universally present (see chapters 2, 5, and 10).

However, as developers and directors increasingly become involved in promoting institutional change, this list of skills and competencies can be supplemented to include knowledge and skill sets more typically related to *organizational development* (OD), which includes the ability to think holistically and systemically outside traditional disciplinary boundaries, awareness of governance processes within the institution, political aptitude, group facilitation skills, knowledge of change theories, strategic planning skills, and broad knowledge of trends in higher education (Morrill, 2007; Ramsden, 1998). Combined, all these sets of typical instructional and organizational development skills and areas of expertise are truly expansive. Additionally a particular set of skills necessary for any given developer may be defined by the institutional culture and priorities at a specific point in time.

Leadership Competency

Leadership development is but one of the many areas of capacity-building that center directors can utilize to help optimize their involvement in institutional change. Center leadership was determined as a significant factor on the survey data in chapter 4 and selected by more than 70% of the participants as a primary factor *enabling* director's involvement in institutional initiatives. Leadership skills are often not fully developed in faculty members who are drawn into administrative positions as directors of TLCs. Unless faculty have served as department chairs or in other administrative positions, they are unlikely to have given much consideration to the development of their leadership skills in a higher education context. In contrast to management skills, which are designed to create order and to solve problems, leadership skills involve creating, communicating, sustaining, and implementing a vision and motivating change (Ramsden, 1998). Leaders have the ability to build consensus around long-term goals and abstract visions and can rally individuals to the tasks necessary to achieve those goals. In the absence of well-developed leadership skills, center directors and other developers may focus on the mastery of managerial and tangible tasks at hand (running a workshop, completing budget documents, writing promotional materials for upcoming programs, conducting a classroom observation, etc.). Exceedingly long work weeks and a sense of accomplishment often result but do not compensate for an inability to achieve or even to articulate a long-term vision for the center. Leadership development can occur in a variety of ways, from mentoring relationships with senior administrators or self-study and reading, to formal training programs, such as Harvard University's Institute for Management and Leadership in Education or the American Council on Education's Leadership Conferences.

Collaborative Skills

Center directors are also uniquely positioned to collaborate with a wide variety of faculty, staff, and administrators on campus. Collaborative activities can extend the reach of the center's services while redistributing responsibility among the center staff for particular center activities. Collaborative ventures further broaden center visibility on campus while capacity-building brings new skills in among center staff professionals. A TLC can often draw diverse groups together in support of its own programing agenda and center goals. But by its very nature, a TLC has the capacity to draw diverse groups together in support of the core *institutional mission* of promoting student learning. In interacting with others to sponsor and host events that are crucial to advancing an institutional initiative or serve on a planning committee, center directors can model how to shift the agenda from narrowly focused programing to *institutional goals*. Directors can also offer a broader perspective on the institution's issues by sharing national and international resources. One example of this involved my joint planning of a Student Success Summit with Academic Affairs and the Division of Student Services. Seated together at the table as coplanners for institutional change and improvement, I brought unique expertise and perspectives at both the institutional and national level. At this level of collaboration, we were able to pool our resources to bring a nationally recognized speaker to campus and reframed our divisional concerns (for classroom success and for whole-person development) within the broader *institutional concern* about student retention. This type of collaborative effort not only disperses the workload but shifts the perspective of the center from instructional development *only* to being viewed as a partner on the institutional radar screen for matters of primary institutional importance.

Center Staff Competencies

For centers who do not have resources to fund additional staff positions, directors can creatively examine ways to capacity-build that have little or no costs associated with them. This may involve developing student internships or hiring graduate students or even work-study undergraduate student assistants. In my case, I managed to do this by utilizing our university's work-study program. I was able to hire three or four talented students each year to work in the TLC, at no cost to the program. The center benefited from the students' talents and skills, and from their ability to staff a front office that otherwise would have been closed much of the time. The students benefited from opportunities to develop new skills and gain experiences that would prove useful to their careers. For example, I hired a graphic art student to develop a logo for the center, to update the center's webpage, and to create marketing materials for our programs—all tasks I could remove from my lengthy "to-do" list. Of course, this effort to capacity-build among the student staff was not entirely "cost-neutral." I had to train and supervise the staff, but the return for my investment was well worth it.

Staff Goal Setting and Performance Evaluation

In many institutions, performance evaluations are a perfunctory activity required of directors. However, a systematic process of goal setting and performance evaluation on an annual basis is a critical way to build the capacity of center staff toward being competent to engage in institutional level initiatives. Instead of simply looking backward and evaluating performance, I encouraged staff to engage with me in mutual goal setting and used these goals as a standard against which to measure performance at the year end. In doing so, the staff had opportunities to inform me of the areas where they felt they needed to enhance their skills, and I had the opportunity to share ideas about how the center needed to grow and develop to fulfill its mission and broaden its scope to integrate involvement at the institutional level. For example, a staff member expressed a desire to learn desktop publishing, a skill that would be increasingly valuable as we ventured into more institution-wide initiatives, and we jointly set the goal for her to take training courses and develop skills in this area over the subsequent calendar year.

Teaching and learning centers that are themselves practicing continuous "learning-centered" professional development and that invest in capacity-building among all of its staff are most likely to have the flexibility and broad skill sets required to move toward intentional involvement in institutional change. Professional development in the competencies needed to fulfill an organizational development mission is essential for all center staff, as are systematic processes of goal setting and performance evaluation that guides progress toward expanding the role of faculty development.

Capacity-building Through Professional Development

All developers must devote time to develop new knowledge and skills on an ongoing basis in order to have the requisite competencies necessary to fulfill changing aspects of even a traditional instructional development role. This is even more necessary when traditional development activities are merged with institutional level involvement. Realigning center missions and units to integrate larger-scale institutional involvement entails making decisions that will ensure all staff are prepared and knowledgeable to sit at the table where larger initiatives involving teaching and learning are planned. Center directors need to be prepared to adjust workload tasks around the shifted responsibilities. Centers that are fortunate enough to have some level of staffing beyond a director clearly have capacity-building opportunities as well. In my case, I was able to hire a part-time administrative assistant after about six months as director. Immediately upon her hiring, we collaboratively set about the task of defining new knowledge and skills she needed to develop in order to fulfill her duties and to help me advance my organizational development vision. We systematically scheduled time for her to enroll in training courses and within six months, she had skills, competencies, and knowledge about the university that far exceeded many administrative assistants who had spent more than a decade on the campus. This laid the groundwork for continuous growth and development as this employee has continued to develop new skills and abilities since that initial training period. She developed competencies in the areas that complemented my weaknesses, such as in financial accounting and procurement, and thus the center operates more effectively as a whole.

Center directors may benefit from a process of self-evaluation that subsequently leads them to systematically seek out additional knowledge or skills in certain domains. The challenge of building the skills and competencies of developers while "on the job" is further complicated by the fact that many center directors are balancing multiple positions, with less than half reporting they are working full time as directors in a recent survey (Brinko et al., 2005).

Efforts to enhance faculty developers' skills can involve consultation or collaboration with other university units and professionals (i.e., financial services staff, assessment coordinators, and institutional planners), mentoring by experienced academic administrators, independent reading on selected topics, or involvement with professional organizations, such as POD, STLHE, or HERDSA (see chapter 1). The time necessary to develop this repertoire of knowledge and skills should not be underestimated.

Center Strategic Planning to Advance Institutional Involvement

Strategic planning refers to a dynamic process that defines an ideal future vision and operating plans to allow achievement of that vision over multiple years (Haines, 1995). Dozens of books outline approaches to strategic planning that are relevant to higher education (e.g., Haines, 1995; Marshall, 2007; Morrill, 2007; Ramsden, 1998). A center director must align center vision, mission, and strategic plans to institutional vision, mission, and strategic plans, and clarify center vision and mission, and define strategic directions.

Once a center director has engaged in a process to clearly articulate a vision for the faculty development program or unit, this vision should be translated into the center's strategic plan. This plan should be fully understood by all staff to guide both the director's and other staff members' decision-making and daily activities. Too often, decision-making is based on short-term goals or established professional relationships rather than on the long-term vision for the center or unit responsible for faculty development. For example, although there are many outstanding programing ideas generated by faculty and campus administrators, no TLC has the resources to act on all of these ideas without overwhelming the staff or losing site of the institution's overall vision for faculty development. The challenge becomes one of defining and communicating a clear vision of academic development and selecting only those activities that directly support that vision. When questions about new programing opportunities arise, directors and staff need to ask themselves, "Does this activity contribute to our long-term vision for faculty development?" Although the answer to this question must invariably be "no" sometimes, developers can work to "capacity-build" in others, to facilitate networking and collaboration among other campus professionals, and can serve in an advisory role rather than taking on the programing responsibilities themselves for ideas that do not fit an institutionally focused vision.

Further, it is essential that center directors and staff regularly examine their activities relative to the center's or unit's long-term strategic plans and visions. It is far too tempting to fall into the trap of focusing on short-term programing goals and finding one never has time to work on the long-term goals that relate to the vision and mission of institutional change. In order to effectively manage the workload, avoid burnout, and remain mission and vision focused, there must be an ongoing process of evaluation and decision making that compares day-to-day activities with long-term visions for institutional change.

It is critically important that all center staff members (and the rest of the campus community, for that matter) are aware of and supportive of the center's vision and how it translates into the center strategic plan. As the director communicates the center's mission and multiple roles of the center and director, an embedded understanding of the center's strategic priorities grows. The strategic plan then becomes a "lived experience," rather than a document that sits on a shelf gathering dust. This understanding then empowers center staff to enact the vision through their day-to-day decisions and activities and prepares them to prioritize accordingly. All center staff become partners in institutional change and less resistant when they are asked to develop new skills because they understand their individual role in fulfilling the center mission.

Reconceptualizing and Letting Go

For faculty developers who have been engaged in traditional center programing to meet the faculty pedagogical needs, the transition to working on larger-scale institutional change projects may require reprioritization of daily activities. Directors often have to give up involvement in and control of some of their previous activities by delegating more authority to others (i.e., other staff, faculty colleagues, student assistants, or collaborators), in order to free up time for new institutional change activities (Ramsden & Lizzio, 1998). Directors who have been particularly "hands on" in program planning and implementation may find they need to step back from intensive planning and implementation (by developing these skills in others) and assume a more administrative role in long-standing programs. In my case, I learned to spend less time providing direct support to teaching grant recipients (and found their projects were usually completed to a high degree, nevertheless). I also significantly reduced the time I spent planning the minutia of a series of technology brown bag discussions by delegating more work to a technology staff member outside the TLC, with whom I continued to collaborate.

Staffing constraints, the most cited obstacle to being involved at the institutional level in initiatives ultimately impacting teaching and learning, can begin to be countered by implementing the range of practical strategies discussed above. Academic leaders and center directors can work through the necessary decisions that will lead to developing the skills and capabilities of existing staff, dispersing workload by entering into collaborative relationships with others, and identifying and communicating the center's strategic plans among the entire center staff.

Optimizing Center Advisory Board Advocacy

What are the potential benefits of having an advisory board working with a faculty development center, particularly, in support of an institutional change vision? Advisory boards provide a mechanism for faculty involvement, ownership and buy-in to centers' institutional change vision. Surprisingly, only 33% of the TLCs surveyed currently have advisory boards (see chapter 4). Several of the case study center directors pointed out the role their advisory board played in *enabling* their involvement in broader institutional initiatives. Might other centers benefit from the addition of an advisory board?

Advisory boards function in a variety of capacities, representing a continuum of authority and engagement with TLCs. At its most basic, an advisory board can be a mechanism to serve primarily as the *voice of the faculty*, and more broadly *all instructional staff*, by providing broad input about how the campus views the teaching and learning enterprise. Center directors may solicit input on a variety of issues from the advisory board to help inform decision-making, but this type of board has no formal power or authority to set a course for the center's activities.

A somewhat more authoritative structure for an advisory board involves charging the board to formally *plan, review, and/or evaluate* the center's work. Boards that operate in this capacity assure that administratively driven perspectives on faculty development do not move forward unchecked. Instead, board members have some very real authority by influencing decisions about the future programing and emphases of the center's work. The work of the center is seen as jointly developed by the center director and the advisory board. The extent to which any specific advisory board utilizes the authority they have been given relates directly to the level of engagement of board members with the center director in the planning, review, and evaluation process.

Even when formally charged, some boards act only in reaction to calls from the center director, while others are more proactive in bringing issues and concerns to the TLC for discussion and action.

A final and most highly engaged model identifies advisory board members as *advocates* and *partners* in defining and communicating the mission of the center. Advisory board members promote the agreed-upon center vision and agenda in their home departments, academic units, and across campus, particularly, with higher administration (where the faculty body, typically have more credibility than would a center director alone). While the authority given to this board is no higher here than in the previous description, advisory board members, in this model, become full partners and collaborators with the director in defining a vision and mission and in communicating that mission and strategic plan to the campus and its administrators. In this scenario where advisory boards are both fully engaged with the TLC and empowered to take action, there is a great potential for advisory boards to act as partners in advancing involvement by the center and director in institutional change.

Given the role that advisory boards and their members can play in supporting the organizational development role of faculty development at an institution, consideration of the advisory board composition is warranted. Typically, members of advisory boards are faculty appointed by a higher level administrator with input from the center director. Sometimes advisory board members are appointed by virtue of having received an institutional teaching award or are given an honorary position on the board. Occasionally board members are elected, much like a standing faculty committee might be. Given this diversity of ways in which advisory boards can be constituted, it is important to consider what arrangements for board constitution and membership may make sense when a center is orienting itself toward the broader vision of involvement in institutional initiatives. For example, it may be advantageous to select individuals who are positively motivated toward faculty development, institutional change, or interested in the broader issues facing higher education. It may be wise to involve faculty who are more senior and influential if one is attempting to create a board to serve as advocates. Further, as a center moves toward engagement in a wider variety of institutional change projects, it is critical to consider a broader constituency when forming an advisory board. Faculty members represent an important, but no doubt, singular segment of the university's constituents. Institution-wide initiatives often dovetail with numerous units that are involved in the teaching and learning mission of the institution. Therefore, potential constituents for teaching center advisory boards may include: other academic and nonacademic administrators, students, alumni, nontenure track faculty, community members, or others with expertise in higher education or the initiatives listed in chapter 4.

Once a board has been constituted, the power of the board to serve as advocates is related to the director's ability to engage in partnership with board members and to utilize facilitation skills to help the group to arrive at a consensus regarding center vision, mission, and strategic plans. The director's work with the advisory board should parallel other work as defined throughout this chapter, in terms of capacity-building, collaborations, and strategic planning. In my case, a number of strategies worked toward engaging the advisory board as an enabling factor for my involvement in broader institutional work.

- I worked diligently to orient new board members to the TLC and its history.
- I worked closely with the board to generate discussion and options for future programing, carefully laying out the organizational change agenda I had developed.
- I listened intently to their concerns and reactions to this agenda.
- We ultimately coauthored a document that defined the center's vision for the future faculty development of the campus.
- We revised the center's mission statement.
- We engaged in systematic strategic planning toward achievement of these goals.

Lessons Learned About Staffing and Advisory Boards in Advancing Involvement in Institutional Change

This chapter has presented a perspective on optimizing staffing and working with advisory boards to promote involvement in institutional level initiatives and change. Rarely are campus efforts as straightforward and linear, or devoid of actual roadblocks as have been described here. For example, I faced challenges as a faculty member still in the tenure ranks, when having to choose between engaging in a few more hours of the important work of the center and engaging in scholarship that would lead to my personal advancement and promotion. I also dealt with the stress created by my own success— that is, demand for collaboration, additional programing, and institutional involvement grew faster than staffing, placing added stress upon all of the existing staff. Sometimes institutional subcultures clashed—there were factions within my institution who had diametrically opposed views regarding how our institution needed to respond to external pressures and change—at times it appeared that efforts to collaborate would devolve into a bitter impasse. If this occurred, I focused subcultures on the common tasks at hand using the institution's vision, mission, and strategic plan. Finally, and perhaps most universally of all of the potential roadblocks, I had to deal with an over-all resistance to change from among many administrators, faculty, and staff alike. However, despite the various and formidable roadblocks that occurred, I persevered, and the TLC has assumed today a new, more central role in institutional change. It is important to expect and even anticipate roadblocks and resistance to changing the role of the TLC on the campus. In anticipating these problems, directors can form alliances with supporters (and advisory boards) and can be better prepared to make the case for reframing faculty development in the larger context of institutional change.

Individual faculty development leaders have an important role to play in responding to demands for institutional change. Faculty developers who dare to engage in institutional change initiatives must be willing to loosen up control and delegate some responsibility for their traditional faculty development work in order to be able to successfully engage in large-scale institutional change processes. This shift in responsibilities requires a considerable attitudinal shift of center directors as much as it requires the development of new skills, knowledge, or competencies. Directors who successfully engage in institutional change initiatives must shift from a focus solely on instructional development to the larger institutional priorities. The entire center staff, under the director's leadership, must guide and balance resources and attention to the individual faculty member *and* the collective, from exclusively short-term goals for programing to include long-term goals for organizational development, from event-level planning to holistic thinking about program-planning over the course of one or more academic years, and from a reactive stance to a proactive one, where national issues in higher education inform local discussion and decisions. Directors who choose to engage institutional change agendas ultimately must strive with colleagues for discontent with the status quo and seek a state of constant restlessness and yearning for improvements in institutional outcomes. Ultimately, they must convince others of the utility of their perspective.

In the future, as in the past, a single framework for faculty development will not be appropriate for all institutions. Instead, twenty-first century educational institutions will need to make choices appropriate for their specific situations in collaboration between faculty developers, senior administrators, and other relevant constituents. Faculty developers, regardless of title or place within the organizational structure of the university, sit in a unique and sometimes precarious place between senior institutional leaders and the faculty. To the extent that faculty developers are successful in "building bridges" between these disparate campus constituencies and in generating clear, coherent, and collaborative plans for institutional change initiatives, faculty developers who are facing unprecedented pressures, and increasingly rapid rates of change will become increasingly valuable to universities.

Strategies for Optimizing Center Staffing and Advisory Boards to Promote Involvement in Institutional Change

1. Reconceptualize Center Staffing
   (a) Loosen up control over and delegate some responsibility for the traditional faculty development work in order to successfully engage in large-scale institutional change processes.
   (b) Model continuous professional development for center staff and advisory boards, and for the campus at large.
   (c) Creatively examine ways to capacity-build or fund additional staff positions with little or no costs associated with them.
   (d) Structure and engage in an active process of goal-setting and performance evaluation with center staff on an annual basis that keeps the role of involvement in institutional change embedded in this process.
   (e) Develop new skills, knowledge, or competencies needed for leadership and organizational development.
2. Develop Leadership Competencies as Director (and Center Staff)
   (a) Develop a clearly defined vision, mission, and strategic plan that emphasize engagement in institution-wide change initiatives.
   (b) Widely communicate a clearly defined vision, mission, and strategic plan on the campus that is transparent to all, rather than operate with a hidden agenda.
   (c) Make sure the clearly defined vision, mission, and strategic plan form the foundation for all capacity-building activities with staff and advisory board members, for new collaborations, for decision-making about future programing, and for fundraising and development activities.
   (d) Expect and even anticipate roadblocks and resistance to changing the role of the TLC on the campus. In anticipating these problems, directors can form alliances with supporters (and advisory boards) and can be better prepared to make the case for reframing

faculty development in the larger context of institutional change.

(e) Ensure national issues in higher education inform discussion and decisions among the center staff, advisory board and institutional level planning.

(f) Regularly engage in the process of review, reflection, and re-evaluation of center vision and mission statements, strategic plans, and work activities, to assure that the day-to-day work of the center supports the center's long-term goals. Define and communicate a clear vision of campus faculty development and select only those activities that directly support that vision. Reprioritize daily activities.

(g) Link your involvement in institutional change efforts to improving institutional effectiveness. Document your involvement and time spent in order to inform advisory boards, supervisors, and center staff. Collect data about both the use of center services and the impacts of those programs on the institution's effectiveness and financial viability.

3. Initiate Collaborations

(a) Form alliances with supporters (and advisory boards) to be better prepared to make the case for reframing faculty development in the larger context of institutional change.

(b) Actively collaborate with research and/or development office to facilitate the identification of good matches between funding sources and institutional priorities.

4. Cultivate a Well-informed and Actively Involved Advisory Board

(a) Consider a broader constituency when forming an advisory board.

(b) Orient new board members to the TLC and its history, vision, mission, and current strategic directions; work closely with the board to generate discussion.

References

Brinko, K. T., Atkins, S. S., & Miller, M. E. (2005). Looking at ourselves: The quality of life of faculty development professionals. In S. Chadwick-Blossey, & D. Reimondo Robertson (Eds.), *To improve the academy, 23, Resources for faculty, instructional and organizational development* (pp. 93–110). Bolton, MA: Anker.

Chism, N. V. (1998). The role of educational developers in institutional change: From the basement office to the front office. In M. Kaplan (Ed.), *To improve* the academy, *17*, Resources for faculty, instructional and organizational development (pp. 141–154). Stillwater, OK: New Forums Press.

Cook, C. E. (2001). The role of a teaching center in curricular reform. In D. Lieberman (Ed.), *To improve the academy, 19, Resources for faculty, instructional and organizational development* (pp. 217–231). Bolton, MA: Anker.

Diamond, R. M. (2002). Faculty, instructional, and organizational development: Options and choices. In K. H. Gillespie (Ed.), *A guide to faculty development: Practical advice, examples, and resources* (pp. 2–8). Bolton, MA: Anker.

Erickson, G. (1986). A survey of faculty development practices. In M. Svinicki, J. Kurfiss, & J. Stone (Eds.), *To improve the academy, 5, Resources for faculty, instructional and organizational development* (pp. 182–186). Stillwater, OK: New Forums Press.

Haines, S. G. (1995). *Successful strategic planning*. Menlo Park, CA: Course Technology Crisp.

Marshall, S. (Ed.), (2007). *Strategic leadership of change in higher education: What's new?* Florence, KY: Routledge.

Morrill, R. L. (2007). *Strategic leadership: Integrating strategy and leadership in colleges and universities*. Westport, CT: Praeger.

Ramsden, P. (1998). *Learning to lead in higher education*. London: Routledge.

Ramsden, P., & Lizzio, A. (1998). Learning to lead: Personal development as an academic leader. In P. Ramsden (Ed.), *Learning to lead in higher education* (pp. 227–252). London: Routledge.

Sorcinelli, M. D., Austin, A. E., Eddy, P. L., & Beach, A. L. (2006). *Creating the future of faculty development: Learning from the past, understanding the present*. Bolton, MA: Anker.

11

ALIGNING AND REVISING CENTER MISSION STATEMENTS

Connie M. Schroeder

M ost teaching and learning centers have a carefully worded mission statement *someplace*. Although perhaps rarely dusted off and reexamined, or hardly ever memorized, the center mission statement serves to articulate the center's purpose to the center, the institution, and beyond. However, rather than continually providing a basis for sorting priorities or guiding center planning, center mission statements often end up merely residing on introductory brochures and nesting inconspicuously on center websites or annual reports. The value of thoughtfully carved-out center mission statements may pale alongside the center's increasingly competing demands and myriad of programs. After all, who really reads it later on (much like a syllabus some would argue, unfortunately)? What impact does it have? This chapter will outline how center mission statements reinforce and position the TLC for involvement in institutional change and development.

The landscape of higher education has shifted significantly since many teaching and learning centers were first envisioned and created. The reach of the center and roles of the director and staff are changing from that of solely providing support, facilitation, consulting, and programs. As institutions seek transformational change and broad-scale improvements, TLCs have broadened their role to partner with, inform, and even lead broader institutional initiatives in ways not anticipated thirty and forty years ago. The typical instructional developer's role now includes bringing leadership, initiative, collaboration, and unique expertise to the table of broad-scale institutional planning. As a result, many original and traditionally worded center mission statements have become outgrown or incongruent with the current scope of teaching and learning center purposes and functions, and wider range of constituents now served. Does this incongruence matter? Have the current mission statements of centers changed as a result? How would a center mission statement reflect a broader role in institutional change? How would a mission statement read that presents the role of a developer as a multilevel change agent (see Figure 1.1, chapter 1)? If this dimension of the director's role is not clearly articulated, the potential for marginalization or diminished support during a budget crises is greatly increased. The changing role of what has been traditionally viewed as "faculty development" requires a careful review of teaching and learning center mission statements and thorough consideration of how this role is communicated.

This chapter provides a research-based analysis of 106 teaching and learning center mission statements from the survey administered to center directors (see chapter 4). Key components of these mission statements were identified by examining the content for common patterns as well as their alignment with an organizational leadership role. The questions addressed by this chapter include:

- What currently are the common themes and content areas among teaching and learning center mission statements? What unique elements of current center mission statements are worth noting?
- How do center mission statements reflect a leadership role in institutional initiatives?
- Do teaching and learning center mission statements impede or enable the center's or director's involvement in institutional initiatives?
- What are the patterns in content among the marginalized to highly involved centers in institutional teaching and learning initiatives?

A look at the organizational literature provides a backdrop for later discussion of the center mission statement findings.

Mission Statement Value

Mission statements have been discussed in the organizational development literature as serving multiple important functions, including, "the overall goal for an organization" and "the organization's vision, its shared values and beliefs, and its reason for being" (Daft, 1998, p. 48). According to Drucker (1992), the "foundation of effective leadership is thinking through the organization's mission, defining it, and establishing it clearly and visibly" (p. 121). Others have explained that mission statements also provide legitimacy to new members of an organization, may enhance performance, and can serve as an organization's guide, motivator, or unifier, (O'Gorman & Doran, 1999). Specific strategic initiatives are often linked to the broader purpose communicated by the mission statement (Abell, 1980). Not surprisingly, as interest in organizational change and strategic planning increased, organizational missions have been given greater attention. By 1994, a study of 500 U.S. managers identified mission statements as the most-used tool out of twenty-five tools (Rigby, 1994).

Unfortunately, much of the discussion in the literature is limited to descriptive accounts of mission statements or advice for the process of writing them (O'Gorman & Doran, 1999), rather than providing an analysis of their content or impact. However, Bart (1998) investigated mission statements and their relationship to the degree of organizational innovativeness. In other investigations, content analysis was used as a method of inquiry to identify mission statement content components and examine their relationship to organizational success (Bart, Tontis, & Taggar, 2001; Bolon, 2005; Fisher & Gitelson, 1983; Pearce, 1982; Pearce & David, 1987; Piercy & Morgan, 1994). Although mission statements may be viewed as anchoring an organization to its origins and founding purposes, they can actually help organizations. Bart (2000) determined they can be a tool for defining and supporting organizational change. Of particular relevance to this chapter, mission statements can eliminate confusion and uncertainty about roles and expectations, reducing role ambiguity and conflict (Bart, Tontis, & Taggar, 2001; Fisher & Gitelson, 1983).

Based on both survey and the case study data (see chapters 4 and 5), the center mission statement is an important factor in enabling involvement in institutional initiatives. Over 51% of the center directors surveyed selected center mission as one of their enabling factors. In addition, this factor was significantly related to the daily work of the director, whether or not the center's primary work focus was individual, department, or institutional development. In further analysis, the type of the director's daily work was significantly related to the level of institutional involvement (see chapter 4). These findings suggest that the congruence between the role of the center and director, the actual daily work performed, and the center mission statement is important and close attention should be paid to center mission statements in order to increase this congruence.

Therefore, based on the broader literature on mission statements and the findings from the *Coming in From the Margins* study, center mission statements play an important role in broadening the organizational role of directors and centers in institutional initiatives. Center mission statements are one step toward building the institutional perception of institutional involvement as a core dimension of centers' and directors' daily work. Directors with an intention to move from a marginalized or lower level of institutional involvement to function as highly involved institutional leaders should consider revising their mission statements in order to:

1. Provide center *legitimacy* to the center's and director's role as institutional leader and change agent for broader-scale change within the institution.
2. *Reduce role ambiguity* by providing clarity in roles and expectations within the center staff and to units with whom the center collaborates (as roles shift from solely traditional faculty development to integrate organizational development responsibilities).
3. Create or increase *alignment* between the institutional strategic plan and the center mission order to *validate and help sustain* the future of the center and its resources in tight budget times.
4. Enable centers and staff to better *handle change.* Centers with missions that embed institutional innovation and change can predict, lead, and inform change at the institutional level rather than merely follow or react to change.

Center Mission Statement Data Collection

Two questions on the Center Director Survey concerned the content and role of center mission statements (see chapter 4). One question asked directors to select which of the 10 factors listed, including their center mission statement, enabled or impeded their involvement in institutional initiatives. In the short-answer portion of the survey, directors were asked to provide their TLC mission statement. Of the 149 completed surveys, 71% (106) of the survey participants elected to provide their actual center mission statements. The center mission statements collected relied on the directors' ability to accurately recall or reproduce a copy of the actual mission statement. Most respondents pasted an electronic copy from an existing source and self-omitted the name of their institution and center, thereby maintaining their anonymity. Any center and institutional references that were included were omitted in order to protect anonymity. Of the 106 statements provided, a total of six were rejected for the sake of accuracy due to the self-admitted partial or vague recall of their center mission statement.

Center Mission Statement Analysis

Frequency analysis, significance testing, and content analysis comprised the three methods used to analyze both the open-ended and multiple-choice survey question formats.

Frequency Analysis

In one survey section, directors were asked whether or not their center mission statement, enabled or impeded their involvement in institutional initiatives. The selection of the center mission statement as an enabling factor was compared with the selection of other factors and reported as frequencies.

Significance Testing

In the survey, one question asked directors to identify their level of involvement in institutional initiatives, as defined by the study (see chapter 4). A significance test examined the relationship between the selection of mission statements as an enabling factor and their identified level of involvement in initiatives. In addition, the significance between the daily work of the center (individually, departmentally, or institutionally focused) and the selection of the center mission statement as an enabling factor was tested.

Content Analysis

As the third method of analysis, content analysis was performed on the content of all mission statements collected. The survey provided a sizeable collection when compared with key studies with smaller sampling sizes in all but one study—103, 83, 64, 44, and 18 (Bart, Tontis, & Taggar, 2001). Content analysis identified patterns in the language used and categorized the mission statements into three main components. Three center mission statement categories were identified for analysis and further comparison:

- Constituency Component (Who): Constituents of the teaching and learning center
- Purpose Component (Why): Purpose(s) of the teaching and learning center
- Goal Component (What): Actions and efforts to fulfill purpose(s)

The following discussion of the results provides evidence and examples of the link between center mission statements and involvement in institutional initiatives.

Quantitative Results

When center directors identified which of 10 factors, including their center mission statement, enabled or impeded their involvement in institutional initiatives, 51.7% of the directors selected center mission statements as an enabling factor. However, only 2.8% of the survey respondents reported that their center mission statement was a factor *impeding* their involvement. Although a significant relationship was not found between mission statements and the level of involvement ($p = .292$) directly, the focus of the daily work selected (individual, departmental, or institutional) was significantly related to the level of involvement, and the type of daily work was significantly related to center mission statements. This suggests a strong relationship between all three variables.

Qualitative Results

Content analysis of the center mission statements identified three major components for further analysis: (a) constituency, (b) purpose, and (c) goals.

Constituency Component (Who)

Each mission statement collected was analyzed to determine the constituenies that the center served (see Table 11.1). The results of the constituency analysis are reported first as frequencies, and second, with mission statement excerpts as examples. Twenty of the respondents did not name any constituency in their mission statement. Faculty was the most frequently identified *sole* constituency in 38 out of the 100 statements analyzed. Considering the historical focus of TLCs exclusively on faculty and how infrequently center mission statements are reexamined, this pattern could be anticipated. However, an additional 28 statements referred to multiple constituencies, including faculty, professors, staff, students, or educators. Therefore, nearly one-third articulated a broad constituency as part of their center mission. Together, these two constituency groups comprised two-thirds of the constituents identified (see Table 11.1).

Sixteen statements specifically described their constituency very broadly and institution-wide, for example, as culture, community, or institutional environment. However, this somewhat weak reference to the entire institution as at least a part of the center's constituency is surprising, given that the 66% of the directors reported being very or highly involved in institutional initiatives (see chapter 4). This may indicate that center mission statements, in terms of their stated constituency, have not integrated the language of institution-wide partnerships or that, despite the institutional-level

TABLE 11.1
Frequency analysis of constituency component (N = 100)

Constituent Component	Frequency	Constituency Component	Frequency
● Faculty	38	Individual Faculty/Depts./ Programs	1
● No constituency specified	20	Faculty/Staff/Administrators	1
● Faculty/Staff	7	All educators	1
● Faculty/Staff/TAs	7	Students/Academic staff	1
● Community of Peers/ Teaching community/ Learning community	7	Learning environment Departments/Faculty	1 1
● Teachers/Instructors	3	All university levels	1
● Culture	2	Students/Faculty	1
● Faculty and TAs	2	Faculty/Staff/Departments/ Programs	1
● Faculty with other educators	2	Faculty/TAs/Instructional units	1
● New professors/ Counselors/Librarians	1	Faculty/Staff/Depts./TAs/ Leaders	1

work performed, the directors do not view the entire institution as their "constituency."

However, this data pattern also reveals that 62 of the 100 statements do not identify faculty as their exclusive constituency (see Table 11.2). This data reflects migration from the earlier, but narrow, circumscription of the role teaching and learning centers play and constituents served. According to recent figures, "The number of full-time tenured and tenure-track faculty members declined from approximately one-third of the instructional staff in 1997 to just over one-quarter in 2007" (American Federation of Teachers, 2009). Just who is it that centers and developers are now serving, and shouldn't this be reflected in their center mission statement as well as in the name the field calls itself? Given that the composition of instructors at many institutions has shifted accordingly over the past several decades, the constituents served by centers of teaching and learning have changed. Institutions are relying more and more on an expanded cadre of adjunct lecturers and teaching assistants that also need "faculty development" and requiring the resources of the center. The integration of multiple constituencies into center mission statements may signal the changing mission of centers, particularly since the majority of the centers participating in the survey were less than 10 years old.

TABLE 11.2
Constituency cluster analysis (N = 100)

Constituent Component	Term Frequency	Cluster Frequency
Exclusively Faculty		**38**
Faculty and Multiple Constituents		**26**
Faculty/Staff/Administrators	1	
Faculty/Staff	7	
Faculty/Staff/TAs	7	
Students/Faculty	1	
Faculty and TAs	2	
Faculty with other educators	2	
New professors/Counselors/Librarians	1	
Individual Faculty/Depts./Programs	1	
Faculty/Staff/Departments/Programs	1	
Faculty/TAs/instructional units	1	
Faculty, Staff, Depts., TAs, Leaders/	1	
Departments/Faculty	1	
Institution-wide Constituency		**16**
Culture	2	
Community of Peers/Teaching	6	
Community/Learning Community		
Teachers/Instructors	3	
All university levels	1	
All educators	1	
Learning environment	1	
Students/Academic staff	1	
Community	1	
No Specified Constituency		**20**

Mission Statement Constituency Examples

The mission statement excerpts in Table 11.3 were categorized into four major clusters of constituents: exclusively faculty; faculty and multiple constituents; institution-wide constituents; and no specified constituency and are reported in Tables 11.1 and 11.2. Only the identification of constituencies is reported in these excerpts.

Purpose Component (Why)

Analysis of the purpose component of the center mission statements revealed even more interesting results and reflected wider variation as well as patterns of commonality. The purpose component results are discussed first as frequencies and followed by brief, interview excerpt examples. Most commonly, center

TABLE 11.3
Center mission statement constituency examples (N = 100)

Constituency Component (Who)	Frequency
Faculty Constituency (exclusively)	38
Examples:	

- ... support faculty to develop outstanding teaching skills ...
- ... support faculty members in their efforts ...
- ... help our faculty members improve student learning ...

Multiple Constituency (including faculty)	38
Examples:	

- ... dedicated to working with individuals, departments, and programs ...
- ... support the faculty, teaching assistants and instructional units ...

Institution-wide Constituency (Community/Culture/Learning Environment)	24
Examples:	

- ... to create a community of peers ...
- ... works collaboratively to create a campus community ...
- ... to foster and support a culture of ...
- ... to promote a diverse and lifelong learning environment ...

mission statements included more than one stated purpose that fit more than one category of analysis. This variation in purpose is consistent with the content analyses of mission statements within other fields, including the healthcare industry (Forehand, 2000). As most center mission statements included multiple purposes, a total of 270 purposes were identified (see Table 11.4). The two most frequently stated mission center purposes were to provide resources, expertise, and information (28) and to align with or support the institutional mission, strategic plan, or university goals (28). The next four purposes most frequently identified were teaching and learning (24); change or innovation (22); faculty (22); and programs (20). Therefore, just over 10% of the statements explicitly identified broad, institutional level purposes as part of their mission. However, given that many institutional initiatives in which directors are involved focus on teaching, learning, and academic programs, at a broader level, it is difficult to determine from the purpose component alone if the mission statements reflect this broader organizational development role. This ambiguity proves to be an important concern. Analysis of the purpose component further identifies the focus of center missions.

TABLE 11.4
Analysis of center mission statement purpose component (N = 270)

Purpose Component	Frequency	Purpose Component	Frequency
Resources; Expertise; Information	28	Community building	13
Institutional mission; Strategic plan; Alignment with mission; University goals;	28	Conversation; Dialogue	13
		Culture; Climate; Environment	12
Teaching and learning	24	Technology	12
Change; Innovation	22	Teaching; Classroom; Instruction	<12
Faculty focused	22	Professional development	<10
Programs	20	Pedagogy	<10
Learning	14	Initiatives	<10
Serving multiple educators	14	Support	<10

Purpose: Provider of Expertise

The most frequently stated center mission statement purposes focused on resources, expertise, and information. This may reflect the growing need for research-based practices at the individual instructional development level as well as the institution's concern with learning outcomes, assessment, general education reform, and retention. If the instructional development role is the sole mission of the center, the resources and expertise mentioned would likely be directed toward that purpose. However, based on the case study interviews, director knowledge and expertise is strongly supported as a primary factor enabling *organizational development*. The specific type of information and unique expertise in knowledge and skills needed are discussed more fully in chapters 5, 6, 7, and 10, and differ significantly from the instructional developer's repertoire of expertise. Center directors became well situated on the institutional radar screen if they were able to contribute, inform, collaborate, and effectively lead with expertise in relevant literature, national trends, change models, and multilevel institutional change processes.

Purpose: Instructional Development Cluster

The combined total of mission statement purposes that identified teaching or instruction, learning, or teaching and learning, totaled just over 38 out of 270. Teaching *and* learning, or simply learning, was used more frequently. It appears that work with teaching as the sole TLC purpose of learning again reflected current trends in higher education. An additional 30 or so teaching related purposes included teaching instruction/classroom (<12), pedagogy (<10), and technology (12). Combined, these instructional development purposes totaled nearly 70. An instructional focus is consistent with how developers have defined as their role since individual sabbatical and grant dispersal responsibilities gave way to instructional development. However, teaching or instruction were rarely stated as the sole purpose (<12). The language used may also reflect migration from a teaching-centered paradigm that was more prevalent when TLCs were first emerging. Many institutions have embraced a learning- or learner-centered mission. This is an important shift in higher education. Learner-centered institutional missions may open the door for broader center mission statements that extend the reach of TLCs beyond an instructional development role.

Purpose: Institution-wide Initiatives

The combined frequency of mission statements that identified broader, institution-wide purposes, innovations, change, or initiatives is nearly 85, which is congruent with the emerging broader role of the centers (see Table 11.5). Interestingly, the *combined* purposes that focus on the entire institution, culture, community, and dialogue outnumbered the resource-based purposes (28) and the the total of combined teaching and learning purposes (<48). However, when all types of identified institution-wide purposes—change and innovation (22); institutional mission, strategic plan, and university goals (28); culture, climate, and environment (12); community building (13); initiatives (<10)—are combined, they total more than the cluster of teaching and learning purposes with approximately 85. Left out of this comparison are purposes that remain ambiguous, for example, programs, dialogues and conversation, and support, since it is not possible to determine if their focus is on teaching and learning, broader initiatives, or both. This ambiguity in purpose language and meaning makes it difficult for the center's role to be fully understood or valued within the institution and easily could be clarified.

In chapter 4, the survey results reported 66% of the directors were *very involved* or *key leaders* in institutional initiatives. The broader institutional purposes identified do not reflect the degree and extent of the broader role performed by the majority of directors surveyed. The examples provided in Table 11.6 further illustrate the scope of purposes among centers.

Center Goals Component (What)

The third content component of the center mission statements identified the goals of TLCs in achieving the purposes articulated in the mission statements.

TABLE 11.5
Frequency analysis of center mission goals (N = 209)

Goals Component	Frequency	Goal Component	Frequency
Support	35	Advance	4
Provide	26	Maintain	3
Promote	26	Coordinate	3
Foster	14	Cultivate	2
Enhance	13	Disseminate	2
Encourage	13	Nurture	2
Help/Assist/Aid	12	Conduct	2
Facilitate	7	Implement	2
Offer	6	Position, Celebrate, Fulfill, Engage	1 (Total 19)
Improve	5	Extend, Conduct, Collaborate,	
Develop	5	Reform Advocate, Play a key role,	
Serve	4	Contribute, Take a leadership role,	
Create	4	Observe, Focus, Advise, Sustain,	
		Inspire, Prepare, Strengthen	

The results of the center goal component analysis are reported as frequencies for comparison (see Table 11.6). Nearly all of the mission statements used multiple goals stated as verb phrases to describe their work. This analysis resulted in identifying 209 goals as verb phrases. For example, "to support faculty" (purpose, constituency) "by providing resources" (goals), indicates support as the purpose accomplished through the goal providing of resources. Since multiple purposes were reported earlier as a separate component of mission statements, it would be likely if not necessary for center mission statements also to state a variety of goals in order to achieve their multifocused center purposes.

Support, provide, and promote were the most frequently stated goals and totaled 87 of the 209 verbs used (see Table 11.6). Although an initial scan may lead one to make distinctions between goals that indicate a stronger leadership role or active versus passive agency, the *object* of a stated goal may link the center mission to direct involvement in institutional priorities at a high level. For example, to assist, help, aid, or encourage sounds like service and on the opposite side of the change agent spectrum, but when coupled with institutional or strategic plans or advancing innovation, along with a broadly named institution-wide constituency, the organizational development role may be firmly embedded.

TABLE 11.6
Frequency and content examples of center mission statements: purpose (why)
(N = 260)

Center Purpose	Frequency
Institutional Goals, Strategic Plan, or Mission Examples:	28

- To support excellence in university instruction. To maximize the effective use of teaching resources and instructional technologies *to meet the university's academic goals and priorities.*
- To support, promote and enhance teaching, provide programs, services and information to [X] University faculty, instructors, adjuncts and teaching assistants *for the support of University strategic planning and academic initiatives . . .*
- *To fulfill the [University] mission* by working with faculty to promote . . .
- . . . *supports [University's] core mission* by promoting excellence in teaching and learning and by encouraging the creation and sharing of knowledge.

Provide Resources, Expertise, Information Examples:	28

- To position the [X] Center as central resources created for faculty . . .
- The resources and activities of the [Center] are focused both on honoring the present needs of instruction and informing the [University] community of the increasing possibilities brought by changing pedagogical theory, innovative practice, and new technologies.

Teaching and Learning Example:	24

- To support teaching and learning.
- To enhance the teaching and learning process . . .

Promote Change, Innovation, Reform Example:	22

- To keep [X] University on the cutting edge of teaching excellence and innovation, both by bringing in the best ideas and strategies for enhancing teaching and learning from the outside and by providing forums for [X] faculty to share their teaching approaches and experiments across the disciplines. . . .
- To support the campus-wide efforts to enhance and reform undergraduate education . . .

(*Continued*)

TABLE 11.6
(Continued)

Center Purpose	Frequency
Programs Example:	20

- the unit offers consultation, classroom observations, and instructional resources to faculty members. Faculty development workshops and seminars are offered . . .
- Offerings include workshops, individual consultations, mid-course student focus groups, and a collection of books, videos, articles, and tip sheets . . .

Learning Example:	14

- To help our faculty members improve student learning by developing teaching strategies to evoke active learning, critical thinking, and writing . . .
- . . . promotes greater understanding of the learning process . . .

Community Building Example:	13

- To be a physical and intellectual space devoted to excellence in teaching; to create a community of peers engaged in reflection, innovation, and improved student learning . . .

Conversation, dialogue Example:	13

- . . . to foster conversation on the art of teaching across campus.
- . . . provides a campus and national forum for examining effective and innovative teaching and learning practices.
- . . . seeks . . . to foster a collegial environment in which faculty engage in professional dialogue that will contribute to their achieving their full potential . . .

Technology Example:	12

- To support excellence in university instruction. To maximize the effective use of teaching resources and instructional technologies to meet the university's academic goals and priorities.

TABLE 11.6
(*Continued*)

Center Purpose	*Frequency*
Culture/Climate Example:	12

- To promote a culture within all of the university [X] in which excellent teaching and learning are valued . . .
- . . . serve as a focal point for efforts to enhance the development of a campus culture that prizes evidence-based teaching, diversity, educational technology, and student centered learning.
- The [X] center . . . advocates and fosters a university-wide culture of academic excellence grounded in scholarship, collaboration, and critical inquiry.

Teaching/Skills Example:	<10

- . . . is committed to providing the services, resources, and support necessary to assist faculty and academic teaching staff in their ongoing efforts to develop and refine their skills as teacher/scholars.

Promote Initiatives Example:	<10

- It promotes initiatives that improve undergraduate and graduate education . . .

Leadership Example:	<10

- . . . to foster quality teaching and learning across the university . . . we take a leadership role in addressing professional development needs . . .
- Providing leadership, advocacy, support, faculty development, and instruction services for teaching and learning excellence.

Relationship of Center Mission to Level of Institutional Involvement

Among the 75 survey respondents for whom their mission statement was a factor that enabled their institutional involvement, the majority (56) had identified their level of involvement in institutional initiatives as being *a key leader* or *very involved*. Although, a cause-and-effect relationship cannot be concluded, further content analysis compared the three components of their center mission statements with their identified level of involvement in institutional initiatives.

Center Mission Statements of Key Leader/Highly Involved Centers

The centers that identified as *key leaders* or *highly involved* in institutional initiatives more commonly named their constituents in very broad language and more often described the level of impact to include the *entire institution.* In contrast, the most common constituency among the *marginalized* centers was solely "faculty." The purpose component showed the greatest pattern of distinction between marginalized centers and those that were *key leaders* or *highly involved* in institutional initiatives and change. The center mission statement purposes of *key leaders* or *highly involved* centers included leadership, impact, innovation, change, and initiatives. These purpose statements also explicitly referred to alignment with the broader institutional mission. Very often, these purpose statements also were accompanied by highly active verbs that described the center goals (what the centers did to achieve the purposes), including "to promote, advance, initiate, or reform," and in some cases, even articulated having a "leadership role."

In comparison, centers that self-identified on the survey as *occasionally involved* or *issue dependent*, emphasized purposes that focused on instructional development solely. Developing teaching and instructional skills, and more frequently used language that reflected a supportive or helping role versus a leadership role. Among the *slightly involved* centers, the purpose component was frequently described as training, mentoring, and networking, or serving as a resource and networking center. The purpose component of *marginalized* centers (6%) focused their center purposes on providing central resources and some variation in serving or nurturing faculty. The evidence reveals a pattern of a traditional, instructional development oriented center based on its mission statement going hand-in-hand with weaker involvement at the institutional level in broader initiatives.

In summary, the centers *least* involved in institutional initiatives had center mission statement purposes that seldom described alignment with the broader institutional culture, mission, priorities, and initiatives when compared with more involved centers and their center mission statements. Centers that were *key leaders* or *highly involved* centers, more frequently used language in their purposes that mentioned the broader institution and alignment with its goals. However, overall, in terms of frequency in language, the purpose component was split between a traditional focus on resources or teaching and learning and a broader role that described alignment with the institutional mission or strategic plan, a focus on change, innovation, or reform. The least involved centers also exhibited the pattern of defining their constituency more exclusively as faculty.

Having analyzed the center mission statements collected according to the three-component categories of center purpose, constituency, and goals, a discussion of revising center mission statements follows with several exemplary center mission statements included.

Revising Center Mission Statements

Based on the literature cited earlier and evidence reviewed, a number of centers may benefit from analyzing and revising their center mission statement components. How should a center mission statement be reviewed and modified to integrate an organizational development role? When should it be revised—before the center or director undertakes involvement in significant institutional change priorities or after? What is the risk of shifting center priorities to encompass a role in institutional initiatives without revising a center mission statement? At what point should a previously marginalized center revise its mission statement? Who should be involved in contributing to the review and modification of the center mission statement?

According to Muliane (2002), it is the process of mission statement formation that provokes more debate than the content. O'Gorman & Doran (1999) found that top-level support and commitment to the mission statement are essential. Their study further reported the importance of integrating the mission statement into all operations, including the performance appraisal, and holding individuals accountable for fulfilling the mission statement. A summary of related studies reported the importance of the number and type of stakeholders involved in the mission process and better outcomes by involving stakeholders from multiple levels within the organization (Bart, 2000). In higher education as well, the mission statement should be "driven by those [who] ultimately have to live with it" (p. 13). Top-down mission statement construction has been replaced by an emphasis on an organization-wide process. For example, the results of an investigation on mission statement processes determined that attention to being "creative" and "flexible" impacted the process positively whereas "top-down/autocratic" approaches resulted in a negative impact (Bart, p. 7). Bart (2000) concluded that involving multiple stakeholder levels and cultivating a process that encourages creativity and flexibility may sacrifice simplicity, but eventually produces a more effective statement. Bart further argues that the process should not try to impose a rigid timetable, as is often the case with linear planning efforts. However, the statement should be considered final when broad agreement has been reached (Bart, 2000). Once developed, the mission statement was communicated most successfully in these contexts through word of mouth and posters or plaques followed by internal documents and newsletters (p. 9).

Clearly, TLCs intent on revising their mission statements should devise a plan for involving multiple levels of the administration and the constituents served. For example, one director pointed out the important role of the center advisory board in the revision process. "So, the advisory board that works with me and I have recently made a change . . . to a more active kind of role (Case study E).

Changing center mission statements to reflect the emerging role of developers in institutional initiatives may risk becoming perceived as an arm of the administration, no longer neutral, or not a safe place. Several directors and supervisors interviewed expressed a desire to avoid any suspicion among faculty of serving at the whim or agenda of the "suspect administration." Interestingly, some directors and their supervisors articulated reluctance in directly referring to their role as a "change agent," even though they fully identified as such. One case study preferred instead to be considered more of an "undercover change agent" (Case study G). Given this reluctance or a particular set of conditions at an institution or center, an explicit organizational role may be important to avoid. However, the fears of centers being viewed as "suspect" or no longer neutral have not been validated by evidence. Negative consequences of bringing center mission statements into congruence with an organizational dimension of this work or aligned with the planning of institutional initiatives has not been supported with evidence. Rather than limit the center mission statement in an effort to maintain faculty trust, the TLC can make explicit their continued focus on faculty while serving other purposes (and constituents) that broadly advance teaching and learning initiatives. For example, centers can continue to cultivate faculty trust through targeted programs, faculty learning communities and teaching academies, advisory boards and faculty fellows, or other center staffing options that encourage faculty to define their own directions of innovation and interest while also meeting their needs and cultivating their voice in center activities.

Furthermore, centers need to consider how integrated and pervasive their organizational role should become before revising the center mission statement. Are centers ready to be evaluated on their involvement in institutional initiatives and held accountable for success in this aspect of their role and mission? Are the center staff prepared with the necessary knowledge and skills to be successful at involvement in institutional change initiatives and is the center prepared to adapt to the necessary change in the distribution of tasks? How would involvement in institutional initiatives be measured or evaluated as a center goal? How should position statements be written to embrace both instructional and organizational development? Finally, centers, supervisors, and directors need to consider why they may be maintaining a center mission statement that does not reflect a sizeable portion of their broader level investment in institutional change, the constituents they actually serve, and the goals and purposes that help advance the priorities of the institution.

Exemplary Center Mission Statements

Several exemplary mission statements included broad constituencies, explicit leadership roles, and instructional purposes, and actively stated center goals that clearly conveyed multiple dimensions of the TLC role (see Table 11.7).

TABLE 11.7
Exemplary mission statements

Exemplary Model Statement A [underlining added]

The mission of the [Center] is to: <u>offer</u> opportunities to instructors for professional development in teaching to <u>enable</u> student learning; <u>play a key role</u> in creating a <u>campus culture</u> that values and rewards teaching; <u>advance</u> new teaching and learning initiatives; <u>foster</u> collegial dialogue within and among faculty; <u>serve</u> as a <u>convener</u> to showcase faculty expertise in teaching; <u>address</u> the needs and interests of the <u>entire academic community</u> in support of the education of students.

Exemplary Model Statement B

The mission of the Center [X] is to <u>support, promote, and enhance</u> teaching, learning and research, and <u>foster innovation</u>. To achieve this mission [center] will <u>provide</u> programs, services and information to [X] University <u>faculty, instructors, adjuncts, and teaching</u> assistants for the <u>support of University</u> <u>strategic planning and academic initiatives</u>; development of a comprehensive and coherent faculty development program; <u>Promotion</u> of scholarship of teaching by <u>engaging</u> faculty in self-reflection, analysis, and sharing of their successful teaching practices with their peers across disciplines . . .

Exemplary Model Statement C

<u>Support</u> the instructional improvement efforts of the University's teaching community . . . <u>facilitate</u> the implementation of programs and activities that enrich and improve teaching and learning . . . <u>promote</u> active engagement and innovation in teaching and learning . . . <u>cultivate an institutional climate</u> that values, rewards, sustains and renews excellence in teaching and learning . . . <u>act as a source</u> of information and research on teaching and learning in higher education.

In each of the exemplary statements, the three components—TLC constituency, purpose, and goals for achieving the stated purpose(s)—uniquely convey a broader constituency, purposes that includes institutional involvement and alignment, and center goals that integrate multiple dimensions of faculty, instructional, and organizational development.

For example, center purposes in Exemplary Model Statement A include teaching, learning, education, and creating a campus culture. This center's mission includes a nod to an organizational development role by including to "advance new teaching and learning initiatives." The goals for achieving these purposes utilize a range of less active to highly active verbs, including: to offer, enable, play a key role, advance, serve, foster, and address. In addition, Statement A identified a broader constituency than faculty alone, including instructors, faculty, and the academic community.

Exemplary Model Statement B actually refers to multiple constituents and states purposes that support, promote, and enhance teaching, research, and innovation. Statement C avoids a narrower instructional focus by referring to teaching and learning in general, although somewhat ambiguously, and highlights the unique expertise of the center staff who cultivate an institutional climate and who act "as a source of information and research on teaching and learning in higher education." Most of the language that reflects a redefined organizational development role in each of the three components is subtle and simply broadens the reach of the center to intersect with the broader initiatives important to the institution.

The centers that have positioned themselves "at the table" and are walking the talk of *organizational development* as redefined in chapter 1, are functioning as organizational change agents—a redefinition of organizational development for developers at this juncture in higher education. Far from producing cookie-cutter mission statements, these center statement mission models retain their unique institutional flavor while reflecting the emerging role of institutional involvement that is clearly merged with the existing instructional development dimension of this work.

Conclusion

In summary, center mission statements provide an opportunity to communicate the multiple purposes, broader constituencies, and organizational level goals of the teaching and learning center. The organizational role of the director can be situated easily within a center mission statement that defines and legitimizes organizational development as an important dimension of the center's daily work.

Since center mission statements are closely linked to the daily work of the center, center leadership, center vision, and alignment with the institutional mission and strategic plan, congruency is essential among all of these aspects of the center. The three-center mission statement content components—purpose, constituency, and goals—provide opportunity to reflect more than the instructional development dimension of this work. The leadership role of the center and director in institutional initiatives and involvement in multiple levels of institutional transformation can coexist within one well-worded center mission statement. The mission statement examples and exemplary models provided evidence that both the instructional development role and the role of change agent can reside within a statement through careful selection of language that addresses all three components with an organizational role. The evidence reported that the language of *key leader* and *highly involved* centers statements differed consistently from the *marginalized* or less involved centers. These results should further encourage centers to review their existing mission statements and have fruitful discussion around the three main components.

It is important to note that the mission statement language does not cause the center or director to become involved as an institutional change agent, nor does it ensure that the campus context recognizes or values this broader purpose. The center mission statement, however, is an important starting point for expanding and legitimizing this role and articulating the broader vision of the center. Particularly important, as both institutional and center leadership may change over time, a broadly stated center mission can anchor the broader role of the director and center during institutional leadership changes and the future planning of budgets or initiatives.

Despite the key finding that the majority of the centers (66%) spend a significant amount of time involved in institutional initiatives, mission statements reflect this emerging role but have not kept pace with the extent of this role change. Based on the literature cited earlier, this incongruity may lead to an anticipated increase in role ambiguity, role conflict, and uncertainty for centers and their directors. This too, was evidenced among the case study directors interviewed (see chapter 5).

Director role conflict and role ambiguity due to the expanding involvement in institutional initiatives were reported by the case study directors already functioning as *key leaders* or *highly involved in institutional initiatives* (see chapter 5). This data suggests the expanded role of the director is producing some workload strain, difficult choices, and differences in expectations along the reporting line. These day-to-day strains can signal that it is time to revise the center mission statement if it no longer matches the multiple roles of the director and center. These growing indications of ambiguity in how center staff see themselves and are seen by others within the institution, although challenging, are typical in the context of changing paradigms and should bring the role of mission statements to the forefront for closer attention.

Center directors and reporting line supervisors need to ask whether or not the work of the center and director is congruous with the roles, expectations, and needs of the institution and the center's mission. Center directors, supervisors, and academic leaders need to collaborate on the most effective application of these findings to redefine the role of developers at each institution. Only then can the conversation among multiple stakeholders take on the task of reformulating the center mission statement to ensure congruence between center mission and practice. This congruity will help create legitimacy and greater clarity in expectations while enabling the center's involvement in institutional initiatives. Center mission statements are a starting point for redefining the work of developers to include instructional, organizational, and faculty development. The recommendations that follow are included as a guide for the collaborative process of reviewing and revising center mission statements.

Strategies and Recommendations

The following center and institution specific questions may serve as touchstones for further dialogue among directors, administrators, advisory boards, and provosts regarding the purpose, constituencies, and goals of TLCs:

In your existing center mission statement (or newly created statement):

1. Scope of Purpose and Level of Alignment
   (a) What purpose(s) of your center are evident?
   (b) Do these purposes reflect what your institution charges your center to do?
   (c) Do these purposes reflect the scope of the work you would like to perform?
   (d) What specific activities, roles, or services are/are not identified?
   (e) How active or passive is the language used to convey these purposes? Is there a stronger way to describe this?
   (f) Toward what level(s) of impact is your center mission statement (individual, department/school, institution) aimed?
   (g) What does your teaching and learning center's mission statement say about its role(s) in the institution? What is its institutional purpose?

    (h) How does your mission statement impact (or limit) what the institution expects from you? How well does this align with the institutional mission?

    (i) How does your budget reflect the center mission purposes?

    (j) How does your daily work reflect the center mission statement purposes? How do center position descriptions align with the mission statement?

    (k) How does your annual report and center assessment reflect the purpose(s) as stated in the center mission statement? Are they congruent?

2. Scope of Constituents

    (a) Which constituents are named in your center mission statement (or should be named)?

    (b) Does this reflect who you serve or interact with (or will serve)? Have you tracked who you serve and can you document this?

    (c) For *each* of the purposes stated, who are your constituencies? Who is left out?

    (d) How are collaborative partnerships and the institution included in your statement as constituents?

    (e) What are the risks and benefits in naming your constituents differently?

    (f) Who does the center serve based on the center mission statement?

3. Scope of Goals and Level of Alignment

    (a) How does the language of the stated goals reflect your alignment with the institution, culture, and community?

    (b) More importantly, what does your mission statement define as the center's role in aligning with the broader institutional mission and key institutional initiatives?

    (c) How might your currently stated mission statement constituencies, purposes, and goals contribute to the marginalization of your center from the institution's mission and priorities? How might your center mission support and advance the center's or director's leadership role in teaching and learning at multiple levels within the institution?

Process of Center Mission Statement Revision

The process of revision should entail a period of data collection, communicating the changed mission, and initiating the implementation of the mission statement. Prepare for the process of revision by first doing considerable homework and gathering information to lay an informed foundation for change.

1. Data Collection
   (a) Discuss at length the revision and the purpose of revising it with your supervisor and advisory board or council and identify the potential resistance and implications at this level and beyond.
   (b) What model center mission statements from like institutions can you provide?
   (c) Collect a log of your daily time spent and summarize the levels of your work for the advisory board and your supervisor.
   (d) Analyze the center budget for expenditures related to involvement with broader initiatives.
   (e) Collect institutional data regarding your actual constituents and the number of TAs, lecturers, and staff that are instructors and their access to your center functions.
   (f) Who might be the most resistant to a change in the center mission or statement?
2. Initiating and Enacting the Change
   (a) Who will you involve in the revision of the center mission statement? Who does your supervisor recommend that you contact?
   (b) How will you create a flexible, creative, and broadly inclusive process of revision?
3. Communicating the Broader Center Mission
   (a) How will you communicate this broader role for the center and its importance in the mission statement revision?
   (b) How do you describe what you do when colleagues ask or when you introduce yourself in committees, to new faculty at orientations, or on your website and how might you need to change this?
   (c) How will the center's broader level of involvement institutional change initiatives be recognized in annual evaluations and reports of the center's accomplishments?

References

Abel, D. F. (1980). *Defining the business: The starting point of strategic planning.* Englewood Cliffs, NJ: Prentice-Hall.

American Federation of Teachers. (2009). *American Academic: The state of the higher education workforce 1997–2007.* Washington, DC. American Federation of Teachers.

Bart, C. K. (1998). A comparison of mission statements and their rationales in innovative and non-innovative firms. *International Journal of Technology Management*, *16*(12–3), 64–77.

Bart, C. K. (2000). Missions statements in Canadian not-for-profit hospitals: Does process matter? *Health Care Management Review*, Retrieved December 5, 2006, from http://proquest.umi.com/pqdweb?did=53323394&sid4&Fmt=3&clientid=1507&RQT=309&Vname=PQD

Bart, C., Tontis, N., & Taggar, S. (2001). A model of the impact of mission statements on firm performance. *Management Decision*, *39*(1), 19. Retrieved December 5, 2006, from http://proquest.umi.com/pqdweb?did=1159232568&sid4&Fmt=3&clientid=1507&RQT=309&Vname=PQD

Bolon, D. S. (2005, Fall). Comparing mission statement content in for-profit and not-for-profit hospitals: Does mission really matter? *Hospital Topics*, *83*(4), 2–8.

Daft, R. (1998). *Organization theory and design.* Cincinnati, OH: International Thomson Publishing.

Drucker, P. (1992). *Managing for the future: The 1990s and beyond*. New York: Truman Talley.

Fisher, C. D., & Gitelson, R. (1983). A meta-analysis of the correlates of role conflict and ambiguity. *Journal of Applied Psychology*, *2*, 320–333.

Forehand, A. (2000). Mission and organizational performance in the healthcare industry. *Journal of Healthcare Management*, *45*(4), 367–377.

Muliane, J. (2002). The mission statement is a strategic tool: When used properly. *Management Decisions*, *40*(5/6), 448–455.

O'Gorman, C., & Doran, R. (October, 1999). Mission statements in small and medium-sized businesses. *Journal of Small Business Management*, *37*(4), 59.

Pearce, J. (Spring, 1982). The company mission as strategic tool. *Sloan Management Review*, *23*(3), 15–24.

Pearce, J., & David, F. (1987). Corporate mission statements: The bottom line. *Executive*, *1*, 109–116.

Piercy, F., & Morgan, N. (1994). Mission analysis: An operational approach. *Journal of General Management*, *19*, 1–19.

Rigby, D. K. (September, October, 1994). Managing the management tools. *Planning Review*, 20–24.

12

EMBEDDING CENTERS IN INSTITUTIONAL STRATEGIC PLANNING

Connie M. Schroeder

Revolutionary in the 1980s (Keller, 1983; Steeples, 1988), strategic planning has become a common planned-change strategy at many, if not all, universities (Dooris, Kelley, & Trainer, 2004; Kotler & Murphy, 1981; Rolfe 2003; Rowland, 2002; Shattock, 2002). Vandament (1989) defines strategic planning as "an active process by which an institution . . . combats the normal drift in the strong currents of the status quo and gains control of its own destiny" (p. 29). A strategic plan functions in similar ways at most institutions in that it determines the priorities, where resources will be directed, and how it will achieve its goals (Daft, 1998). As one of many planned change strategies, strategic planning processes are used to identify goals and outline steps to achieve them. Most often, "upper management" determines the strategic priorities and develops policies that are passed down to middle management. Midmanagers commonly identify departments and managers to delegate responsibility for the tactical planning. These "first-line managers" implement the actual plan or "how to accomplish specific tasks with available resources" (Kinicki & Williams, 2006, p. 146). However, despite the increased focus on strategic planning over the past decades, studies have produced uneven results regarding the effectiveness of strategic planning. These results have led to questions concerning how effective strategic planning efforts are in accomplishing goals and implementing change (Mintzberg, 1994).

Not surprising, goals, vision, mission, and strategic planning may be terms vaguely familiar to center directors. Depending on their disciplinary or professional background, many have come from faculty ranks where their exposure to management has been the academic department. Although they may have served as a department chair or dean, they may have little or no background in management strategies and techniques that have infiltrated higher education in the current climate of improvement. Not necessarily versed in the particulars of organizational knowledge or key definitions of vision, mission, and strategic planning, directors often begin and continue their roles while learning from experience and experienced colleagues. However, evidence from the case study interviews revealed strategic planning involvement as one of the most important aspects of becoming an organizational change agent. Therefore, developing knowledge and skill in strategic planning is a pivotal area to focus ongoing professional development.

Although vision, mission, and strategic planning are interconnected, they are distinct. Levin (2000) neatly distinguished vision from strategy. Strategy, he points out, "is the path that an organization chooses to pursue its future, while vision should describe a future in which goals and strategy are being successfully achieved in lock step with the organization's guiding philosophy and values" (p. 95).

Strategic Planning as a Primary Enabling Factor

Involvement in the institutional strategic plan was discussed by directors and their supervisors as involving two important aspects: as an important *process* of planning in which directors were involved, as well as a key *document* in which centers were embedded directly. Being at the planning table at some level during which institutional initiatives are discussed happened quite frequently among the case study directors. Additionally, embedding the TLC in the strategic planning *document* continuously linked the center to institutional priorities and initiatives, and therefore served as an essential center-based factor. Both aspects of strategic planning were proven essential in enabling an organizational role in key institutional initiatives. Therefore, strategic planning is discussed in this chapter both as director and as center-based factors that enabled directors to establish higher levels of involvement in institutional initiatives. Rather than an overview or introduction to strategic planning, this chapter examines the evidence of and strategies for embedding the center and director in both the institution's strategic planning process and strategic planning document.

Evidence of Strategic Planning Process Involvement

Five of the eight case study directors discussed their involvement in the institutional strategic planning process and how this impacted their leadership role. As is the case with all of the center and director-based factors, this enabling factor requires action on the part of the director in order to exert its impact on the level of involvement in institutional change. The factors are not existing entities waiting to be hijacked into duty as enablers. In fact, they most always needed to be created and initiated on the part of the directors. An organizational role did not emerge from passively waiting to be invited to play a more central institutional role. Involvement in both the strategic planning process and being embedded in the strategic planning document requires the director's intentional efforts and actions. Three examples from the interviews that follow will illustrate how the directors gained access to this important "table" and how involvement in institutional strategic planning enhanced the director's role in institutional change.

Accessing the institutional strategic planning process is critical in order to elevate the role that the center and director will play in larger initiatives that ultimately dovetail with teaching and learning. Most institutional priorities are outlined in the strategic initiatives, and gaining a seat at this planning table gives directors a heads up in terms of what is on the institutional radar screen and provides ongoing information on the strategic directions as they are being planned. In turn, their presence creates opportunities to provide valuable expertise and leadership skills to the planning team. The supervisor may be the sole advocate for appointing the center director as a member or chair of a strategic initiative committee or subcommittee, based on the director's expertise. The supervisor's help with accessing this planning process should be discussed often.

When a center director has functioned outside the strategic planning process, it may seem impossible to gain entry. Institutional planning habits, expectations, and norms become "the way it is done," and the culture may dictate a process that appears inflexible and insistent on hierarchy versus collaboration. If access to the planning process is not available, the director should maintain in-depth knowledge of the planning process through reading publicly posted minutes on the academic affairs website or conversation with his or her supervisor. In order to become a key player in broader issues of teaching and learning beyond the instructional development level, knowledge of and involvement in the framing of the institutional priorities and strategies are essential. In some institutions, the planning process may involve numerous steps and multiple smaller committees. Connection and involvement with these subcommittees are essential as is evidenced in the following three examples.

Example 1. (Case Study B)

The supervisor of one case study director (small, liberal arts institution) fully supported the role of the center in strategic initiatives and strategic planning:

> We do have a center for teaching and learning that I helped to develop as part of our last strategic planning effort.... My role in the strategic planning process was to design and direct it.... We are now thinking about the next generation of the center since it has been through one review cycle, and so the questions on the table are currently involving its relationship to assessment of student learning outcomes, and to what degree the center could be expanded to include more of the technological presence ... the college is gearing up for another strategic planning phase, and there may be things that come out of that that do belong to the mission of the center for teaching and learning. (Case Study B)

In discussing the role the director would play in future strategic planning committees, the director's supervisor admitted:

> Well, I would imagine the center director will be a member of any strategic planning committees that are developed out of the next initiative.... I could see in the next strategic planning process that, if the institution wants to expand its commitment to global education, then one role of the center might be to help us look at the pedagogy in bringing global perspectives into the classroom.... If we are wanting to transform the curriculum and be more intentionally global, at least in the general education program, then we see the center playing an important role in helping us develop the language [and] learning outcomes. (Case Study B)

From these comments, it is apparent that the founder and immediate supervisor of the center held similar views of the center's role in institutional level strategic planning.

Getting onto the institutional radar screen rather than hovering at the institutional margins clearly was due to the constellation of many factors that the directors identified, such as vision, mission, and knowledge of change processes interacting in a dynamic way (see chapters 4, 5, 8, 9, 11, and 13). One of the most powerful and sustaining factors that enabled both the center and director to function with greater involvement at the institutional level was being involved in the institutional strategic planning process for these broad level initiatives. This involvement entails the director being at the table, in some form, whether it is being a member on the smaller subcommittee, leading a task force, or serving on the strategic planning committee itself. This often required volunteering, initiating access, or being appointed. Institutional leaders may appoint the director, or the center director's supervisor may place the director into the planning process.

Once seated at this planning table, or a subcommittee of the strategic planning group, the director learns more about the institutional culture, emerging priorities and leadership styles, and key initiatives when they first become designated as priorities from the top-down. However, if absent from these levels of involvement in the strategic planning processes, the director often hears of the initiatives much later and, as a reactionary response, makes effort to align programing and resources accordingly. Reactionary efforts by the center and director are appropriate and critical in order to remain aligned with the institutional priorities. However, involvement at the strategic planning table (and/or subcommittee and task force tables) situates the center and director in the process of initiative formation, delegation, research, data gathering, and collaboration in a proactive manner.

It is at these strategic planning tables that the unique expertise of developers should be made available to help shape or influence the issues closest to student learning and teaching. The director may have opportunity to provide resources, expertise, skills, knowledge, and data regarding campus events, comparable models, strategies at other institutions, and national initiatives underway, or bring pertinent research to bear on the issue at hand. In one case study that follows, the director was invited to bring his knowledge, expertise, and writing skills to the table in developing the strategic planning document.

Example 2 (Case Study H)

I was a part of that group and also one of the authors of the report, the person whose job is to draft the teaching and learning and curriculum section of that report. But it is likely to be a major kind of statement for the university to set the strategic directions to us.

I think also the closer we get to strategic conversations the more I want to be working with the faculty so we are collaboratively cultivating a mission of where we should be going. I want the Center for New Directions in Learning and Scholarship (CNDLS) to be an important strategic and intellectual dimension. (Case Study H)

Another director provided a consultative role in preparation for the strategic planning process.

Example 3 (Case Study F)

> He [chancellor] really used us, kind of, as a think tank with him to help
> lay the groundwork for the strategic learning plan, and even calling it a
> "strategic learning plan" was huge for us as opposed to the "comprehensive
> development plan" or something where the executives did it.

The case study directors' organizational development and leadership skills,
in addition to her or his instructional development skills, became more widely
known and valued at this level of planning. These highly visible efforts enabled
the director's involvement in initiatives to be accepted and even perceived as
the norm, and helped shift the way others saw the director's and center's
role. In each of the case studies identified above, involvement in the planning
of strategic initiatives evolved into additional invitations, appointments, or
opportunities for continued involvement at the institutional level, thereby
working as a factor that further enabled additional, broader-level involvement.

Gateway to Large Institutional Initiatives and Change

Five of the eight case study directors discussed their involvement in the institutional strategic planning process and the role this played in enabling
their role in broader initiatives. Through strategic planning involvement, the
role change from solely instructional developer to organizational developer
evolved in the context of planning the very initiatives in which the TLC would
likely be involved eventually through instructional development efforts. This
mutual reinforcement of two dimensions of the director's role was described
repeatedly by directors as advantageous to both roles. In chapter 6, Catherine
E. Frerichs and colleagues describe a multiyear, institution-wide liberal education initiative planned by a collaborative leadership team. Initiating this
institutional change simultaneously moved the center and the director to the
core of the institutional agenda *through* the advancement of the initiative.
Similarly, Phyllis Blumberg, in chapter 7, expanded her role as organizational
change agent within the larger institutional agenda with her leadership and involvement in several tactical planning level groups while also maintaining her
instructional development role. Susan Gano-Phillips described advancing her
organizational development role through involvement with general education
reform in chapter 10. Institutional perceptions of the center and director were
altered by acting in the role of institutional change agent.

For these case study center directors, involvement in key initiatives and
the planning of institutional change through strategic planning processes
established this organizational dimension of their role in a very visible manner

among key institutional leaders. The following two examples from the case study interviews make evident both the role of the TLC director and director's supervisor in situating the center within the strategic planning process and document. The chapter will conclude with a series of recommendations and strategies for advancing the director's involvement in the strategic planning process and integrating the TLC within the institutional strategic planning document.

Example 1: (Case Study D)

Phyllis Blumberg, University of the Sciences, Philadelphia

Student-centered Learning Strategic Initiative

During the 2001–2002 school year, administrators identified six strategic imperatives, which include to develop a culture of student-centered learning and living and to direct the university's planning. The Tactical Planning Group on Student-Centered Learning and Living defined objectives, developed future action steps, and outlined outcome indicators. As the director of the Teaching and Learning Center, I was an *appointed member* of this tactical planning group, and I served as their key educator/informant and resource. The academic's side translated the strategic imperative of student-centered learning and living into learning-centered teaching and [the] student affair's side translated it into learning-centered students. When we made strategic plans regarding who would do what and where it would happen, I was picked for doing it.

This director's supervisor confirmed the director's key involvement:

> The TLC was a very, very key player in the last round of strategic planning or . . . the tactical planning groups that came with the strategic planning. So, that is where we got this student-centered learning and living. That was one-fifth of the new initiatives. Then she cochaired that committee. So she had a lot of input on that one. (Case Study D)

Example 2: (Case Study E)

This director's role in the strategic planning process entailed significant leadership for one of the subcommittees.

> I think it was a 30-person committee that was charged with doing [the] strategic planning process and I chaired one of the subcommittees. . . . I honestly think that this was the first time in our institution's strategic planning history that administrators actually thought the teaching and learning center should probably be there.

The director's supervisor commented that the director has been more involved in larger-scale projects, such as strategic planning and general education reform. The director and center's role as an organizational developer and leader within the institution's change initiatives had become embraced by the president of the college.

> One of the things that the chancellor really pushes [in] the strategic plan was student centeredness and [he] sees the teaching/learning [center] as really a way to get faculty to understand the importance of students and how important it is to focus on students in the teaching process, etc. (Case study E)

Embedding Centers Within the Strategic Plan Document

Some centers originated out of their institution's strategic planning process, nesting the original design and mission of the center from the start within the strategic planning process and document at that time. Embedding the TLC into the strategic process from its very inception provides the *opportunity* for the center to maintain continual mention and integration in the future strategic plan documents. Being embedded explicitly in the institution's strategic planning document was a prominent factor enabling the case study directors to position and sustain their involvement at the core of institutional priorities. For example, in one case, the strategic plan itself had been renamed the Strategic Learning Plan, bringing learning into the core language of the strategic plan. With this shift in language, "the center was positioned within the new strategic plan" (Case study F).

However, the obvious connections between the TLC and institutional strategic planning are often missed opportunities because of how narrowly centers have defined themselves. If TLC work is cast exclusively at the individual level (see chapter 1, Figure 1.1) or primarily as instructional development, it may never be obvious to include the TLC in discussions and planning of broader institutional initiatives. Being caught up in the enormous load of day-to-day consultations, programing, and services is necessary, but no director can afford to be unaware of their institution's strategic plan and the key priorities as stated in the actual strategic planning document. Neither can they afford to have their work and expertise defined only in terms of course development.

It is important to nurture and maintain clear connection to the institution's strategic priorities in the center's own strategic planning goals and objectives, mission, and daily work. Additionally, annual center reports are a potential point of connection between the institution's strategic planning process and documents and the center. Whenever possible, the center should name which strategic planning document and item or page is reflected in its center planning, budget, and annual center reports, and make an effort to use the language that communicates the institutional priorities and objectives. This internal congruence between the TLC language in all its documents and its institutional planning documents that advance change, is critical. Directors who have not read the institutions' strategic planning documents are at a significant disadvantage when trying to ramp up their role in broader-level planning. Very often, the center's supervisor may have to position the center within the planning document and continually advocate for the language that embeds the center within these initiatives. These recommendations leave little room to rely simply on an implicit understanding of the role of the center, especially when institutional leadership changes—one of the primary impeding factors noted by directors.

Conclusion

Being on the fringes, marginalized, or off of the institutional radar screen very often go hand-in-hand with being absent in the institutional strategic planning document and uninvolved in the institutional planning process. Whether this absence on institutional level committees and planning efforts is a sign of the administration's or institution's limited view of the center and director's role is uncertain, but it may be an important red flag. It may be best to choose selectively which larger-scale planning groups would benefit most from center and director involvement. Likewise, it is important to be aware of how this involvement benefits the center by increasing understanding of the organizational development role of the center and director. The director and supervisor must consider which strategic planning initiatives and committees align best with the center vision and mission and how the center vision and mission are stated to reflect an ongoing role in strategic initiatives (see chapter 8 and 11). Once involved in the strategic planning *process*, the relationship is reciprocal, in that the director and center benefit from early access to the key initiatives that are being planned, and the planning group benefits from unique knowledge and expertise that the developer brings to the table. Ultimately, the institution gains from bringing more stakeholders to the table in order to advance change.

Strategies and Recommendations

1. Research the Center Origins
   (a) Locate the origins of the center within any strategic planning documents. Determine if the existing mission of the center reflects

      the originally intended vision and mission that created the center. When there is discrepancy, investigate how this occurred.

2. Align and Embed Center
   (a) Embed the center into the strategic planning documents on matters broadly related to teaching and learning and instructional development, specifically. Analyze key institutional initiatives for their intersection with teaching and learning matters in the broadest and narrowest sense.

3. Volunteer Committee Involvement
   (a) Volunteer or ask to be appointed to the strategic planning committee or subcommittees.

4. Stay Informed
   (a) Request updates and notes or minutes, if appropriate, of strategic planning committee meetings through the supervisor if the director is not on committees.

5. Create Language Alignment
   (a) Align language of the center strategic plan with institutional strategic initiatives.
   (b) Ensure that the center website reflects partnerships, collaborations, or involvement with institutional strategic plans and key initiatives.

6. Acquire Knowledge/Expertise
   (a) Maintain a literature base on institutional key initiatives outlined in the strategic plan.
   (b) Identify trends in higher education regarding strategic initiatives and collect exemplary institutional models.
   (c) Know the national associations geared toward strategic initiatives and upcoming conferences.
   (d) Research strategies, successful roles, and approaches of TLCs involved in these issues.
   (e) Seek additional professional development at conferences on these issues; read articles and books; forward relevant materials to supervisor, committees, and task forces.

References

Daft, R. (1998). *Organization theory and design* (6th ed.). Cincinnati, OH: Southwestern College Publishing.

Dooris, M. J., Kelley, J. M., & Trainer, F. (2004). Strategic planning in higher education. *New Directions for Institutional Research, 123,* 5–11.

Keller, G. (1983). *Academic strategy: The management revolution in higher education.* Baltimore, MD: Johns Hopkins University Press.

Kinicki, A., & Williams, B. (2006). *Management: A practical introduction.* Boston: McGraw Hill/Irwin.

Kotler, P., & Murphy, P. (1981). Strategic planning for higher education. *Journal of Higher Education, 52*(5), 470–489.

Levin, I. M. (2000). Vision revisited. *The Journal of Applied Behavioral Science, 36* (1), 91–107.

Mintzberg, H. (1994). *The rise and fall of strategic planning.* New York: Free Press.

Rolfe, H. (2003). University strategy in an age of uncertainty: The effect of higher education funding on old and new universities. *Higher Education Quarterly, 57*(1), 24–47.

Rowland, S. (2002). Overcoming fragmentation in professional life: The challenge for academic development. *Higher Education Quarterly, 56* (1), 52–64.

Shattock, M. (2002). Re-balancing modern concepts of university governance. *Higher Education Quarterly, 56* (3), 235–244.

Steeples, D. W. (1988). *Successful strategic planning: Case studies.* New Directions in Higher Education No. 63. San Francisco: Jossey-Bass.

Vandament, W. E. (1989). *Managing money in higher education.* San Francisco: Jossey-Bass.

PART FOUR

NEXT STEPS

13

RECENTERING WITHIN THE WEB OF INSTITUTIONAL LEADERSHIP

Connie M. Schroeder

T
he evidence presented in this book confirms an increasing institutional leadership role for developers. The voices and models of directors and leaders in the field as well as numerous practical recommendations provide enough understanding for systematically integrating this role into "faculty development." Conceptualizing an organizational development dimension of the field has become increasingly important considering the critical issues higher education institutions are facing. Similar to the transformation of early "faculty development" to become instructionally focused development due to dramatic shifts in higher education, this field cannot afford to neglect the inescapable need for ongoing involvement in institution-wide change processes.

Higher education may not change quickly, nevertheless, it is changing and we are not in Kansas anymore. This field of educational or faculty development has yet to come to terms collectively with the current landscape of higher education. The scope of institutional changes needed and underway are complex and are both broad and deep, many of which result in institutional initiatives that are now bringing new people to the table. In the past few decades, the expansion of the instructional development dimension of this field has taxed developers to their limits in order to keep up with the paradigm shifts in teaching and learning and widespread growth of assessment and technology. That work will continue to expand and demand more as faculty retire and there is less resistance to innovation, active learning, and assessment. There is little leftover time to catch one's breath and consider where this field is headed or needs to go.

If this field is to be forward thinking and proactive in appraising the current climate of institutional change, the organizational role of developers could not be more needed. It prevails upon the field to define itself in areas left murky, step up to the calling for expertise and leadership, and integrate core roles into new expectations of developers. It is in this climate of change and greater need for collaborative leadership and problem solving that traditional "faculty development" needs to gather itself and address the current landscape in higher education. Developers have sat in the institutional blind spot for too long, surfacing only when obvious instructional development gaps have required filling.

Professional organizations, such as the Professional and Organizational Development Network (POD) and the *International Journal of Academic Developers* (IJAD) have been discussing ways to identify the missing "O" in POD and define a broader role through articles, conference themes, and presentations (Gillespie, Gardiner, Lee, & Tiberius, 2007; Schroeder, 2007). The earliest framework for this field (Gaff, 1975) included ideas of both faculty and organizational development, but the vision and language were situated in a particular time and place. Although an initial and somewhat temporary alignment with the formal field of organizational development became weaker and less defined as the field solidified, an organizational role for developers remains a critical dimension that warrants being reexamined and defined based on what is currently happening. This book provides an invitation to step back and critically examine the history, current conditions, and future directions possible for the role of developers in order to transform along with higher education.

However, despite our best efforts, some will believe this additional role will diminish the work and role of current centers and directors and devalues instructional or faculty-focused development. Contrarily, it is a call to collectively integrate the type of institutional change work already being done as the recognized third dimension of this role using existing models and evidence to map this emerging terrain.

Characteristics of Development Work in Relation to Change

The developer's organizational and leadership role is consuming significant time and making important contributions to the process and outcomes of institutional change. This is a significant change and yet it is barely talked about. How is it that this field is so active regarding instructional design change and so passive regarding changing its own field? I suspect that it is less about outright resistance and more about the following widespread characteristics of our field that are relevant to advancing this role change:

1. **We value variety.** We value variety to the detriment of our field. Anyone and any type of center can do this work in just about any way imaginable. We have patted ourselves on the back too much for having many formats for centers and types of director roles. We use inclusivity and the culture of the institution too often to explain great divergence in this field and the professionals in it. Some place between a confining one-size-fits-all and loosely defined all-things-to-all-types lies a definition of this field with an established set of expected skills and competencies that could be relied upon by institutions, and thereby, bring greater credibility to the field.

2. **We are busy.** We *are* overwhelmed and understaffed. This seems like a catch-22. How do we do more with the same resources? In a number of cases, if not all, this broader role eventually resulted in staffing strains as well as in bringing more funds, staffing, grants, or resources to the center. Sometimes the center director had to initiate seeking the expanded resources; involve the advisory board and supervisor extensively; and track expenditures, time spent, and staff needs in order to accommodate the new organizational development responsibilities.

3. **We are afraid.** We are afraid of drawing too much attention to ourselves. We are afraid of being held accountable for something we were not trained to do. We are afraid of the added workload stress, of change, and of doing it differently. We like what we do and do well. Do not steal our cheese!! I think we should be more afraid of the marginalization of centers, of the closing of centers, and of appearing peripheral to the major priorities of the institution.

4. **We don't like it.** We fully embrace the work we already do and derive great satisfaction and intangible but palpable reward from working at the individual change and instructional development level. Most instructional development contacts involve people seeking change, expertise, and help. The payoffs are far more immediate and measurable than with longer range institutional change. Some may hate the idea of more meetings and task forces that never seem to do anything. Given the organizational resistance to change, identify the initiatives that have momentum and leaders that you admire and make connections.

One instructor told me, "Ride the horse that is already saddled." Sidle up to the saddle that looks most interesting and get on board.

5. **We underestimate what we do.** We do not toot our own horns often or easily. Some prefer working behind the scenes just off of the institutional radar screen and are content on the fringes. The contributions developers make to planning teams for large-scale initiatives are either small nudges here and there by providing timely literature, models, resources, and recommendations or they are significant but become buried in the many incremental changes performed by multiple hands on deck. Given the collaborative nature of institutional change initiatives, the impact of the expertise lended is less direct and noticeable. Although less immediate and rarely recognized, the work of a change agent over time is no less influential than that of work with individual instructors and their courses. However, making this dimension of development work more explicit may seem to be taking credit for what had been dismissed as an extra meeting or two developers need to document efforts at broader level involvement and include these contributions in center reports, evaluations, and notes to supervisors. It takes time to acquire the lens to see these incremental efforts as *organizational development* and noteworthy.

6. **We may underestimate this role because what we *have* brought to the table really is not significant.** Perhaps a number of developers are not prepared to link broad-scale institutional initiatives to national conversations, provide relevant literature, and investigate other relevant models for initiatives. Being seated at the institutional initiative planning table might be uncomfortable if one does not have a clue about how to bring change in this broader context and knows little about organizational change, national trends, or the initiatives being planned. It is not a given that a developer is competent to be involved in institutional planned change, at least at this point. In addition to being underprepared for this role, a negative attitude toward changing and expanding the developer's role may be evident by not being prepared for meetings, forgetting to read the minutes or do the work in between meetings, and seldom volunteering to be involved. Those who dread committee and task force meetings, hoping they will end quickly in order to get back to the *real* work of the center may not recognize the organizational dimension of their role and their potential contribution. It is not impossible to ramp up one's knowledge of the institution, national trends, and higher education literature.

Developers can create a professional development plan for increasing their organizational development skill set and discuss it with their supervisor.

Toward a Grounded Theory of Processual Role Transformation

The directors all demonstrated a proactive approach to creating and managing conditions that would enable their organizational role to emerge and be sustained. This constant vigilance toward managing the complexity of a multilevel role was central to successfully leaving the fringes of the university, moving to the center, and staying there. In other words, the right factors or conditions and role change did not come *to* the directors and TLCs! How would a director then use the results of the study to venture into broader involvement at the institutional level? How could a director committed to engaging in institutional change initiatives make sense of and actually use the results of the study to become a multilevel change agent? To answer this final question, I approached the results with the intent to make the study's findings more practical and transferrable.

Chronological Time Line Models of Linear Change

During analysis of the interview data, I had reconstructed a time line of key events concerning the director, their role and the TLC, institutional initiatives, and identified the timing of primary factors that occurred within the context of their unique institutional change processes. I provided the time line to each interviewee for confirmation of events. Mapping the process of this role transformation for each director onto a chronological time line situated the factors and role change progress within the perspective of a linear time frame. At that point, I merely used the timelines to examine how fast or slow the role transformation took place and to get a sense of how long the institutional change initiatives took in which directors were invested. I proceeded with the content analysis of the interview transcripts and comparison with the quantitative results (see chapters 4 and 5).

As directors set about to construct this dimension of their role, it seemed plausible to identify some factors more important to focus on as preliminary steps toward involvement or as preparation for involvement, others factors as better cultivated and essential when acting as an institutional change agent, and still other factors as more likely during an advanced stage in developing this role. I clustered the factors into a sequence of three stages—preliminary, implementation, and advanced—into which I placed the three categories of factors—director-, center-, and institution-based. At first glance, and to some extent, this staging could prove helpful (see Figure 13.1) and might serve to prioritize events.

Although I documented the significant dates accurately for each TLC and director, and produced a detailed time line of events that identified when key factors were impacting their role, I soon realized the manner in which the organizational role transformation occurred was not reflected in a linear time line of events. This provided one perspective or lens for viewing the factors, but did it really describe the process of developing this role? Although the directors and their supervisors clearly demonstrated intentionality in raising the level of their visibility and involvement, the role change process was not simply a series of steps that controlled the final transformation. For example, some factors were easier to initiate and cultivate while others were outside of the director's control. Although the key events, such as the opening of the center, hiring of a director, and commencing of an institutional initiative or task force, could be recorded and placed precisely on a time line, the role itself did not function in similar linear, sequential, or staged manner. How then might the process of role change be analyzed and portrayed?

Processual Models of Dynamic Change

Several theoretical frameworks draw attention specifically to the process of change, known as *processual change*, and the dynamic nature of interaction between an environment, the individual, and the actions taken to evoke change. In the past, a number of change studies have focused on the product of change, satisfaction with and effectiveness of change, measurement of change, organizational variables, structures, and contexts (Baldridge & Birnham, 1975; Haige & Aiken, 1967; Hefferlin, 1969; Lindquist, 1978), as well as individual characteristics. In contrast, processual frameworks look at the manner in which the change occurs (Kozma, 1985). For example, Bandura's (1977) social learning theory describes how behavior factors and environmental factors "all operate in interlocking determinants of each other" (p. 10). His work prompts consideration of how "both people and their environment are reciprocal determinants of each other" and how both "select, organize, and transform the stimuli that impinge upon them" (Bandura, 1977, p. vii). According to Bandura (1977), "Behavior partly creates the environment and the environment influences the behavior in a reciprocal fashion" (p. 203). Bandura (1989) and others (Davis, Strand, Alexander, & Hussain 1982; Pettigrew 1985), provide alternative theoretical foundations for understanding the reciprocal

FIGURE 13.1
Attempted staging of enabling factors for developer role change

Stages of Change Agent Role Implementation	Director-based	Center-based	Institution-based
Preliminary Change Agent Steps	• Envision role • Discuss with supervisor	• Discuss with center staffing, reprioritize	
Implementation Change Agent Steps	• Select and initiate committee involvement • Build and expand relationships and collaborations • Build expertise, knowledge, skills • Expand knowledge of institutional culture, governance systems • Examine institutional strategic plan • Explore grant funding • Develop regular contact with faculty and institutional leaders • Develop knowledge of national initiatives • Develop knowledge of higher education literature in alignment with strategic plan • Expand knowledge of change process/models in higher education	• Examine center mission • Align programing with institutional mission • Involve center advisory board • Cohost institution-wide dialogues	• Cultivate support from center founder and upper-level institutional support
Advanced Implementation Steps	• Build partnerships • Align center and institutional initiatives with national associations	• Embed center in institutional strategic plan and planning process • Explore new institutional structures and positions for the TLC and this work	

and dynamic nature of how the developer's role was transformed in a complex process rather than as a staged, linear progression.

Processual change advocates strongly argue that organizational members can, in fact, change the context, roles, and organization (Dawson, 1997, 2003; Pettigrew, 1985; Wilson, 1992). Social learning theory emphasizes that the organizational context is itself a complex set of interactions rather than an "ad hoc back drop" (Bandura 1977, p. 37) and a dynamic potential versus a "fixed property" (Bandura, 1977, p. 195). The reciprocity in action among factors can be explained by Heider's (1958) suggestion that there are times when the environmental factors in change exercise powerful constraints on behavior and other times when personal factors dictate the environmental events (i.e., director vision or expertise). For example, when translated into higher education, environmental events such as a new provost or new in-stitutional mission mobilizes a host of other factors, and the personal traits, values, expertise, or vision of a university president or dean may set in motion or constrain other factors. In doing so, "the individual and the organization play approximately coequal roles as they interact with one another to produce the final product . . . innovation is shaped by the interaction of the individ-ual and the organization" (Davis et al., 1982, p. 584). This was exactly the case, confirmed by the directors and supervisors, who readily identified envi-ronmental (institution-based), individual (director-based), and organizational (center-based) factors interacting at all times.

Therefore, based on the analysis of the data collected for this book, the role change toward integrating instructional and organizational development seems best and more deeply understood as a "process in which context comes to be involved in the production of action . . . aspects of context are mobilized or activated by actors and groups as they seek to obtain outcomes important to them" (Pettigrew, 1985, p. 37), not as a series of steps or stages. After reviewing the processual change literature, it was apparent that the director-, center-, and institution-based factors could not be approached as merely a list of factors to be achieved and checked off. In other words, the factors did not line up in a linear progression with one factor following another. The variables and details of each context were too great and too much in motion. One could conclude that it is an impenetrable experience defying descripton, or delve further for gaining some understanding.

Further analysis brought me closer to revealing how this role forms and is enacted, and the *contingent* nature of the way enabling factors interacted with one another to further enable directors to enact this role. As TLC directors constructed an organizational development role, one might imagine multiple seeds being planted and watered at different times, fireworks going off in different intensities at different times, and dominoes toppling over a sequence of other dominoes. One action on the part of the center director (or supervisor) triggered another enabling factor that was *contingent* on that factor coming in to being while other factors took on a life of their own once set in motion and "mobilized" by both actors and contexts.

This dynamic nature of the developer's role fits well with the kinds of interactive and interconnective images and metaphors the directors used to describe their OD role and the TLC's involvement in institutional change (see chapter 8). For example, case study H spoke of his center as a hub, layering levels of involvement and empowering pockets of innovation all through the institution. Similarly, Hall, Harding, and Ramsden (2001) describe an institutional change project in which the educational developers facilitated an interdependent network and effected "links between policy, culture, and support" (p. 157) that allowed sites to innovate.

Using processual change and social learning theory frameworks for describing this role change may be frustrating for those that prefer obtaining a list of steps to take in a specific order to effect change. However, based on the evidence, that type of role change process does not describe what took place among the case study directors and will not lead to the type of sustained, dynamic, and interactive role these directors created.

The Process of Coming in From the Margins: Toward a Grounded Theory

Based on the evidence I collected and analyzed, and the wide range of literature I investigated to better understand this role, coming in from the margins for TLCs and developers is a *processual* change process for both the center and director. I reexamined the data for evidence of the process, dynamic interactions, and reciprocal actions. With the processual theoretical frameworks guiding me, I constructed the theoretical groundwork for this process of role change by first identifying ten common themes or characteristics that described the process of seeking and achieving the many factors that will enable an organizational role and arranged descriptors into two clusters. The first five descriptive words, Cluster A, clarify the way we can think about this role and conceptualize the answer to—what is it like? The second five characteristics, Cluster B, provide five words to better understand how to operationalize this role.

Cluster A: Conceptualizing. What is this organizational role like?

- *Intentional*
- *Dynamic*
- *Integrated*
- *Distinct*
- *Contingent*

Cluster B: Operationalizing. How is this role enacted and sustained?

- *Congruent*
- *Aligned*
- *Scaffolded*
- *Flexible*
- *Collaborative*

Cluster A: Conceptualizing. What is this organizational role like? How should we think about this role?

1. **Intentional:** The factors that enable this role are created, carved out, and the result of *intentional* decision making on the part of the center director and the director's supervisor. Center mission statement revision, center staffing adjustments, collaborative relationships, knowledge of national initiatives, and investigation of relevant research and literature, all happened because the center director and supervisor chose to take specific and intentional action. The consistent exceptions to this intentionality are the antecedent conditions, most often the institution-based factors, that existed prior to the director's efforts to develop an institutional leadership role, and are largely outside of the director's control and often long-lasing. Occasionally, center- and director-based factors were preexisting, as in staffing limitations, center mission, and so forth, but they are changeable and not fixed conditions. **The organizational dimension of a developer's role continually unfolded as directors made new factors clame into play, and was reinvented or constrained by alchemy of intentionality and serendipity.**

2. **Dynamic:** The factors are dynamic in that they ebb and flow, influence one another, trigger other enabling factors, counter impeding factors as they arise, and stimulate other impeding factors. Cultivating this role is an *intentional* and *dynamic* dance of institution-, director-, and

center-based factors in motion that spins and percolates, bursting in pockets of energy and momentum that fizzles, simmers, or retreats to fermenting "petri dishes" (Case Study B). Managing the dynamic factors that enable this role, while intentional, is not a linear process and amounts to keeping lots of balls in the air at once or irons in many fires that unexpectedly change shape along the way.

3. **Integrated:** Embarking on this role change is a process of *integrating* multiple dimensions of the developers' role. The developers' instructional development role is not eliminated. The expertise acquired for instructional development work feeds and informs the organizational dimension, and similarly, organizational involvement raises the effectiveness of the instructional development efforts of the director and center. The reciprocal nature of each dimension, when integrated, underscores the need to avoid dividing this role into separate units and creating more silos, but rather, challenges this field to find ways to redirect and integrate the work, merging instructional and organizational development as never before.

4. **Distinct:** The process of integrating multiple dimensions of the developer's role must happen while maintaining distinctions within the role. The organizational development dimension challenges centers to identify the skills and expertise *distinct* to this broader role and claim this role as part of this field by incorporating it into position descriptions, evaluations, reports, and mission statements. The day-to-day blurring of the roles signal successful integration but could erode the intentionality or distinctions of the role itself, rendering it invisible and void of value. **Its distinctiveness needs to exist alongside of its integration, without sacrificing the benefits of either.**

5. **Contingent:** We all know that titles singularly do not make the role happen. It is in the messy, moment-to-moment acts that are *contingent* on the act just prior—the planned and surprise acts—that evoke this role to its fullest sense. We grow into the title and create, as much as acquire, the role. So too, the role of the institutional change agent is one that developers transform and that transforms the developers over time into multilevel change agents. Directors who had initially viewed their centers as marginalized (Case Study A), demonstrated an active role in intentionally creating the center- and director-based factors in order to change the environment. Another case study director was able to initiate and build a center that was significantly involved in the strategic directions of the institution. This director was committed to this role change by cultivating a wide range of director- and

center-based factors repeatedly and consistently over five brief years (Case Study H). The extent and pace of role change would not have happened using a staged, linear model and attempting to follow pre-scribed steps in order. Much of the opportunities to advance the role of the TLC and director were both planned and unplanned, often seized and maximized, contingent on one unexpected door opening, and opportunity triggered by another factor. Successfully involved di-rectors interacted dynamically with their environment to advance an organizational development role and recognized these opportunities.

Cluster B: Operationalizing. How is this role enacted and sustained?

6. **Congruent:** The way the role is lived must be *congruent* with the center and director's resources, capacities, and resources or such variables as potential limitations must be changed. Greater congruency can be achieved through professional development of the director and center staff (see chapter 10), discussions with supervisors, securing grants (see chapter 6), and collaborating (see chapters 6, 7, and 10). To avoid severe workload constraint and role identity confusion, the extent of the role integration should not advance beyond the constraints of these variables, or the credibility is likely to diminish as both instructional developers and organizational developers.

7. **Aligned:** Closely related, the redefined developer's role must become *aligned* with the center's documents, including the center mission statement and strategic plan, as well as the institution's strategic plan-ning documents. This ensures that the role is sustained beyond indi-vidual director, supervisor, or administrative leadership and personal-ity, as well as changing institutional or reporting line leadership.

8. **Scaffolded:** Organizational development, as reenvisioned in this book, is done through *scaffolding* actions, much the way course assignments are redesigned in smaller increments that build toward higher learn-ing. Small decisions, conversations, e-mail exchanges, articles located, and collaboration with other developer colleagues, all contribute to developing this role over and over again. It is never "developed" and never done. It is not one heroic grand gesture, but rather, a series of opportunities seized and created through a mindset that enacts the role of instructional, faculty, and organizational development at the same time. Developers assert that assignments and assessments cannot be "added-on" effectively by creating a separate and parallel universe, similarly then, this role cannot thrive as a once in a while *other* activity

one does outside of instructional development. Occasionally, the level of opportunity for institutional involvement may be large and the responsibility nearly consuming.

9. **Flexible:** Certainly, a *flexible* stance is necessary when performing any multidimensional role. How often does an instructor shift a research task for a student who walks in, e-mails, or paper that needs more feedback, or an article that needs revision? How often will the developer stay late to prepare for a consultation the next day because a meeting about broader-level change ran over? At some point, the tradeoffs are too much, but the point is, the maximum limits usually have to be reached (and surpassed) before resources are brought to bear on it. This in turn may require the staff to be flexible in order for the roles to be integrated over time. The integration of instructional and organizational development in some forms may continue for a considerable length of time. It is important to avoid territorialism, rigid ownership of tasks, and a step back to envision how best to achieve the work needing to be done.

10. **Collaborative:** Finally, directors and supervisors reported an enormous need to *build relationships, partnerships, and collaboration* over time in order to do this role effectively. The formal committee work, informal conversations after meetings, staying in touch with faculty and institutional leaders, and initiating contact are part of the organizational developer's role. Just as faculty development or instructional development cannot be done well without knowing faculty, organizational development cannot be practiced effectively without getting out there and knowing the organization, its leaders, structures, history, and pulse. Colleagues in Australia encourage developers to form "influential partnerships at all levels within the institution" (Fraser, 2006, p. 6) and to initiate the conversations that are critical for fundamental curricular change. To this end, they encourage evolution from a one-way model in which developers transmit expert knowledge to that of "partnerships that are ongoing . . . and critically reflective . . . throughout all levels of the institution" (Fraser, 2006, p. 14).

These descriptive words, far more than a linear progression from preliminary to advanced stages, further provide the groundwork for explaining the nature of how developers, as institutional change agents, transform their instructional development role into multidimensional change agents. Circumstances and variables, some under the director's control and others not, can be evoked and constructed in such a way that a director, armed with knowledge of this role change and the primary factors that enable it, can leverage opportunities to enact their involvement, moving far from the fringes of the institution. In effect, directors, along with their supervisors, embark on an intentional *process* of role change.

A Web of Leadership

The changes facing higher education call for leadership that draws on the expertise of many, creates many tables of planning, and convenes expertise that crosses traditional boundaries and silos within institutions. The hierarchical structures and governing bodies play an important role and will continue providing and approving policies and enacting mandates for change. However, the deep commitment, hard work, and analysis required at each institution to carve out effective change initiatives call for leadership of the many seated around real or virtual tables for problem solving and planning. How these multiple tables and collaborative circles of expertise are assembled and who is at them is of great importance. Earlier models of individuals as an organizational change agent have been expanded to include a group, or change sponsors, having power and influence as well as vision (Lick & Kaufman, 2000).

Coming in from the margins is not an allusion, or illusion, for that matter, that all issues of institutional importance revolve around one center or the assumption that faculty development need only crawl to the center and catch its breath there. Although the university may seem to have a purely hierarchical structure with one top leader, in fact, there are multiple centers and hubs of decision makers—fluid webs that convene temporarily and wield great influence—and porous structures that shift and move with events and memberships that change. TLCs must constantly recenter themselves with the priorities and demands in constant flux around them and within multiple institutional centers of decision making.

This conceptualizing of leadership in institutions is occurring as complex problems are not getting solved with top-down plans. Leaders are becoming frustrated with meetings that produce talk but no change and with plans that never become fully implemented. Bensimon and Neuman (1993); Kezar, Carducci, and Contreras-McGavin (2006); and others have pointed higher education toward new models of leading and new ways of collaborating and making change happen. Helgesen (1995) discusses power that is maintained not by control and top-down models but "influence and maintained by communication" (p. 6). Involving more of the university community in identifying issues, brainstorming solutions, and creating shared visions embodies a new structure, a web of inclusion, that is circular rather than pyramidal and in which connections bind the web in coherence (Helgesen, 1995). These models of leadership, as they are adapted more and more into higher education, create the type of organizational development landscape in which many can participate and improve the whole. It is imperative that the leaders of what is still termed *faculty development* prepare developers to move within these circular webs of change as leaders and change agents.

The conditions are ripe for faculty development to expand its role collectively and to stake a claim in helping institutions transform. With such wide variation among centers and director responsibilities, one could imagine this period in faculty development as a "liminal" stage (Czarniawska & Mazza, 2003; Tempest, 2009; Turner, 1967; Turner & Turner, 1978; Van Gennep, 1977). In such a stage, roles are no longer what they were, and in the liminal space, "novel configurations of ideas and relations may arise" (Turner, 1967, p. 97). For example, the ambiguity of the liminal space is demonstrated by confusion of roles. Similarly, developers are no longer primarily instructional developers but uncertain and ambivalent about stepping through the threshold of organizational development and leadership roles. This "betwixt and between" stage of faculty development brings with it the opportunity for play or for experimentation with new ideas, structures, entities, and behaviors.

This can be seen in the wide variation in position descriptions for center directors that describe very traditional, instructional development roles to those positioned well within the institutional radar screen. For example, center director position descriptions currently list a range of qualifications and experiences required, but rarely mention organizational change process knowledge. Most often, this list entails expertise that is appropriate for instructional development as well as the administrative role of center director. Occasionally, the description reads with a nod to a broader role, one that incorporates leadership and involvement in the institution's initiatives surrounding teaching and learning. When listed, this set of knowledge and skills makes evident the expanded role of the developer by emphasizing expertise in institution-wide collaboration, initiation and planning of broad initiatives, and facilitating and leading implementation of initiatives. In position descriptions that combine instructional and organizational development, the knowledge and facilitation of organizational change processes appears integrated in the role and alongside instructional development–oriented expertise. For example, in position descriptions on the POD Network Listserve between January 2008 and January 2010 (September 17, 2008; electronic mailing list message. Retrieved from http://www.podnetwork.org/listserv.htm), several director or newly designed positions and titles indicated involvement in institutional initiatives and broad-level leadership and contained the following excerpts:

> Senior Advisor on Teaching and Learning to the Office of the Provost . . . you will support the development of a vision and an implementation strategy that works toward greater synergy among teaching and learning initiatives distributed across UBC Vancouver . . . experience **collaborating with multiple stakeholders and 6) an awareness of issues facing higher education today** . . . a commitment to **provide innovative leadership** in instructional and faculty development. Successful candidates will have an earned Ph.D. and experience in **innovative curricular initiatives** and can provide evidence of an ability to build collaborative relationships with faculty, staff, and campus constituents . . . the Director will create a culture of teaching, respond to individual faculty members for development of teaching skills, advance innovation and new initiatives in the curriculum (including the use of technology to enhance learning), and **act as an institutional change agent**.

With small but careful changes such as these to an instructional development–focused position, the expectation of a leader involved in institutional change initiatives begins to emerge. The directors looking to begin or expand upon this role need to consider carefully the implications for themselves and the center staff. After reading this book, it should be impossible to make such a significant change with complete naïveté. The paths to this role have been carved out in this book and lifted up for discussion as a field. The strategies and recommendations at the end of each chapter can guide the new and seasoned developer toward successful integration of this broader role.

One could argue that all of higher education is in the middle stage of a rite of passage—in a liminal state, passing between the traditional model of delivery of knowledge to active learning-centered teaching and assessment. Culture, policies, structures, and practices are being realigned to transition higher education across the current threshold.

Sorcinelli, Austin, Eddy, and Beach (2006) have coined this faculty development period as the *Age of the Network* and affirm that institutions "will require a collaborative effort among all stakeholders in higher education" (p. 5). They predict that the "future offers more opportunities for faculty development than ever before" (p. 158). They explain,

> The opportunity for faculty development to contribute to the broader success of institutions has never been greater, and we envision that faculty development efforts will become associated even more clearly than at the present with institutional commitment to excellence and quality. (p. 158)

The opportunity is here and conditions may be ripe for this role, but as Sorcinelli and colleagues (2006) reported,

> Faculty developers are highly influenced by the needs of individual faculty members and considerably less influenced by the departmental and college needs, or by the critical needs and strategic goals defined by their institutions. (p. 169).

This then, is the question: Will faculty development remain where it is, with some at the periphery, with some centers closing, and others at the core of the institution, or will it step up to confront the indications of new institutional leadership models, the need for collaborative expertise, and enlist their expertise as change agents, collectively? The missing dimension of this role is being enacted by active leaders, who are creating the organizational dimension of this role. As subjects, they are not only impacted by their environment and the factors within it. They are impacted by the factors they create impediments for themselves as well. As Bandura (1977) explains, "Subjects . . . are at least partial architects of their own destinies . . ." rather than "pawns of external influences." (p. 206). As subjects, they are not only impacted by their environment and the factors within it. They are impacted by the factors they create. Subjects can create impediments for themselves as well.

Will this field once again embrace the challenges facing higher education that signal a paradigmatic role change for developers and become architects of their role? Or, will it resist new structures, titles, and professional development that could dramatically change the status quo—content with the niche it has created and sustained for several decades?

References

Baldridge, J., & Birnham, R. (1975). Organizational innovation: Individual, organizational, and environmental impacts. *Administrative Science Quarterly, 20*, 165–176.

Bandura, A. (1977). *Social learning theory.* Englewood Cliffs, NJ: Prentice Hall.

Bensimon, E., & Neuman, A. (1993). *Redesigning collegiate leadership: Teams and teamwork in higher education.* Baltimore: Johns Hopkins University Press.

Czarniawska, B., & Mazza, C. (2003). Consulting as a liminal space. *Human Relations, 56*(3), 267–290.

Davis, R. H., Strand, R., Alexander, L. T., & Hussain, M. N. (1982). The impact of organizational and innovation variables on institutional innovation in higher education. *Journal of Higher Education, 53*(5), 568–586.

Dawson, P. (1997). Beyond conventional change models: A processual perspective. *Asia Pacific Journal of Human Resources, 34*(2), 57–70.

Dawson, P. (2003). *Reshaping change: A processual perspective.* Routledge.

Fraser, S. P. (2006, May). Shaping the university curriculum through partnerships and critical conversations. *International Journal for Academic Development, 11*(1), 5–17.

Gaff, J. (1975). *Toward faculty renewal: Advances in faculty instructional and organizational development.* San Francisco: Jossey-Bass.

Gillespie, K., Gardiner, L., Lee, V., & Tiberius, R. (2007, October). *The "O" in POD: Organizational development–retrospective and new perspectives.* Presentation at the annual POD Network Conference. Pittsburgh, PA.

Haige, J., & Aiken, M. (1967). Program change and organizational properties: A comparative analysis. *The American Journal of Sociology, 72*(5), 503–519.

Hall, R., Harding, D., & Ramsden, C. (2001). Priming institutional change through effective project management: A case study of the Chic project. *The International Journal for Academic Development, 6*(2), 152–161.

Hefferlin, J. (1969). *Dynamics of academic reform.* San Francisco: Jossey-Bass.

Heider, F. (1958). *The psychology of interpersonal relations.* New York: John Wiley & Sons.

Helgesen, S. (1995). *The web of inclusion.* New York: Paulist Press.

Kezar, A., Carducci, R., & Contreras-McGavin, M. (2006). Rethinking the "L" word in higher education: The revolution in research on leadership. In K. Ward, & L. Wolf-Wendel (Eds.), *ASHE Higher Education Report: 31*(6). San Francisco: Wiley Periodicals.

Kozma, R. (1985, May/June). A grounded theory of instructional innovation in higher education. *Journal of Higher Education, 56*(3), 300–319.

Lick, D. W., & Kaufman, R. (2000). Change creation: The rest of the planning story. In J. V. Boettcher, M. M. Doyle, & R. W. Jensen (Eds.), *Technology-driven change: Principles to practice* (pp. 25–38). Ann Arbor, MI: Society for College and University Planning.

Lindquist, J. (1978). *Planned change.* New York: Harcourt, Brace, and Co., Inc.

Patternson, J. (2004). Organisational learning and leadership: On metaphor, meaning making, liminality and intercultural communication. *Organization Studies, 25*(4), 507–527.

Pettigrew, A. (1989). *The awakening giant.* Oxford: Basil Blackwell, Ltd.

Schroeder, C. (2007, January). Countering SoTL marginalization: A model for integrating SoTL with Institutional Initiatives. *International Journal for the Scholarship of Teaching and Learning, 1*(1). Retrieved from http://www.georgiasouthern.edu/ijsotl

Sorcinelli, M., Austin, A. E., Eddy, P. L., & Beach, A. L. (2006). *Creating the future of faculty development: Learning from the past, understanding the present.* Bolton, MA: Anker.

Tempest, S. (2009). The effects of liminality on individual and organizational learning. *International Journal of Learning and Change, 3*(4), 382–393.

Turner, V. (1967). *Betwixt and between: The liminal period in rites de passage Ithaca.* New York: Cornell University Press.

Turner, V., & Turner, E. (1978). *Image and pilgrimmage in the Christian Culture: Anthropological perspectives.* Oxford: Columbia University Press.

Van Gennep, A. (1977). *The rites of passage.* Translated by M.B. Vizedom & J. G. Chaffee. London: Routledge.

Wilson, D. C. (1992). *A strategy of change: Concepts and controversies in the management of change.* London: Routledge.

ABOUT THE AUTHOR AND CONTRIBUTORS

Phyllis Blumberg is director of the Teaching and Learning Center at the University of the Sciences in Philadelphia and a professor in the departments of Social and Behavioral Sciences and Mathematics, Physics and Statistics. Dr. Blumberg has developed a model for teaching learner-centered teaching that was published in the book, *Developing Learner-Centered Teaching: A Practical Guide for Faculty* (Jossey-Bass, 2009). Her recent projects include developing a series of rubrics for faculty to evaluate their teaching and research on problem-based learning. She holds a PhD in educational psychology from the University of Pittsburgh (1976). At the University of the Sciences, she has worked to create a culture where excellent teaching is valued and teaching practices and concerns are shared. More than two-thirds of the faculty attend at least one Teaching and Learning Center event annually and about one-third of the faculty are present at these events and programs. Under Phyllis's direction, many faculty members are beginning to do SoTL and present at educational conferences.

Catherine E. Frerichs is professor of writing at Grand Valley State University in Allendale, Michigan. She has 30 years of experience in faculty development, including serving as director of the Pew Faculty Teaching and Learning Center at Grand Valley from 1997 to 2009. Prior to that, she taught English and did administrative work at Albion College, serving as associate provost and founding and directing a women's center. Besides her work in faculty development, she has published in composition studies and women's studies. She has recently published a memoir, *Desires of the Heart: A Daughter Remembers Her Missionary Parents* (Cold River Studio, 2010). She is currently exploring the possibility of teaching and doing faculty development work in Papua New Guinea, where she grew up. Dr. Frerichs earned her Doctor of Arts in English at the University of Michigan (1974).

Susan Gano-Phillips is an interim assistant dean in the College of Arts and Sciences and an associate professor of psychology at the University of Michigan–Flint. She is the former director of the Thompson Center for Learning and Teaching at University of Michigan–Flint, where she initiated an ongoing faculty development program for new faculty and broadened the scope of the center's activities to include organizational development through strategic planning activities and general education curriculum reform. Her research interests involve general education reform and processes associated with Institutional Change. In 2008, she published, with coauthor Robert Barnett, "Against All Odds: Transforming Institutional Culture," in AAC&U's *Liberal Education*, and she has a forthcoming edited book titled, *A Process Approach to General Education Reform: Transforming Institutional Culture in Higher Education*. She is also engaged in research on students' expectations and experiences of general education curriculum across cultures. Dr. Gano-Phillips was named a Fulbright Scholar to Hong Kong during the 2008–2009 academic year, where she taught, consulted, and engaged in research at the City University of Hong Kong. She earned her PhD in clinical psychology from the University of Illinois at Urbana–Champaign.

Devorah Lieberman is provost and vice president for academic affairs at Wagner College in New York City. She assumed this position in January 2004 having been the vice provost and special assistant to the president at Portland State University in Portland, Oregon. While at Portland State University, she was presented the institution's "Distinguished Faculty Award" and the Carnegie Foundation for the Advancement of Teaching "Professor of the Year-State of Oregon" award. Dr. Lieberman received her PhD in intercultural communication and certification in gerontology (1984) from the University of Florida. She works closely with the president of the institution, advocating for faculty, students, and staff while furthering the mission and goals of the institution. Her national involvement with initiatives addressing liberal education, faculty development, student development, internationalization, diversity, and institutional transformation help to keep the campus involved with current trends in higher education. She authored and received the National Hesburgh Award for Outstanding Undergraduate Education at both Portland State University and Wagner College. She is the principal investigator on major grants that further campus-based initiatives, received from the Corporation for National Service, the Teagle Foundation, and AAC&U. As an educator, she continues to teach in her discipline. As an academic and a scholar she continues to publish in the higher education literature and to present in higher education venues. Her publications include edited books, book chapters, edited journals, and journal articles which address institutional change, assessment, civic engagement, international studies, intercultural communication, diversity, faculty development, and gerontology. Her most recent publications have focused on academic institutions as learning organizations, institutional transformation, issues of diversity in higher education, and creating community-based learning opportunities locally, nationally, and internationally.

Diana G. Pace has been associate dean of students at Grand Valley State University since 2003, and she teaches in the student affairs masters program. From 1985 to 2003, she was director of the counseling center at Grand Valley. She is a licensed psychologist in the state of Michigan and holds a PhD from the University of North Dakota. Her research interests include student affairs administration and counseling concerns of college students, and she is author of *The Career Fix-It Book.*

Tamara Rosier serves as the academic dean at Kuyper College in Grand Rapids, Michigan. Prior to her current position, Dr. Rosier provided support for faculty as they developed their teaching skills at Grand Valley State University and Cornerstone University. While at Cornerstone University, Dr. Rosier was the founding director of the Center for Excellence in Learning and Teaching where she also taught in the Teacher Education Department. She earned her PhD in leadership in higher education from Western Michigan University in 2004. Dr. Rosier has provided workshop sessions and keynote conference presentations in the areas of teaching and learning, motivation, and leadership.

Connie M. Schroeder is the assistant director of the Center for Instructional Development at the University of Wisconsin–Milwaukee and teaches graduate courses within the Certificate of Teaching and Learning, including distance education, adult learning, and higher education. She works with general education task force efforts, departmental program assessment, and instructional development at the individual and department level with emphasis on high impact practices and the AAC&U *Essential Learning Outcomes.* Dr. Schroeder has a PhD in educational leadership–higher education and a minor focused on organizational behavior from the University of Wisconsin–Madison and an MS in higher education student affairs from Indiana University, Bloomington. Dr. Schroeder has been involved in higher education administration since 1984 at both research universities and liberal arts colleges. As an associate dean at Beloit College for nearly a decade, she worked closely with student affairs, first-year seminars, and academic affairs. She has served on the governing board for the Professional and Organizational Development (POD), Network and received the POD Robert J. Menges Research Award in 2002 and 2007. Her research centers on change in higher education and levers for organizational change at institutional and department levels, including SoTL programs, teaching and learning centers, and departments. Her doctoral research examined change in academic departments through faculty as change agents, and identified the factors and conditions that enable or impede faculty involvement in departmental change. Her recent international and national presentations focus on clarifying and defining the role of organizational development for educational developers, redefining the mission of teaching and learning centers, and identifying the conditions and program and institutional factors that sustain scholarship of teaching and learning (SoTL) programs.

Nancy Van Note Chism is professor of higher education and student affairs at the Indiana University School of Education, Indiana University Purdue University Indianapolis (IUPUI). Dr. Chism advises doctoral students in higher education and teaches courses in professional and organizational development, the professoriate, college teaching and learning, and qualitative research methods. From 1999 to 2006, she was associate vice chancellor for academic affairs and associate dean of the faculties at IUPUI. She is past president of the Professional and Organizational Development Network in Higher Education. In 1998, she received the Bob Pierleoni Spirit of POD Award of that association and in 2009 the Robert J. Menges Research Award. She previously served as director of faculty and TA development at the Ohio State University. She has consulted on professional development or college teaching and learning at more than 50 campuses in the United States. She is active in international educational development projects in several countries, such as Thailand, Kenya, Saudi Arabia, and Singapore. She served as a Fulbright Scholar in Thailand in 2008. She has authored or coauthored more than 80 additional publications on professional and organizational development and college teaching and learning.

Note: Page numbers followed by t indicate tables.

AAHE, 210
AAC&U
  Greater Expectations Institute, 153, 156
Accreditation, process, 71
Academic Affairs, 48, 65, 70–71, 83, 96, 101,
    130, 137, 147, 159
Academic development, 9, 32, 78, 226
Academic programs
  new, 64, 171–172, 243
Academic Vice President, 122, 137, 209–210
Accountability, and centers, 26, 60
Action learning, approach to change, 53
Administration, upper level, 65
Administrative advocacy, 52, 62, 130, 133,
    220, 228, 249
Advisory board(s), 11, 81, 83, 93–94, 96, 183,
    194
  and center programming, 80, 117, 132, 227
  appointed, 11, 81
  as advocates, 229–230
  as collaborators, 29–30, 39, 63, 67
  as partners, 229
  authority, 228–229
  center, 91, 93, 127, 194
  composition, 55, 68, 229, 241, 293
  constituency, 229
  elected, 93–96
  empowered, 229
  groups, 218–219
  orienting, 229
Advocate(s), center, 2
Alignment
  center, 158
  need for, 206–207
  with mission, 244t
  with strategic plan, 165t
Allies (Alliances), center, 158, 181t

American Council on Education, Leadership
    Conferences, 223
A Nation At Risk, 25, 44
Antecedent conditions, 90, 115, 282
Assessment
  culture of, 62–63
  student learning, 5, 12–13, 20, 25, 27, 40
Associate Dean, 48, 64, 67–68, 128–129, 133,
    159, 295–296
Associate Provost for Teaching, 67, 70, 71,
    188, 293
Associate Vice Chancellor, 48, 296
Attributes, 54, 103, 178–179
Australia, 19, 31, 37, 214

Bass, Randy, 33
Broad-scale initiatives, 5, 10

Canada, 19, 32, 143
Capacity-building, 221–222, 225, 230–232
Center
  accountability, 63
  advisory boards, 220
  advocates, 158
  age of, 91
  alignment, 158
  alliances, 203
  annual report, 193, 235
  assessment, 103
  budget, 258
  champion, 183
  closings, 13
  collaborations, 232
  constituencies, 208
  council, 50
  credibility, 131
  daily work, 182

Center (*Continued*)
  establishment, 61
  evaluation, 31, 48, 50, 114, 150
  financial support, 149, 195
  focus, 1
  founder, 84
  geographic location, 70
  goals, 94
  grant funding, 126, 156, 183, 279
  highly involved, 236
  key leader, 250
  leadership, 222
  marketing, 222
  mission, 2
  mission statement, 103
  marginalized, 13
  marginalization, 13
  names, 27, 55–56
  neutrality, 28, 54
  occasionally involved, 84
  openings, 278, 284
  origin(s), 81t
  partnerships, 127
  performance evaluations, 224
  position descriptions, statements, 10,
    29–30, 103, 123, 156, 192
  positioning, 62–64
  proactive, 4, 13, 49–50, 132, 171
  programming, 6, 98, 132
  programming goals, 227
  purpose, 32–60
  recognition, 9, 12, 37, 57, 62
  as remedial service, 28
  reporting line, 91t
  reputation, 119t
  resources, 18, 21
  size, 40
  staffing, 40
  strategic plan(ning), 22, 28, 30–31, 54, 63,
    66, 96t, 100, 114t
  structural designs, 192
  supervisors, 163
  support, 2
  value, 1–2, 10, 18–19
  very involved, 80, 84, 85t, 88t, 93, 95,
    108
  visibility, 135, 162

  vision, 100
  workload, 11, 27, 50, 78, 115
Catalyst, for change, 211
*Center for New Directions in Learning and
  Scholarship* (CNDLS), 264
Champion, 48, 183
Chancellors, 99t
Change
  and adaptation, 39
  alliances, 203, 231–232
  bottom-up, 206
  action learning, 53
  catalyst, 22, 191t
  coalitions for, 203
  and collaboration, 130
  conceptual, 286
  cultural, 149
  diffusion model, 167, 209
  and discrepancy, 213
  epidemic, 213
  evolutionary, 203
  first–order, 203
  grassroots, 2, 134, 167, 207, 209, 212
  and growing dissonance, 147, 211
  individual, 275
  initiators, 149, 152
  institutional, 139
  need for, 145
  leveraging, 165, 208
  levers, 212, 295
  life cycle, 36, 202
  linear, 25, 203, 252, 277
  model(s), 202–204
  message, 153
  mobilizing for, 203
  motivate, 149
  opposition, 203
  organizational, 124–125
  pitfalls, 212, 214
  planned, 22, 36
  process(es), 1, 18, 21–22
  processual, 278
  reciprocal, 278
  resistance, 77
  second order, 212
  social cognition, 202
  structural, 38

systemic, 211
teleological, 203
theory, 49
top-down, 206
transformational, 157
transformative, 57
virus, 152
Change agents
developer, 1–2, 4–12, 19, 27–28, 37–39
faculty, 21
institutional, 10–11
multi-level, 35–39, 236, 244, 277, 283
role, 33
undercover, 8, 12–13, 252
Chief
academic officer, 65, 70, 168–169
learning officer, 210
Chronological timeline, 277–278
CIRP (Cooperative Institutional Research
Project), 145–148
CLA (Collegiate Learning Assessment)
instrument, 151
Claiming a Liberal Education (CLE), 144–145
Climate, campus, 66, 72, 98, 244
Collaborative, 285
culture, 138
relationships, 127
constellation of, 127
structure, 1, 67
Collaborators, 29–30, 39, 63, 67
Collaboration
building, 2, 9
formal, 207, 213
leadership style, 122, 127–128, 184, 264
relationships, 127–129
Committee(s)
ad hoc, 194
appointed, 56
appointments, 123
Ex officio member, 170
formal, 163
governance, 49
informal, 50
institution-wide, 119
involvement on, 120–121
large scale, 162
membership, 130

representative, 194
strategic planning, 263
task forces, 115
volunteering, 175
Connectors, 153–154
Consultant(s), informal, 163
Consultations, with key administrators,
194–195
Continuum of Center Involvement, 80
Credibility, 119t, 149
centers, 131
directors, 10, 130
Culture, of assessment, 62
Cultural
components, 216
transformation, 209
values, 185
Curriculum
reform, 124
revision, 168, 175

Dean, 5, 57
dean's council, 48, 99t
Decentralized, faculty development, 68
Decision making, 38, 41
groups, 52
Department chairs, 21, 24, 64, 69, 121, 127,
133, 154, 166–168, 193
Department change, 122
Diffusion strategies, 200
Director
background, 5, 7, 10, 31
burnout, 195–196, 227
expertise, 8–10, 13, 19–20
founding, 20–21, 82, 84, 100, 178, 183,
184–185, 187
knowledge, 5–6, 8, 10, 25, 30
skills, 8–9, 13, 18, 30, 32, 37, 52, 54–55, 57,
60
workload strain, 255
Director role, 255
change agent, 37
collaborator, 29, 36, 67, 149
conflict, 7, 39, 50, 109
convener, 165
disseminator, 173
educator, 165–166

Director role (*Continued*)
  expertise, 8–10
  facilitator, 137, 165
  initiator, 30
  investigator, 294
  representative, 146, 154, 168, 170
  status, 7–8
Directorship
  length of, 81t, 83t, 84, 91t, 96–98, 101t
Distance education, 80t, 90t, 114t

Educational development, 23–24, 31, 38, 123, 296
EDUCAUSE, 72
Environmental scan, 193, 195
Exemplary
  mission statements, 253t
  models, 253–254
Expertise
  cross unit, 181t, 202
  unique, 9

Faculty
  change agents, 4, 12–13, 28–29, 33–36
  Council, 50, 56
  fellows, 104, 220, 252
  governance, 7, 49–50, 156
  learning communities, 47, 127, 132, 156, 175
  scholar(s) for, 67–68
  teaching and learning, 2, 4–11
  senate, 96t, 146, 148t, 155
  status, 47–48
  turnover, 117, 132, 137–138, 214
  virtues, 57
  voice of, 228
Faculty development
  definition, 2–4
Funding
  external, 72
  grant, 96t, 116

General education
  Institute, 187
  program, 174
  reform, 89t, 106
Georgetown University, 184

Gladwell, Malcolm, *The Tipping Point*, 152, 211
Globalization, initiative, 69
Governance
  faculty, 49
  institutional, 123t
  structure, 123t
Grand Valley State University, 210–212, 295
Grant
  center, 117
  funding, 96t, 156
  institutional initiatives, 41, 135
  Title III, 127, 209
  writing, 116
Grassroots, change, 2, 134
Grounded Theory, 86–87, 142, 277, 281

Harvard University Institute for Management and Leadership in Education, 223
Hierarchy, institutional, 64
Higher education
  environment, 35
  national issues, 116, 231
  organizations, 125
  trends, 174, 176t
Hot button issues, 55

Initiatives
  institutional, 249–250
  student learning, 20, 25, 27, 40, 48–50
  internationalization, 64, 69–70, 294
Instructional, development, 6, 26–27, 32, 166
Institution-wide
  committees, 243t
  dialogues, 116–117
Institutional
  beliefs, 22, 30, 170, 199, 215, 236
  blind spot, 274
  change, 1–4
  committees, 120
  conflict, 214
  context, 11, 138
  culture, 64
  environment, 240
  fringes, 2, 9
  goals, 223
  history, 1–4

infrastructure, 64–65
initiatives, 49, 64
leadership, 8–9
leadership turnover, 214
levels, 1–4
margins, 13
mission, 11
norms, 262
periphery, 30
planning, 9
policies, 51
priorities, 7, 11
processes, 21
radar screen, 2, 9, 17, 27, 29–30, 40, 112,
    120
research, 145
stakeholders, 12
structures, 122
subcultures, 230
transformation, 37, 67
values, 126
vision (ing), 71
Involvement
    extent of, 35, 87–88, 111
    highly, 82, 88, 101t-102, 250, 255
    key leader, 88
    level of, 6
    marginalized, 13, 28
    occasionally, 80, 88t, 92t, 113

Key leaders, 84, 92
Knowledge of
    areas, 222
    campus, 194
    literature, 12, 18, 26, 34–35, 56, 65, 77, 82,
        123–124, 126, 140, 146
    organizational change, 125
    specialist, 124
    trends, 54, 123
    unique, 30

Leader
    institutional, 3
    visionary, 189, 196
Leadership
    collaborative, 1
    development, 223
    director, 273

from the middle, 149, 151
    institutional, 3
    support, 132
Learning
    -centered teaching, 89, 90, 114, 165–168,
        170, 174, 208–209
    community, 50, 55, 66, 71–72, 89, 156
    individual, 2, 22, 200
    learner-centered teaching, 89, 90, 105, 114,
        166
    organization, 34, 64–65, 70–72
    organizational, 4–5, 199
Learning Reconsidered, 147
Liberal education, 145–148, 150–155, 210–211,
    294
Liminal, 287
Lumina Foundation, 148, 151

Macquarie University, 37
Margins, 4, 9, 35, 41, 75, 78, 101, 157, 164,
    220–221
Marginalization, 32–34
Mavens, 152
Metaphors, 190–191, 281
    center, 190
Mission
    center, 2
    -critical, 68
    institutional, 13
Mission statement(s), 61, 236
    center, 252
    communicating, 179, 257
    components, 254
    constituencies, 257
    exemplary, 253–254
    formation, 236
    goal(s), 68
    institutional, 255
    instructional focus, 178, 245
    instructional development focus, 1, 30
    learner-centered, 6, 166, 192, 245
    of college, 295
    purpose(s) of, 60, 62
    revising, 252

National
    associations conversations, .
    dialogue, 63
    initiatives, 282

National (*Continued*)
  Institute for New Faculty Developers, 204,
    213
  organizations, trends, 204, 213
Need, for change, 145–146
Neutral
  centers, 28
  politically, 28, 50
New Zealand, 31–32
Niche, center, 29
North Central Association (NCA), 121, 157
NSSE, 150–152, 155, 158

Online, distance education, 63, 89, 90, 106,
    114, 295
Organization(s)
  international, 73
  national, 73
Organizational
  behavior, 18, 21
  culture, 22
  development, 57
  development role, 6
  development literature, 34, 236
  dynamics, 33
  learning, 70
  structure(s), 23–24
  studies, 18
  theories, 199
  in use, 199
  vision, 179
Organizational change
  knowledge of, 102
  life-cycle models, 203
  models, 204
  political (dialectical) models, 203
  processes, 199–200
  social cognition, 203
  strategies, 212
  theories, 199
  transformation, 22
  vision, 181

Paradigm
  higher education, 7, 9, 12, 18, 20, 23, 25–26
  learning, 4–7, 11, 19–20, 22, 24, 26, 28–30,
    32–34

old, 11, 13, 95, 144, 196
  shifts, 7, 26
Partnership(s), building, 24, 47, 206–207
Perry, William, 124
Persuaders, 153, 155
PEW FLTLC, 144
PEW Grant, 144
Planning table, getting to, 7, 9
POD
  Conference, 41
  New Faculty Developers' Institute, 204, 213
  Organizational Development Institute, 215
Policy (cies), 37, 50
Position
  definitions, 62
  descriptions, 62
Positive restlessness, 206–208, 213
Power, 9, 52
Presidents, institutional, 99t
Primary factors
  enabling, 81
  impeding, 76, 79
  director-based, 10, 75, 86
  institution-based, 5, 75–76
  center-based, 10, 90
  antecedent, 90, 115
Proactive, 49–50
Profession, faculty development, 19
Professional development: organizations,
Program assessment, 89t, 90t, 114t, 175
Programming, center, 132
Promotion and tenure, 47–48, 63–64
  guidelines, 50, 64
  policies, 175
Processual change, model, 278, 280–281
Provost (s): Council, 67

Qualitative data, 5, 76, 83, 111, 120, 201
Quantitative data, 5

Readings, Bill, 124
The University in Ruins, 124
Reform
  general education, 114t
  undergraduate, 114t
Reporting line
  center, 81t

Resource
    center limitations, 134, 219
Retention, 68, 89t, 90t, 105, 114
Revenue-positive, 61
Role(s):
    ambiguity, 238, 255
    blended, 116, 173
    blurred, 166
    of centers, 191
    change, 289
    combined, 171
    conflict, 118, 134, 255
    confusion, 284, 287
    definition, 165
    dimensions, 30
    educator, 242
    faculty development, 18
    informant, 165, 208
    influential, 51–52, 175, 229, 285
    integration, 284–285
    leadership, 82, 124, 131, 133, 135, 173, 190
    legitimacy, 237–238, 256
    merged, 164
    merge(ing), 112, 116
    multidimensional, 285
    multilevel, 277
    stress, 119t
    traditional, 6
    transformation, 9
    transparent, 12
    undefined, 7, 78

Skills
    and abilities, 60
    facilitation, 157, 166
    leadership, 19
    refinement of, 53
    sets, 19, 163–164, 222, 225
    visionary, 180
Social cognition, 36, 200, 202–205
Social Learning Theory, 280
SoTL, 27, 114,1 32, 200, 296
South Africa, 19, 31
Sticky Message, 153, 203
Staffing
    capacity building, 221–222
    center, 219

    competencies, 224
    goal-setting, 224–225
    patterns, 215
    professional development of, 196
    reconceptualizing, 227–228
    size, 101t
    supervision of, 222
Strategic
    institutional, 267
    plan, 226–228, 232, 247, 251
    plan and mission, 267
    planning-center
    planning committee, 31, 120, 122, 137, 164, 264, 269
    planning document, 261–262, 266–268
    planning process, 63, 260
    priorities, 28
Status
    director, 85t, 113t
STLHE, 23, 226
Student Affairs, 146–148, 152, 156, 295–296
Student-centered learning, 164–165, 208, 266
Student retention, 48, 68, 224
Supervisor
    advocacy, 130
    center, 100
    center founder, 100, 112, 116, 119, 138, 179, 183, 279
    conduit, 9, 28, 130
    connections, 130
Survey, 79, 92t
Systems Thinking, 153, 158, 203

Tables
    virtual, 286
Task forces, 51
Theoretical
    proposition, 82–83, 86, 88, 92, 98, 100–101
    sampling, 83
Title
    center, 105
    director, 105
Trust, in director, 28, 65

United Kingdom, 31, 38, 214
The University in Ruins, 124

University of MI-Flint, 192–194
University of Nevada, Las Vegas, 112
University of the Sciences in Philadelphia
    (USP), 208, 266
University's purpose, 145

Vigilant opportunism, 56
Virtual, centers, 71
Visibility
    center, 223
    cultivating, 52
Vision
    alignment, 255
    center, 268

Change Model, 180–181
    as change strategy, 180–182
    communicating, 189–190
    enacting, 190–192
    embedding, 195–196
    formulating, 195–196
    and metaphors, 281

Wagner Plan, 66
Wagner College, 65–69, 294
Web(s)
    of change, 287
    of inclusion, 287
Workload, strain, 255

Also available from Stylus

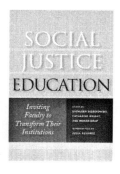

Social Justice Education
Inviting Faculty to Transform Their Institutions
Edited by Kathleen Skubikowski, Catharine Wright and Roman Graf
Introduction by Julia Alvarez

This book grew out of a project – involving deans and directors of teaching centers and diversity offices from six institutions – to instigate discussions among teachers and administrators about implementing socially just practices in their classrooms, departments, and offices. The purpose was to explore how best to foster such conversations across departments and functions within an institution, as well as between institutions. This book presents the theoretical framework used, and many of the successful projects to which it gave rise.

This book provides individual faculty, faculty developers and diversity officers with the concepts, reflective tools, and collaborative models, as well as a wealth of examples, to confidently embark on the path to transforming educational practice.

Building Teaching Capacities in Higher Education
A Comprehensive International Model
Edited by Alenoush Saroyan and Mariane Frenay
Foreword by James E. Groccia

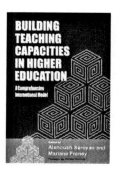

The outcome of a three year project involving teams of faculty developers, professors, and graduate students from eight institutions in five different European and North American countries this book conceptualizes what an internationally-appropriate, formal academic program for faculty development in higher education might look like, taking into account differing national contexts. It begins with five case studies that describe current practice in Belgium, Canada, Denmark, France and Switzerland.

It also defines a common curriculum, or core course with common foundations, for faculty and graduate students, based on a distributed learning model. This book offers practitioners around the world with a framework and model of educational development that can serve a number of purposes including professional development, monitoring and assessment of effectiveness, and research, as they meet increasing demands for public accountability.

22883 Quicksilver Drive
Sterling, VA 20166-2102

Subscribe to our e-mail alerts: www.Styluspub.com